# NEW FRONTIERS
# IN THEOLOGY

*Discussions among Continental
and American Theologians*

## VOLUME III

## THEOLOGY AS HISTORY

# NEW FRONTIERS
# IN THEOLOGY

*Discussions among Continental
and American Theologians*

---

VOLUME III
## *Theology as History*

*Edited by*

JAMES M. ROBINSON   ·   JOHN B. COBB, JR.
*Claremont Graduate School*    *School of Theology at Claremont*

HARPER & ROW, PUBLISHERS

New York, Evanston, and London

THEOLOGY AS HISTORY. *Copyright © 1967 by James M. Robinson. Printed in the United States of America. All rights reserved. No part of this book may be used or reproduced in any manner whatsoever without written permission except in the case of brief quotations embodied in critical articles and reviews. For information address Harper & Row, Publishers, Incorporated, 49 East 33rd Street, New York, N.Y. 10016.*

FIRST EDITION

LIBRARY OF CONGRESS CATALOG CARD NUMBER: 67-14936

E-R

# CONTENTS

# NEW FRONTIERS IN THEOLOGY

## I. THE LATER HEIDEGGER AND THEOLOGY

*Contributors:*

Heinrich Ott
Arnold B. Come
Carl Michalson
Schubert M. Ogden

## II. THE NEW HERMENEUTIC

*Contributors:*

Gerhard Ebeling
Ernst Fuchs
John Dillenberger
Robert W. Funk
Amos N. Wilder

## III. THEOLOGY AS HISTORY

*Contributors:*

Wolfhart Pannenberg
Martin J. Buss
Kendrick Grobel
William Hamilton

## IV. PROCESS THEOLOGY (in preparation)

*Contributors:*

Schubert M. Ogden
Gerhard Ebeling
Ernst Fuchs
Heinrich Ott
Wolfhart Pannenberg

# Foreword to the Series

Continental, and especially German, theology has played a leading role in the creative theological thinking of modern times. American theology has shown a characteristic openness to hearing, adapting, and assimilating the significant movements of European theology.

As long as this relationship was characterized by a considerable time lag in the translation and introduction in America of theological trends from the Continent, the American role was of necessity often that of receiving the results of a largely terminated discussion, so that the ensuing American discussion could hardly affect the ongoing discussion abroad. In recent years the greatly increased number of personal contacts among Continental and American theologians, and the steady flow of translations, indicate the possibility of a more direct interaction.

This series of "discussions among Continental and American theologians" is intended to provide a means for such a theological interaction. Rather than translating the finished systems of mature scholars, it proposes to identify future trends at the germinal stage of programmatic essays, and by means of critical discussion to share constructively in their development. Accordingly, each volume presents in translation such a programmatic essay, which has been introduced by Professor Robinson with an analysis of the situation in which it emerged and in terms of which it has its significance. This is followed by constructive and critical contributions to the issue by American theologians of promise. Finally, reappraisals of the issue in the light of these American contributions are presented both by Professor Cobb and by the author of the essay under analysis.

Indicative of the rapidity with which the dialogue is becoming a two-way affair is not only the fact that a German edition of the series is appearing (*Neuland in der Theologie,*

Zürich and Stuttgart: Zwingli-Verlag, Volume I, 1964, Volume II, 1965), but also the fact that as Volume IV a "reverse" volume is planned, in which a promising young American theologian, Schubert M. Ogden, will provide the lead essay, with an introduction by Professor Cobb, to which Continental theologians will respond.

# Editors' Preface

The synonymous terms *Traditionsgeschichte* and *Überlieferungsgeschichte* have become sufficiently focal in the Pannenberg circle to call for an analysis from which the translation, "history of the transmission of traditions," emerges. One of the problems of the role played by German theology in English-language theology derives from the ambiguity inherent in the German ability to run one noun on to the next. This creates a technical term of a very vague nature, so that the only thing the translator has initially to go on is the sensitivity that the first noun is something like a genitive phrase modifying the second. Hence, if one does not succumb to the easy temptation to avoid the problem with a sort of transliteration ("tradition history"), and thus renounce the translator's interpretative responsibility completely, one is inclined to translate woodenly: "history of tradition." But already this translation involves interpretive decisions in need of improvement. For the German words *Tradition* and *Überlieferung* retain some of the dual meaning of the Latin term *traditio*, which means both "tradition" and "transmission." In order to make clear that *Traditionsgeschichte* and *Überlieferungsgeschichte* do not suggest simply tracing a packaged and hence unaltered tradition, but rather intend to do full justice to the varying acts and situations of transmission which shape the tradition as it grows (or shrinks or changes), one should translate *Traditions*—or *Überlieferungs*—as "transmission of traditions." "Transmission" as a verbal noun is singular in number, and as such is sufficiently heard in the German term to prevent a plural formulation in German (which would be the rather cumbersome *"Traditionengeschichte" "Überlieferungengeschichte"*). Yet *Traditionsgeschichte* or *Überlieferungsgeschichte* has to do with many traditions, so that when in translation the meaning "tradition" can be distinguished from the meaning "transmission," the plural understanding of tradition inherent in the concept should be brought to expression, so as to distinguish this descriptive historical method from the dogmatic claim of a single harmonious "capital-letter" tradition. From these considerations emerges the hermeneutical translation of *Traditionsgeschichte* and *Überliefer-ungsgeschichte* as "history of the transmission of traditions."

The translation of Professor Pannenberg's essay was prepared for publication by Professor Kendrick Grobel shortly before the latter's death. Both it and his valuable contribution to the discussion in the volume are eloquent testimony to the loss to theological scholarship that his premature death represents. We wish also to express our indebtedness to Professor William A. Beardslee of Emory University, who, in conjunction with Professor Thomas Oden and Miss Carol Fellows, prepared the translation of Professor Pannenberg's response to the discussion.

Scriptural quotations are from the Revised Standard Version except in instances where the author's interpretation was better brought to expression in his own translation.

We wish to express our appreciation to the Divinity School of Vanderbilt University, and especially to Professor Gordon D. Kaufmann and Dean William C. Finch, who made the arrangements at the time, for being host to a meeting of all the participants in the volume, at which time early drafts of the material were discussed. The published form represents extensive revision subsequent to the Vanderbilt meeting, with the three American essays reaching their final form by 1965.

Without the support of President Ernest C. Colwell of the School of Theology at Claremont this Series would not be possible. To him we would express our continued and renewed gratitude.

To Mr. Larry Rose and Mr. David Griffin we express our appreciation for their assistance in editing the materials in this volume for consistency and clarity. And to Mrs. Frances Baker we express our appreciation for her help as a capable typist.

# PART I. The Issue

## 1. Revelation as Word and as History

JAMES M. ROBINSON

*Claremont Graduate School and University Center*

German theology between the two World Wars was dominated by what was initially a united movement called "dialectic theology," but which polarized into a Barthian position,
usually called the "theology of the word," and a Bultmannian
position, often referred to as "kerygmatic theology"—terminologies that suggest the common orientation to the concept
of the word of God. That brilliant theological epoch is now
drawing to an end, and new theologies are beginning to
emerge. One alternative is to pick up dialectic theology's
focus upon the word of God as a point of departure, and to
bring it into coordination with newly emerging understandings
of language, such as the understanding of language as event,
as performatory language. The result is the new hermeneutic
analyzed in Volume II of *New Frontiers in Theology*. Another alternative is to "forsake" "the context of the 'theology
of the word' that has determined theological thinking in one
form or another for more than a generation,"[1] and to find instead a focal orientation in an understanding of history. It is

---

[1] Wolfhart Pannenberg in *Offenbarung als Geschichte* (*Kerygma und
Dogma* [abbreviated *KuD*], *Beiheft* 1; Göttingen: Vandenhoeck und
Ruprecht, 1961; 2nd ed., 1963), in his "Postscript" to the second edition,
p. 132.

I

this alternative that is to be analyzed in the present volume.[2]

It is not surprising that titles in the literature related to this development have reflected from time to time such a juxtaposition of word and history. An advocate of the new position has defended it in an article entitled "History and Word in the Old Testament,"[3] and a critic has entitled his treatment, *Theology of the Word of God and the Hypothesis of Universal History.*[4] Similarly the leader of the new movement has presented a comparison of the two positions in an essay entitled "Hermeneutic and Universal History."[5] The title of the present essay is intended to reflect this usage present in the discussion itself.

Such terminologies are not intended to suggest an either/or relationship between language and history. Rather the discussion has to do with the question: Which provides the more adequate overarching category for bringing to expression their correct relationship? "Hermeneutic," by interpreting language as *event* that recurs in the ongoing translation of meaning, provides an approach to a theological understanding of history. And "universal history," by interpreting events in the context of the history of the transmission of *traditions,* provides an approach to a theological understanding of language. Yet by the nature of the case each would tend to be more adequate in bringing to expression that pole which it has used as the model for the overarching category. Hence the debate between the two positions has often followed the pattern of

[2] The attentive reader will note that the introduction has been written by one more oriented to the first alternative. Yet an effort has been made, without losing a participant's sensitivity for what the issues are and where the problems lie, to reduce so far as possible elements that would hinder the reader's open access to the new and creative theological position this volume seeks to introduce as one of the living options in theology today.

[3] Rolf Rendtorff, "Geschichte und Wort im Alten Testament," *Evangelische Theologie* (abbreviated *EvTh*), XXII (1962), 621–649.

[4] Günter Klein, *Theologie des Wortes Gottes und die Hypothese der Universalgeschichte. Zur Auseinandersetzung mit Wolfhart Pannenberg* (*Beiträge zur evangelischen Theologie,* 37; Munich: Christian Kaiser Verlag, 1964).

[5] Pannenberg, *"Hermeneutik und Universalgeschichte," Zeitschrift für Theologie und Kirche* (abbreviated *ZThK*), LX (1963), 90–121.

criticizing the other side of the discussion for its inadequate treatment of the pole that is one's own point of departure, and of claiming to do more justice to total reality by using that pole as a model: the linguisticality of all reality, or all reality as history.

## I. The Theological Experience of Contemporary History

If it is true that reflection upon history emerges in the wake of great historic events, then, conversely, the ways in which such events are themselves experienced should foreshadow the understanding of history operative in the historical study that follows. The contours of Wolfhart Pannenberg's distinctive position in the Christian understanding of history can thus be anticipated by contrasting the divergent ways in which leading German theologians experienced the two World Wars.

In 1920 *The Christian World,* the leading religious weekly of German Christendom, comparable to *The Christian Century* in America, carried a shocking article that repudiated all that the journal stood for, especially the program of *Kulturprotestantismus* its title expressed. This article by a village pastor, Friedrich Gogarten, was significantly entitled "Between the Times." It began: "It is the fate of our generation that we stand between the times. We never belonged to the time that is today reaching its end. Will we ever belong to the time that will come? And even if we for our part could belong to it, will it come so soon? Thus we stand in the middle between the two—in an empty space."[6] The defeat and dethroning of the Kaiser, and now the ruinous inflation, brought to an end a culture that had proudly inscribed its self-understanding on the buttons of its soldiers, "Gott mit

[6] "Zwischen den Zeiten," reprinted from *Die Christliche Welt* in *Anfänge der dialektischen Theologie,* II, ed. by Jürgen Moltmann (*Theologische Bücherei: Neudrucke und Berichte aus dem 20. Jahrhundert,* 17; Munich: Christian Kaiser Verlag, 1963), 95–101.

uns." This grinding halt is seen by Gogarten as a welcomed liberation from an empty theology that had only provided a false security. The final external collapse was all that was to be expected in a view of the inner hollowness. Albert Schweitzer's dramatic discovery of primitive Christian apocalyptic eschatology, which prior to World War I had been shocking only in demonstrating how irrelevant Jesus' position was to modern theology, was now followed by a second shock wave: this eschatology, rather than modern liberal theology,[7] seemed to fit the contemporary situation, seen now as the "interim" following upon the collapse of the "present evil aeon." Gogarten argued that it was not yet the time to set up new programs for the future to fill in the void (where Communism and then Nazism would be the live options), but rather the time finally to pause, unburdened by the vested interest of a culture comprised of man's achievements, and for once to listen to what God has to say.

Now, it is significant to Gogarten that the inner hollowness had become visible prior to the external collapse. His generation had caught sight of it by means of critical historical method, in terms of which the great historians of the day had taught the theological student to understand Biblical and church history just as other history is to be understood, i.e., as man's doing. *Heilsgeschichte* had been unmasked as simply a part of the long story of human self-assertion. "All these things [of Christian culture] have long since disintegrated. They have long since been explained in terms of the evolution of history, long since embedded in the stream of general his-

---

[7] For example, the leading theological journal of liberalism prior to World War I, the *Zeitschrift für Theologie und Kirche,* in spite of its programmatic intention to carry on theology as a constant hermeneutical translation of the point of the gospel into the contemporary situation, failed to do precisely that between the two World Wars. Cf. the survey of the history of that journal in my introductory essay, "For Theology and the Church," *The Bultmann School of Biblical Interpretation: New Directions? Journal for Theology and the Church* (abbreviated *JThC*), I (1965), 1–19, esp. p. 16. Cf. also Paul Schempp, "Randglossen zum Barthianismus," *Anfänge der dialektischen Theologie,* II, 305: "Barth has a following because his theology corresponds better than do other theologies to the present intellectual climate."

tory. This happened in the moment in which they were
worked over scientifically. This could not have been done a
moment earlier. A thing is dead when science (should I say
'our' science?) can turn its attention to it and grasp it. And
what does our day still have that science may not yet work
over and grasp? . . . On no side do we see any formation of
life that had not disintegrated. Have you not taught us to see
in everything man's work? Was it not you who sharpened our
eyes for the human, by putting for us everything within history
and evolution? We are grateful to you for doing that. You
created our tool; it is for us now to use it. We now draw the
consequence: Everything that in any way is man's work not
only arises, but also fades away. And it fades away when
man's work overgrows everything else—when science grasps
it, as I said earlier. And it can do that precisely at the moment in which man has succeeded in having his way. Today
is the hour when the sun sets. . . . We have achieved the
finest sensitivity for what is man's. . . . And in all seriousness
we are wrestling with the question as to whether there is anyone at all today who can really think God."[8]

Here the theology that we know today in terms of the
"post-Christian era," in which "God is dead" and theology
accordingly must be "honest to God," was launched at the
moment when the secular approach to history implicit in critical historical method was finding its dramatic vindication in
current events: The Christian service of the Kaiser in building God's kingdom on earth was unmasked as just a typical
instance of the nationalism, militarism, and colonialism of the
twentieth century.[9] It is not surprising that this theology interpreted Franz Overbeck's classification of primitive Christianity as "pre-historic" with regard to the history of Hellenistic literature and culture as a normative statement of what

---

[8] Gogarten, *ibid.*, pp. 97 f.
[9] For an analysis of the "unmasking" function of critical historical
method, cf. Robert W. Funk, "The Hermeneutical Problem and Historical
Criticism," *The New Hermeneutic* (*New Frontiers in Theology;* New
York: Harper & Row, 1964), II, esp. pp. 185 f.

Christianity should be,[10] made a "system" of Kierkegaard's "infinite qualitative difference" between time and eternity,[11] and elevated the name of Gogarten's article to the name of its journal, *Zwischen den Zeiten*.[12] And it is not surprising that when the Barthian wing of dialectic theology gradually moved toward *Heilsgeschichte*, it was challenged from within the dialectic theology context itself in the aftermath of World War II by the translation of Paul's phrase in Rom. 10:4, "Christ the end of the law," as "Christ the end of history."[13] Yet, in the decisive first years after World War II, with Bonhoeffer silenced,[14] postwar theology hardly begun,[15] and the

[10] Karl Barth, "Unerledigte Anfragen an die heutige Theologie," written 1920, republished in *Die Theologie und die Kirche, Gesammelte Aufsätze II* (Zollikon-Zürich: Evangelischer Verlag, 1928), pp. 1–25 [*Theology and Church: Shorter Writings, 1920–1928,* tr. by Louise Pettibone Smith, intr. by T. F. Torrance (New York: Harper & Row, 1952), pp. 55–73].

[11] Barth, *Der Römerbrief* (2nd ed., 8th reprint; Zollikon-Zürich: Evangelischer Verlag, 1947), p. xiii [*The Epistle to the Romans,* tr. by Edwyn C. Hoskyns (London: Oxford University Press, 1933), p. 11]. The quotation is from the Foreword to the 2nd ed., written September, 1921.

[12] Karl Barth, Friedrich Gogarten, and Eduard Thurneysen were in charge of this organ of their school from 1922–1933. It was edited by Georg Merz.

[13] Rudolf Bultmann, *Das Urchristentum im Rahmen der antiken Religionen* (Zürich: Artemis-Verlag, 1949), p. 209 [*Primitive Christianity in Its Contemporary Setting,* tr. by R. H. Fuller (New York: Meridian Books, in the series Living Age Books, 1956), pp. 187–188]. Similarly, Bultmann in *New Testament Studies,* I (1954–55), 13, reprinted in *Glauben und Verstehen,* III (Tübingen: J.C.B. Mohr [Paul Siebeck], 1960), 103. Also Ernst Fuchs, "Christus das Ende der Geschichte" (review of Oscar Cullmann, *Christ and Time*), *EvTh,* VIII (1948–49), pp. 447–461; reprinted in *Zur Frage nach dem historischen Jesus, Gesammelte Aufsätze II* (Tübingen: J.C.B. Mohr [Paul Siebeck], 1960), pp. 79–99.

[14] Killed in April, 1945, Bonhoeffer began his new posthumous influence on theology only with the publication of *Widerstand und Ergebung, Briefe und Aufzeichnungen aus der Haft* (Munich: Christian Kaiser Verlag, 1951) [*Prisoner for God: Letters and Papers from Prison,* tr. by R. H. Fuller (1st ed., 1953; 2nd ed., New York: The Macmillan Company, 1954)].

[15] The currency reform of 1948 marked more than did 1945 the beginning of postwar German activity. Only then can one note real signs of new theological vigor, such as the publication in 1948 of the first fascicle (Vol. I of the English edition) of Rudolf Bultmann's *Theologie des Neuen Testaments* (Tübingen: J.C.B. Mohr [Paul Siebeck]) and the resumption in 1950 of the publication of the *Zeitschrift für Theologie und Kirche.*

occasional attempts to speak to the situation often more well-meant than fully adequate,[16] many were ready for someone to provide a new orientation.

When the University of Heidelberg opened after the war, the first Rector to be elected from the Theological Faculty presented in his Rectoral Address an attempt to provide a theological reinterpretation of the history that was taking place. Hans von Campenhausen spoke on "Augustine and the Fall of Rome."[17] His description of the end of the first Roman Empire, from the raping and looting of the eternal city that left it in ashes (like most German cities in 1945), to the stream of pitiful refugees in regions (like Heidelberg) that had not themselves been devastated by the war, certainly drew into sharp focus the parallel to the fall of the Third Reich. Then von Campenhausen outlined in impressive terms the way in which Augustine, in the face of the catastrophe which seemed to deny *ad oculos* any meaning to history and any value to Christianity, had presented in *De civitate dei* the "last, greatest apology of Christian antiquity,"[18] "a refounding of Christian faith itself by developing a concrete theodicy that speaks to the concerns and needs of the day."[19] This apology is not really an attempt to prove Christianity; it is rather an appeal to believe that, in spite of the apparent arbitrariness and hence meaninglessness of what happens, there will be on the last day, before God's judgment throne, a solving of the

[16] Günther Bornkamm's pamphlet of 1946 quoting Jean Paul's "Speech of the Dead Christ from the Firmament that there is no God" succeeded in bringing to expression what many Germans felt at that time. His own "Postscript" may have sounded like the same language of Zion one heard the last time one went to church. Reprinted in *Studien zu Antike und Urchristentum: Gesammelte Aufsätze* II (*Beiträge zur evangelischen Theologie,* 28; Munich: Christian Kaiser Verlag, 1959, pp. 245–252).

[17] "Augustin und der Fall von Rom," first published in *Weltgeschichte und Gottesgericht* (*Lebendige Wissenschaft,* 1; Stuttgart: Kreuz-Verlag, 1947), pp. 2–18; reprinted in the volume of Campenhausen's Collected essays entitled *Tradition und Leben: Kräfte der Kirchengeschichte: Aufsätze und Vorträge* (Tübingen: J.C.B. Mohr [Paul Siebeck], 1960), pp. 253–271.

[18] *Ibid.,* p. 256.

[19] *Ibid.,* p. 259.

puzzle, a vindication of God's justice and of Christian faith.[20]

Von Campenhausen's concern is to correct a "pietistic and individualistic"[21] understanding of Augustine, in terms of which his response "could be understood as a wholly resigned retreat from the world of reality and its political decisions, as the final founding of a purely individualistic, ascetic stance toward life, which gives up forming world history at large and turns it over without a struggle to the purely earthly demonic forces."[22] Rather Augustine confronts the *civitas terrena* with the *civitas dei*, with "reality and real community."[23] "Augustine feels that the pagan appeal to the nation's greatness and to its past has brought into play a moral power and a passion that the church cannot bypass and simply turn over to its pagan opponents, having condemned them without examination. One must speak to the issue, and the religious apology thus becomes a critical revision of the dominant historic consciousness, a struggle for the proper possession of one's own past and of political history as a whole."[24] Augustine opposes "the dominant national ideology of pagan historians and philosophers" and recognizes in the pride that separates the individual from God the driving power behind the Roman state, which led to its fall.[25] In this way Augustine achieves a Christian understanding of the history of Rome from Romulus' murder of his brother down to the degeneracy of Augustine's own time. And to this view of past history there corresponds a new Christian society of the future in which

[20] *Ibid.*, p. 261.
[21] These are also the terms with which von Campenhausen had described a position falsely identified as Christian "since Augustine," in his address at the University of Heidelberg on the four hundredth anniversary of the death of Martin Luther, Feb. 18, 1946, "Gottesgericht und Menschengerechtigkeit in der Geschichte," in *Vom neuen Geist der Universität: Dokumente, Reden und Vortrage 1945–46,* ed. by K. H. Bauer (*Schriften der Universität Heidelberg,* 2; Berlin and Heidelberg: Springer-Verlag, 1947), pp. 64–73, esp. p. 65. The position of Luther presented in this address is similar to the position of Augustine as presented in the Rectoral Address.
[22] *Tradition und Leben,* p. 262.
[23] *Ibid.*
[24] *Ibid.*, p. 263.
[25] *Ibid.*, pp. 263 f.

"political virtues emerge again in a new spirit."[26] Thus Augustine rose to the occasion created by the fall of Rome, presented the gospel in terms of the situation he confronted, and thereby became "the first universal historian and theologian of history in Western civilization."[27]

Von Campenhausen concluded his address with a program for orienting contemporary theology to Augustine's Christian philosophy of history. "At least the *church* historian has no reason to give up today the task Augustine posed. He has only to take it up again with new means. Of course, it is a long road before we shall possess a total history of the church that meets the requirements of modern research in church history and history of religions and that nonetheless relates each epoch directly to Christ and measures it by Jesus' original proclamation, as is called for by what 'church' means. Furthermore it would be necessary, in order to have a real whole, to achieve a corresponding theological grasp of Israelite and Near Eastern history as a movement toward Christ, at whose center would of course be the presentation of primitive Christianity and of Jesus, a presentation that points both backward and forward. Only so would the disciplines of historical theology be able to perform theologically in their unity and totality that which the single individual Augustine once called for and accomplished."[28]

At the time this program would seem to have had its implementation in such a work as Oscar Cullmann's *Christ and Time*.[29] Von Campenhausen had spoken of *Heilsgeschichte*, and, though his teachers had been Bultmann and Hans von

---

[26] *Ibid.*, p. 266.
[27] *Ibid.*, p. 270.
[28] *Ibid.*, p. 271.
[29] *Christus und die Zeit: Die urchristliche Zeit- und Geschichtsauffassung* (Zollikon-Zürich: Evangelischer Verlag, 1946) [*Christ and Time: The Primitive Christian Conception of Time and History*, tr. by Floyd V. Filson (Philadelphia: The Westminster Press, 1950)]. The objective validity of this work in its historical aspects seemed in a way verified by the use made of it, though with a different ideological orientation, by Karl Löwith, *Meaning in History* (Chicago: University of Chicago Press, 1949) [German ed., *Weltgeschichte und Heilsgeschehen* (Stuttgart: Kohlhammer, 1953)].

Soden, he could present his understanding in language rem-
iniscent of Cullmann. "All the lines of history from the beginning on converge toward a point in time and meet at Jesus
Christ, in whom the meaning and goal of the whole movement are mysteriously unveiled. Here begins the history of our
present, which flows irresistibly toward the same Christ, i.e.,
his return at the end of time for the consummation and the
judgment."[30] Yet this *Heilsgeschichte* was soon replaced by
Rudolph Bultmann's concept of the "saving event," and the
nascent philosophy of history gave way to existentialism's historicness of existence as the current partner to theology.

Meanwhile the impact of von Campenhausen's Rectoral
Address continued to work among the theological students,
who crowded into Heidelberg until there was standing room
only in the reading rooms of the University Library and Theological Seminar. The systematic theologians Peter Brunner
and Edmund Schlink, with their strict Lutheran dogmatics,
seemed at the time to present a bold Christianity that did not
seek to curry favor with the cultural fads and the modern
mind but was content to give an unambiguous witness. And
the Old Testament theology of Gerhard von Rad began working out on a grand scale the basic Old Testament segment of
the thesis that theology is ultimately an interpretation of
history.

A group of young graduate students, drawn together by
such influences, crystallized into a small but lasting discussion
group that gradually became visible as dissertations and *Ha-
bilitationsschriften* (second dissertations prerequisite in Germany to entering the academic career) began to appear in
print. Wolfhart Pannenberg,[31] now Professor of Systematic

---

[30] *Tradition und Leben,* p. 271.

[31] Pannenberg (born 1928), came to Heidelberg as a student in 1951
after a year in Basel, where he had received strong influences from Barth
but had reacted against him at two points: He recognized, in a constitutive way Barth did not, the need for critical historical study of the
Bible (with a modified methodology) and was thus directed to the historical disciplines in Heidelberg; and he recognized, in distinction from
Barth, the need to involve oneself more seriously in general, nontheological thought. He had studied philosophy under Nicolai Hartmann in

Theology at the University of Mainz, published his *Doctrine of Predestination in Duns Scotus*[32] in 1954, the same year in which Rolf Rendtorff, now Professor of Old Testament at the University of Heidelberg, published his *Laws in the Priestly Document: A Study in the History of Gattungen.*[33] The latter's brother, Trutz, now *Dozent* of Systematic Theology at the University of Münster, published in 1958 *The Social Structure of the Congregation: The Ecclesiastical Forms of Life in the Social Change of the Present.*[34] In 1959 Klaus Koch, now Professor of Old Testament at the University of Hamburg, followed up Rolf Rendtorff's work on the Priestly Document with his own work, *The Priestly Document from Exodus 25 to Leviticus 16.*[35] Ulrich Wilckens, now Professor of New Testament at the *Kirchliche Hochschule* in Berlin, published the same year his dissertation, *Wisdom and Foolishness: An Exegetical and Comparative Religious Investigation of 1 Cor. 1 and 2,*[36] and two years later his *Habilitationsschrift,* entitled *The Missionary Speeches in Acts: Investigations in Form Criticism and the History of Traditions.*[37] Mean-

---

Göttingen in 1948–49 and under Karl Jaspers while in Basel in 1950–51, and he continued these studies under Karl Löwith in Heidelberg from 1951 to 1953. Indeed Pannenberg's own road to Christianity had been more one of rational reflection than of Christian nurture or a conversion experience.

[32] *Die Prädestinationslehre des Duns Skotus (Forschungen zur Kirchen- und Dogmengeschichte,* abbreviated *FKDG,* 4; Göttingen: Vandenhoeck und Ruprecht).

[33] *Die Gesetze in der Priesterschrift: Eine gattungsgeschichtliche Untersuchung (Forschungen zur Religion und Literatur des Alten und Neuen Testaments,* abbreviated *FRLANT,* 62; Göttingen: Vandenhoeck und Ruprecht).

[34] *Die soziale Struktur der Gemeinde: Die kirchlichen Lebensformen im gesellschaftlichen Wandel der Gegenwart (Studien zur evangelischen Sozialtheologie und Sozialethik,* 1; Hamburg: Furche-Verlag).

[35] *Die Priesterschrift von Exodus 25 bis Leviticus 16 (FRLANT,* 71; Göttingen: Vandenhoeck und Ruprecht).

[36] *Weisheit und Torheit: Eine exegetisch-religionsgeschichtliche Untersuchung zu 1. Kor. 1 und 2 (Beiträge zur historischen Theologie,* 26; Tübingen: J.C.B. Mohr [Paul Siebeck]).

[37] *Die Missionsreden der Apostelgeschichte: Form- und traditionsgeschichtliche Untersuchungen (Wissenschaftliche Monographien zum Alten und Neuen Testament,* abbreviated *WMANT,* 5; Neukirchen: Neukirchener Verlag, 1961, 2nd ed. 1962).

while Dietrich Rössler published in 1960 his dissertation in the department of New Testament at Heidelberg, entitled *Law and History: Investigations in the Theology of Jewish Apocalypticism and Pharisaic Orthodoxy;*[38] and in the same year Martin Elze, now *Dozent* in Church History at the University of Tübingen, published his dissertation, *Tatian and His Theology.*[39] Rössler has shifted into Practical Theology with a small volume entitled *The "Whole" Man: The Concept of Man in More Recent Pastoral Counselling and Modern Medicine in Relation to Anthropology in General,*[40] and is now Professor of Practical Theology at the University of Tübingen.

Lest one overlook the inner unity in this series of scattered monographs reaching from the Old Testament to the social structure of the church and to psychiatry in the present, a programmatic essay by Pannenberg on "Redemptive Event and History"[41] appeared on the crest of this wave of monographs in 1959, with a footnote to the title: "The following discussion is a slightly revised lecture given in Wuppertal on January 5, 1959, at a meeting of teachers from the theological schools of Bethel and Wuppertal. Especially in the first part, it deals with a theme on which a theological circle originally from Heidelberg has worked regularly for seven years. Although I am responsible for the following considerations, many of them could not be expressed as they are without my continuing conversations with M. Elze, K. Koch, R. Rendtorff, D. Rössler, and U. Wilckens."[42] A new school had been

---

[38] *Gesetz und Geschichte: Untersuchungen zur Theologie der jüdischen Apokalyptik und der pharisäischen Orthodoxie (WMANT, 3;* Neukirchen: Neukirchener Verlag, 2nd ed., 1962).

[39] *Tatian und seine Theologie (FKDG, 9;* Göttingen: Vandenhoeck und Ruprecht).

[40] *Der "ganze" Mensch: Das Menschenbild der neueren Seelsorgelehre und des modernen medizinischen Denkens im Zusammenhang der allgemeinen Anthropologie* (Göttingen: Vandenhoeck und Ruprecht, 1962).

[41] Cf. below, note 44.

[42] *KuD,* V (1959), 218 [*Essays on Old Testament Hermeneutics,* p. 314]. Compare the opening footnote of Ulrich Wilckens' essay "Die Bekehrung des Paulus als religionsgeschichtliches Problem," *ZThK,* LVI (1959), 273: "Inaugural address presented on December 10, 1958 in

launched. This new movement, usually referred to as the "Pannenberg circle,"[43] is the first to emerge from the German generation that was born well after World War I had passed, was raised in the throes of the Third *Reich,* World War II, and the collapse of 1945, and has reached maturity in the *Bundesrepublik.* It is also the first theological school to emerge in Germany within recent years that is not in one form or the other a development of the dialectic theology of the twenties.

## II. THE LOCATION OF THE NEW POSITION WITHIN THE THEOLOGICAL SPECTRUM

The position emerging from this movement was first presented as such in the programmatic essay by Pannenberg entitled "Redemptive Event and History."[44] That essay includes

Heidelberg and on December 12, 1958 in Marburg. The thesis which is intentionally only sketched here originated in connection with theological work shared over a period of years with Martin Elze, Klaus Koch, Wolfhart Pannenberg, Rolf Rendtorff and Dietrich Rössler." Robert L. Wilken, "Who is Wolfhart Pannenberg?" *Dialogue,* IV (1965), 140, says the group consisted initially of only Wilckens, Rössler, Koch, and Rendtorff. Lothar Steiger, "Offenbarungsgeschichte und theologische Vernunft. Zur Theologie W. Pannenbergs," *ZThK,* LIX (1962), 89, comments: "The Old Testament scholar Klaus Koch, and in the area of Church History, Martin Elze, give less clear indication of belonging to this group." However, Koch's essays, "Spätisraelitisches Geschictsdenken am Beispiel des Buches Daniel," *Historische Zeitschrift,* CXCL (1961), 1–32, and "Der Tod des Religionsstifters," *KuD,* VIII (1954), 100–123, and Elze's essay, "Der Begriff des Dogmas in der Alten Kirche," *ZThK,* LXI (1964), 421–438, are oriented to Pannenberg's position. The brother of Rolf Rendtorff, Trutz Rendtorff, identified himself with the group in the symposium, *Offenbarung als Geschichte* (*KuD, Beiheft* 1; Göttingen: Vandenhoeck und Ruprecht, 1961), with his essay "Das Offenbarungsproblem im Kirchenbegriff," pp. 115–131. August Strobel's book, *Die apokalyptische Sendung Jesu. Gedanken zur Neuorientierung in der kerygmatischen Frage* (Rothenburg a.d. Tauber: Martin-Luther-Verlag, 1962), indicates that he has adopted the new position with the uncritical zeal characteristic of the convert, as Ulrich Wilckens' somewhat cool review, *Theologische Literaturzeitung* (abbreviated *ThLZ*), LXXXIX (1964), 670–672, indicates.

[43] Pannenberg refers to the movement as a "working circle" and their position as a "theological conception of history." *Grundzüge der Christologie* (Gerd Mohn: Gütersloher Verlagshaus, 1964), p. 9 of the Preface.

[44] "Heilsgeschehen und Geschichte," *KuD,* V (1959), 218–237, 259–288. The first part was reprinted in slightly shortened form in *Probleme*

both a critical assessment of the then current theological options in Germany and the main lines of an alternative to them. And indeed one can best begin an evaluation of the importance of this new movement and of the role it is currently playing in German theological discussion by clarifying where its first thrust lies in relation to these alternate positions. The discussion was initially hampered by overhasty assumptions on both sides in this regard. For the older positions have available certain rejected categories in terms of which it is all too convenient to classify any and all divergent opinions. And the younger movement, not having experienced the older views in their original vigor and excitement of discovery, but as "safe doctrine," handed down and watered down, may not do full justice to the theologies it is opposing. Hence it is the purpose of this section to work through such initial assessments to a more accurate identification of the points of divergence.

The programmatic essay began by setting out its location within the spectrum as follows:

"History is the most comprehensive horizon of Christian theology. All theological questions and answers are meaningful only within the framework of the history that God has with humanity and through humanity with his whole creation —the history moving toward a future still hidden from the world but already revealed in Jesus Christ. This presupposition of Christian theology must be defended today within theology itself on two sides: on the one side, against Bultmann and Gogarten's existential theology that dissolves history into the historicness of existence; on the other side, against the thesis, developed by Martin Kähler in the tradition of redemptive history, that the real content of faith is supra-

---

alttestamentlicher Hermeneutik, Claus Westermann, ed. (Munich: Christian Kaiser Verlag, 1960), pp. 295–318 [Essays on Old Testament Hermeneutics, tr. by Shirley C. Guthrie, Jr., ed. by J. L. Mays (Richmond: John Knox Press, 1963), pp. 314–335]. (It is odd that pp. 233–235 of the original essay, in which Pannenberg expresses most agreement with the other side, in this instance Kierkegaard and Gogarten, are omitted from the reprint, which resumes where the criticism, in this instance of Bultmann and Fuchs, resumes.)

historical. This assumption of a suprahistorical kernel of history, which was in substance present already in von Hofmann's delimitation of a theology of redemptive history (*Heilsgeschichte*) over against ordinary history (*Historie*), and which is still alive today especially in the form of Barth's interpretation of the incarnation as 'prehistory' (*Urgeschichte*), necessarily depreciates real history, just as does the reduction of history to historicness. Both theological positions, that of pure historicness and that of the suprahistoric ground of faith, have a common extratheological motive. Their common starting point is to be seen in the fact that critical historical research as the scientific establishment of events did not seem to leave any room for redemptive events. Therefore the theology of redemptive history fled into a harbor supposedly safe from the critical historical flood tide, the harbor of suprahistory, or, with Barth, of prehistory. For the same reason the theology of existence withdrew from the meaningless and godless 'objective' course of history to the experience of the significance of history in the 'historicness' of the individual. The historical character of the redemptive event must therefore be asserted today in debate with the theology of existence, with the theology of redemptive history, and with the methodological principles of critical historical research."[45]

This position would seem to oppose equally the Barthian and Bultmannian alternatives. However, the concept of *Urgeschichte*, "prehistory," was limited to the early Barth, so that the quotation is not as direct a criticism of the Barthians of today as it might seem. To be sure there does seem to remain in the later Barth a vestige of a supernatural precinct.[46] Yet

[45] *KuD*, V (1959), 218 [*Essays on Old Testament Hermeneutics*, p. 314].

[46] Cf. Bornkamm, "Die Theologie Rudolf Bultmanns in der neueren Diskussion: Zum Problem der Entmythologisierung und Hermeneutik," *Theologische Rundschau* (abbreviated *ThR*), N.S., XXIX (1963), 88 f.: "In Barth on the other hand it seems as if the revelation not only calls upon us for faith but also for the concession of another advantage, namely the separating out in advance of an area of mysterious things that, as was customary in the orthodox tradition, I exclude in advance with the help of a formal concept of scripture and canon and that I may no longer

the emphasis in the Barthian movement has moved in the direction of a view of revelatory history nearer to that out of which the Pannenberg movement arose. Thus Barth could express his approval of such Old Testament views with regard to "faith and history"[47] as that of von Rad, from which Pannenberg's view of history emerged, and that of Walter Zimmerli, who provided a basic ingredient for the theology of the Pannenberg group and found it difficult to distinguish his position from theirs, as the next section of this introduction will indicate. Hence, when the Barthian journal, *Evangelische Theologie,* called a meeting of its editorial board in September, 1961, to carry through a reorganization along more scholarly lines and to appraise critically "a theology of history emerging again in somewhat different form,"[48] the series of papers presented for discussion more nearly revealed the extent to which the two movements were converging.[49] The

make the object of critical inquiry." In note 1 on p. 89 he comments that he had already registered this criticism in 1951, and that in the interim his hopes of having misunderstood Barth have "become fainter." Pannenberg senses in Barth's neglect of critical historical method a continuation of his "prehistory" position.

[47] Cf. Barth, "How My Mind Has Changed," *The Christian Century,* LXXVII (1960), 75: "To me it is significant that present-day Old Testament scholars, especially in regard to the old yet always new theme of 'faith and history,' are on the whole on much better ground than the authoritative New Testament men."

[48] Cf. *EvTh,* XXI (1961), 529 f. The editor, Ernst Wolf, expressed the personal dissatisfaction of the Barthians with this new movement by thus suggesting a parallel to the theology of history presented by the notorious "German Christians," an innuendo subsequently retracted, *EvTh,* XXII (1962), 223 f.

[49] The reorganized journal opened with a double issue for January–February, 1962, which included the papers discussed at the meeting: Günther Bornkamm, "Geschichte und Glaube im Neuen Testament. Ein Beitrag zur Frage der 'historischen' Begründung theolokischer Aussagen," XXII, 1–15, which did not address itself directly to the position of Pannenberg; Walter Zimmerli, " 'Offenbarung' im Alten Testament. Ein Gespräch mit R. Rendtorff," XXII, 15–31, which will be discussed in the next section; Jürgen Moltmann, "Exegese und Eschatologie der Geschichte," XXII, 31–66; Rudolf Bohren, "Die Krise der Predigt als Frage an die Exegese," XXII, 66–92. It was only a supplementary article by another participant at the meeting, Hans-Georg Geyer, that brought out any extensive divergence from Pannenberg: "Geschichte als theologisches Problem. Bemerkungen zu W. Pannenbergs Geschichtstheologie," XXII, 92–104. In his "Postscript" to *Offenbarung als Geschichte,* 2nd

main theological paper was presented by Jürgen Moltmann, known as the editor of the collection of important articles from the twenties reprinted as the *Beginnings of Dialectic Theology* as well as for his own *Theology of Hope*. His presentation parallels very closely the thought of Pannenberg, and only in a somewhat peripheral way echoes the "theology of the word of God."[50] And Bohren's application of Moltmann's paper to the homiletical problem, while sensing in Pannenberg's emphasis that facts speak for themselves "a complete defeat for preaching,"[51] goes on to affirm that over against the other alternatives this emphasis is "simply liberating,"[52] and then to sketch a concept of preaching oriented to remembering and narrating history that could well be a homiletical implementation of Pannenberg's theology.

Dialectic theology had originally waged its polemic against an objectivizing idealistic interpretation of history in favor of an encounter with history in which history is not ultimately under man's control but rather opens up access to that which is not at his disposal, and for that reason encounters him as a real, irreplaceable, and authoritative event.[53] It was that

---

ed., p. 147, note 35, Pannenberg relativizes the difference between their positions.

[50] In his preface to *Anfänge der dialektischen Theologie* (*Theologische Bucherei*, 17; Munich: Christian Kaiser Verlag, Parts I and II, 1962), I, p. XII, Moltmann argues that "theology of the word" is the only "appropriate" designation for dialectic theology. In *EvTh*, XXII (1962), 58, one finds a passing echo of that theology: "The revelation of the special history that grounds faith in Christ takes place in the word that effects history. . . . Thus history does not become revelation, but it does become the sphere of revelation." But this is then led in a direction nearer to Pannenberg, p. 59: "The eschatological proclamation effects and provokes the experience of reality as history, . . . makes the reality in which men live together a historical process." In Moltmann's *Theologie der Hoffnung* (Munich: Christian Kaiser Verlag, 1964; 2nd ed., 1965), p. 49, he defends Barth against Pannenberg's association of Barth's understanding of the word of God with gnosticism and personalism.

[51] *EvTh*, XXII (1962), 78.

[52] *Ibid.*, pp. 82 f.

[53] Cf., e.g., Bultmann's criticism of his predecessors, "Das Problem einer theologischen Exegese des Neuen Testaments," *Zwischen den Zeiten*, III (1925), 334–357, reprinted in *Anfänge der dialektischen Theologie*, I, 51: "The coordination of the *existing* subject to history does not take place at all—at least not if man's existence does not lie in the general, in

new understanding of history that came to expression more adequately in terms of a historic concept of word, to which it was then coordinated.[54] Now this coordination seems to be fading among the Barthians, with the result that the concept of the word tends to merge with that of the interpretation given in the tradition—which Pannenberg includes within his concept of history. Thus the Barthian tends not to realize how much his own position has become like that of Pannenberg, with the result that he is able to mark the difference only by presenting Pannenberg's view as nearer to that of positivism than in reality it is. For example, Eduard Schweizer summarizes critically: "With [the Pannenberg circle] the revelation of God is to be found exclusively in history. It is not the interpreting word of the prophet or of the witness in [the] early church; it is the course of history itself which reveals God to anyone who is not blind. . . . We cannot deal extensively with this [position]. It may suffice to say that accord-

---

rationality, but rather in the individual, in the concrete moments of here and now. It is for this reason that the idealistic observer sees nothing in history that can lay a claim on him in the sense that here something new is said to him that he does not already potentially possess and have at his disposal by means of his participation in reason in general. He finds nothing that encounters him as authority, he finds in history only himself, in that the content of history is reduced to the movement of ideas coordinated to man's rationality. Thus all along he has at his disposal all possibilities of historic occurrence."

[54] *Ibid.*, p. 53: "In all these cases [sc. of idealistic exegesis] the word of the text is not able to speak to the interpreter in any real sense, since he all along and on principle has at his disposal all possibilities of what can be said, namely on the basis of the principle implicit in his approach. Yet without a doubt the original and genuine meaning of the word 'word' is that it points to a subject matter lying outside the speaker, opens this up to the hearer, and thus is designed to become an *event* for the hearer. The possible rejoinder of idealistic exegesis, to the effect that it meets this requirement, is based on the fact that it does indeed conceive of the speaking individual not as a psychic subject or just as environmentally conditioned, and hence can interpret his expressions as pointing to trans-subjective subject matters. But these subject matters are not those meant here, for they cannot become for the hearer an event at all. Rather, in that their content is the system of reason that is the essence of the rational spirit, they contain only what the interpreter as rational subject has all along at his disposal. Hence [our] exegesis in terms of subject matter intends to take seriously the original and genuine meaning of the word 'word,' by understanding it as pointing out the subject matter."

ing to the Old and New Testament God's acts [in] history are
not at all visible to everybody. It is the word of the prophet;
it is the preaching of the Apostles; it is the special instruction
of Jesus granted to the disciples, which solves the riddles; and
it is, above all, always the miracle of God's Spirit, which
opens hardened hearts. With Pannenberg, the fundamental
difference between scientific perception and faith as a gift of
God becomes blurred. . . . Stressing with Pannenberg exclusively the mere facts leads us astray. The mere fact is a
birth, and nobody could see its relevance, its real meaning,
without the interpretation of faith."[55] Yet in actuality the
Pannenberg group does not[56] maintain a revelation in historical fact apart from the context of traditions and interpretations in which it took place. Their divergence from dialectic
theology is in the area of history as present address, and when
on this topic the Barthian, much like the traditional Lutheran
Althaus,[57] speaks simply of "the miracle of God's Spirit," Pannenberg can with some justification feel such a view is in need
of demythologization. That is to say he is at least in part to
be understood as reacting in his way, i.e., in terms of a theology of history, against the same symptoms of decline within

[55] "Some Trends in European New Testament Research of Today,"
*The Chicago Theological Seminary Register,* LIV (1963), 5, 7. For the
extent to which Schweizer's position is actually like that of Rendtorff, cf.
below, note 184. For the extent to which the Barthians have in general
been moving away from the original understanding of the word characteristic of dialectic theology, one may compare an exchange between Heinrich Ott and Bultmann. In his pamphlet *Die Frage nach dem historischen
Jesus und die Ontologie der Geschichte* (Zürich: EVZ-Verlag, *Theologische Studien,* No. 62, 1960), p. 40, Ott appeals, in his opposition to
brute-fact positivistic historiography, to Martin Buber for the fact that
"saga," the meaning of events, goes back to the inspiration with which
the events themselves were experienced. To this Bultmann replied in a
letter: "Your quotations from Buber show how much he is still stuck in
historicism. For the inspiration whose function he perceives in the historical tradition is after all a phenomenon thoroughly visible to the
positivistic historian. The kind of encounter which is the presupposition
of genuine understanding of historical reality is surely my own encounter
as I question history, expose myself to it; but it is not the encounter of
various reporters."
[56] Apart from an occasional remark, later by implication withdrawn;
cf. below, nn. 155, 156, 183.
[57] Cf. below, pp. 64–68.

the "theology of the word" as is Ebeling in his, i.e., in terms of a hermeneutical understanding of language.

There is, on the other hand, some degree of justification for Oscar Cullmann to sense a convergence between his and Pannenberg's views of history. For although Cullmann is hardly a dialectic theologian, his position is in fact that toward which the Barthian school has been moving. In the "Retrospect on the Effect of the Book in Theology since the War" that Cullmann uses in the place of a preface to the third German edition of *Christ and Time* (1962), he finds himself in the propitious moment "where the theological situation seems to be developing such that in the future one can perhaps expect even in Germany more understanding for what I was at, than was the case in the period now coming to an end, characterized by the inroads of existentialism into New Testament exegesis." This hope is documented in a footnote with the remark: "I have in mind, e.g., the circle around W. Pannenberg (without yet assuming a position with regard to it)."[58] Even this reservation is removed in Cullmann's new book, whose title, *Salvation as History*,[59] stands in striking parallel to that of the symposium of the Pannenberg group, *Revelation as History*,[60] of which Cullmann says: "To be sure [it] does not play up the term '*Heilsgeschichte*,' but in spite of all deviation in detail its position comes near to that advocated by myself in *Christ and Time*."[61]

[58] *Christus und die Zeit*, 3rd ed., pp. 9 f.

[59] *Heil als Geschichte. Heilsgeschichtliche Existenz im Neuen Testament* (Tübingen: J.C.B. Mohr [Paul Siebeck], 1965).

[60] *Offenbarung als Geschichte* (*KuD, Beiheft* 1; Göttingen: Vandenhoeck und Ruprecht, 1961; 2nd ed., 1963). Since this is the first *Beiheft* to *Kerygma und Dogma,* there is prefaced to it a brief note by the "editors" of the journal, of whom Cullmann is one, to the effect that the value of the essays in the volume led them to introduce the series format for this symposium and similar materials.

[61] *Heil als Geschichte*, p. 39. Cullmann recognizes here that his soteriological focus is a "quite different perspective" from the focus of the Pannenberg group on revelation, a distinction that becomes quite explicit in Pannenberg's *Grundzüge der Christologie,* esp. Ch. 2 on "Christology and Soteriology," pp. 32–44. The Cullmannian concept of the Christ event as "the center of *Heilsgeschichte*" emerges in the Pannenberg group, e.g., Dietrich Rössler, *Göttinger Predigtmeditationen* XVI (1962), 159,

If however there is hardly a sharp line of demarcation between the Pannenberg group and the place at which the Barthian movement has in fact by and large arrived, so that the Pannenberg group may in retrospect seem more its heir than its opponent, a clearer alternative would seem to exist with regard to the Bultmannian position; for this position has retained more of the original correlation of history and word by means of which dialectic theology had distinguished itself from the antecedent idealistic view of history. Unfortunately the version of this position prevalent at Heidelberg,[62] and apparently sanctioned by the fact that it had been propagated by the Bultmannian on the faculty,[63] was in fact misleading. Yet Pannenberg appeals to Bornkamm's criticism of Bultmann[64] as "showing convincingly that Paul is not concerned with a new self-understanding, but with a 'new history and existence,' in which I am taken up into Christ's history."[65]

Johannes Körner had already challenged the validity of the interpretation of Bultmann implicit in this either-or formulation. For if it does not advocate a dualistic view of history,

---

although Pannenberg subordinates it to the futurity of eschatology, *Grundzüge der Christologie,* pp. 405 f., and prefers to speak of Jesus as the "proleptic end" of history, *KuD,* V (1959), 224. The focus of Ernst Fuchs's review of *Offenbarung als Geschichte,* entitled "Theologie oder Ideologie? Bemerkungen zu einem heilsgeschichtlichen Programm," *ThLZ,* LXXXVIII (1963), 257–260, is to draw the parallel between the Pannenberg circle and Cullmann.

[62] On the general breakdown of real communication between the leading positions in Germany, the rigidifying of fronts, the misrepresentation, and hence the general degeneration of the relevance of the discussion between groups (in contrast to the more accurate and profound interpretation and discussion especially of Bultmann currently coming from Roman Catholic and English language theology), cf. Günther Bornkamm's survey, "Die Theologie Rudolf Bultmanns in der neueren Diskussion. Zum Problem der Entmythologisierung und Hermeneutik," *ThR,* N.S., XXIX (1963), 33–141.

[63] Günther Bornkamm, "Mythus und Evangelium. Zur Diskussion des Problems der Entmythologisierung der neutestamentlichen Verkündigung," in the pamphlet including an article by W. Klaas and published under the title, *Mythos und Evangelium* (*Theologische Existenz Heute,* N.S., 26; Munich: Christian Kaiser Verlag, 1951).

[64] *Mythos und Evangelium,* p. 25.

[65] *KuD,* V (1959), 224 [*Essays on Old Testament Hermeneutics,* p. 322].

which Bornkamm hardly intended, it presupposes a misunderstanding of Bultmann.[66] However, Pannenberg maintains
that Körner's interpretation is "automatically refuted"[67] by
Bultmann's own presentation in *The Presence of Eternity,*
where Bultmann says: "But although the history of the nation
and the world has lost interest for Paul, he brings to light
another phenomenon, the historicity of man, the true historical life of the human being."[68] Körner argues that Bultmann

---

[66] *Eschatologie und Geschichte. Eine Untersuchung des Begriffes des
Eschatologischen in der Theologie Rudolf Bultmanns* (*Theologische
Forschung: Wissenschaftliche Beiträge zur kirchlich-evangelischen
Lehre,* 13; Hamburg: Herbert Reich, Evangelischer Verlag, 1957), p.
124. "But what is meant by this new history of Christ? That is the problem. Does this call for a historic dualism to the effect that there is an old
history, world history, and alongside of it a new history of Christ different in content? Does that mean that first two kinds of history are shown
objectively to exist, of which one is mine, the other Christ's, histories that
I can observe even before being taken up into them? That would correspond, e.g., to the dualism of Manicheeism or Mardionitism, or Flacius'
doctrine of justification, and would necessarily contradict every scholarly
view of history, which can only be monistic. Or does it merely mean that,
in believing, reality all at once appears to me as completely new, that [in
this sense] Christ takes me into his history and hence prior history is now
indeed 'no longer mine'? But Bultmann himself means the same thing—
and Bornkamm himself [*ibid.,* p. 27] concedes that Paul speaks of the
new history 'to be sure not in a descriptive way, but only indirectly,
through a renewed exposition of what now comprises man's being in
faith.' " In a blurb attached to Körner's book, Bultmann is quoted as regarding it as "one of the most important recent publications in the field
of theology," which "will advance the theological discussion fruitfully."
Bultmann wrote me: "my view [on the relation of the ontological to the
ontic] is accurately presented in the excellent book of Johannes Körner."
Bornkamm (*ThR,* N.F., XXIX [1963], 69, note 1) has expressed reservations concerning his previous formulation of Bultmann's position in this
regard, and (orally) specifically of the use Pannenberg made of it. Cf.
Bultmann's "Answer to Ernst Käsemann": "Käsemann may criticize the
fact that this constant (sc. between Jesus and the kerygma) is seen in the
self-understanding. But he does so obviously because he conceives of the
self-understanding as an anthropological phenomenon visible to a distancing, objectifying view. The self-understanding in Braun and Robinson's
sense includes in any case a self-understanding of man in his relation to a
transcendent reality confronting him." *Glauben und Verstehen* (Tübingen: J.C.B. Mohr [Paul Siebeck], IV, 1965), p. 195.
[67] *KuD,* V (1959), 225, note 13 [*Essays on Old Testament Hermeneutics,* p. 322].
[68] *The Presence of Eternity: History and Eschatology* (New York:
Harper & Row, 1957), pp. 41 ff. The quotation is on p. 43, and is quoted
by Pannenberg in *KuD,* V (1959), 224 [*Essays on Old Testament Herme-*

does occasionally speak of a "new history," a "God-led history," and is indeed not replacing history with anthropology. Rather Bultmann's reserve in referring to eschatological existence as history and his preference for referring to it as a possibility of man's existence is to prevent much the kind of thing Pannenberg seeks,[69] namely the understanding of that history in its revelatory nature as demonstrable to the historian

---

*neutics,* p. 322]. The quotation from Bultmann continues: ". . . the history which every one experiences for himself and by which he gains his real essence." Thus Bultmann's talk of man's historicness would not seem to replace or "dissolve" history. In such statements Bultmann is contrasting a relation of salvation to the history of a whole nation or people, Israel, with the Christian understanding of salvation for which "there is neither Jew nor Greek." Cf. Bultmann, "History and Eschatology in the New Testament," *New Testament Studies,* I (1954), 5–16, esp. p. 13, reprinted in *Glauben und Verstehen* (Tübingen: J.C.B. Mohr [Paul Siebeck], III, 1960, 91–106, esp. p. 112; *The Presence of Eternity,* p. 31. Thus Bultmann's point in the quotation under discussion is that salvation is independent of the course of international political history. Of course, this is not meant in the sense of the common distinction between "particularism" and "universalism," where preferring the latter to the former would move in the direction of Pannenberg's own position. Rather Bultmann is here distinguishing the Christian understanding of history not only from an understanding oriented to the national history of Israel, but also to an understanding in terms of world history. This latter distinction is to be understood in Gogarten's sense: "A person's relation to history will differ, depending on whether one holds the whole breadth of its development for the real revelation of God, or whether one sees the real revelation in the original deed of God that does not flow into its effects and consequences, to be modified by them and hence recognized in them, but rather that must again and again be grasped in its pure originality beyond its historical effects and formations, however important these may also be." "Vom heiligen Egoismus des Christen (Eine Antwort auf Jülichers Aufsatz: 'Ein moderner Paulus-Ausleger')," *Die christliche Welt,* XXXIV (1920), 548, reprinted in *Anfänge der dialektischen Theologie,* I, 101.

[69] In connection with a (valid) use made by Pannenberg of an exegetical insight from Bultmann's *Theology of the New Testament,* Georg Muschalek, S.J., comments: "Bultmann's real concern in Section 37, which Pannenberg quotes in support of his thesis, is a diametrical contradiction of Pannenberg's thesis to the effect that 'the truth (of revelation) lies so patently before everyone's eyes that the natural and only possible result, in terms of the matter itself, is that it would have to be perceived.'" Cf. Georg Muschalek, S.J., and Arnold Gamper, S.J., "Offenbarung in Geschichte," *Zeitschrift für katholische Theologie,* LXXXVI (1964), 180–196, of which Parts 1 and 3 are by Muschalek, Part 2 by Gamper. The quotation is from p. 192.

apart from (even though presumably leading to)[70] faith as one's own commitment.[71]

Bultmann himself expresses his view as follows: "Faith also speaks of God acting in his control of nature and history, as Creator and Ruler. Indeed faith must so speak. For if man in his existence knows himself both called into life and sustained by God's omnipotence, then he knows also that the nature and history within which his life takes place are permeated by God's action. But this knowledge can be expressed only as confession and never as a general truth such as a theory of natural science or a philosophy of history. Otherwise God's action would be objectified to a worldly transaction. The statement of God's creatorship and dominion has its legitimate ground only in man's existential self-understanding."[72] In reply to a critic advocating an interpretation of him analogous to that of Pannenberg, Bultmann has said: "He over-

---

[70] Cf. the "Postscript" to *Offenbarung als Geschichte,* 2nd ed., p. 147; *ThLZ,* LXXXVIII (1963), 86, 90 f.; and below, pp. 86–89; and Pannenberg's lead essay, pp. 129–131.

[71] Körner, *Eschatologie und Geschichte,* p. 123: "But since this 'history' is exclusively a fact to faith, a fact that in principle can never be demonstrated as a factual event, which is what historiography has as its objective—since otherwise it would become rigidified into an empirical condition and then would no longer have anything to do with eschatological occurrence—hence Bultmann usually avoids the term history. This history is to be made intelligible only ontologically as a possibility. Hence it is more fitting to speak of it as 'authentic historic being' or as 'eschatological existence.' By means of this circumlocution the indirectness of the revelation is brought to expression . . . , i.e., the fact that man as a being in history has no unmediated relation to God in which he could have definitive hold of his authenticity. The ontological formulation is more suited as a scholarly means to this purpose than is history, because the intention of the ontological talk is to give up any pictorial description of a so-called Christian history and to point only to the possibilities of Christian existence in terms of man's being. . . . It is possible . . . to speak this way . . . because Bultmann roots history ontologically in historicness, i.e., every human actualization of being always must in some way be 'history' and the 'new history' is basically history in general, under the promise of faith."

[72] "Zum Problem der Entmythologisierung," *Kerygma und Mythos, VI, 1. Entmythologisierung und existentiale Interpretation (Theologische Forschung,* 30; Hamburg-Bergstedt: Herbert Reich, Evangelischer Verlag, 1963), p. 26. Cf. similarly *Glauben und Verstehen* (Tübingen: J.C.B. Mohr [Paul Siebeck], 1952), II, 101–104 [*Essays Philosophical and Theological* (New York: The Macmillan Company, 1955), pp. 115–118].

looks the fact that existential understanding is not subjectivity, and that the nature of revelation as encounter is not denied in that it is designated as inaccessible for objectifying historical research. He fails to see that revelation is not thereby separated from history because he does not see the paradox that dominates the whole presentation of the Gospel of John, namely that the historical activity of Jesus is at the same time eschatological occurrence."[73]

Bultmann has recently addressed himself explicitly to the question of his own view of history as distinguished from that of von Campenhausen, which lies in the background of that of the Pannenberg group. For a Czechoslovakian pastor, J. A. Dvoracek, had been corresponding with von Campenhausen on this point, and sent their correspondence to Bultmann, who replied in a letter of October 6, 1961: "You understand correctly that it is my opinion that historical research can only produce data that can be objectively established, and this only with relative certainty. Demonstrating the origins of the Christian message by means of historical research would only establish this message as an historical phenomenon, and would not, however, establish it as the authentic, faith-producing 'message,' as the word of God addressing me. Further, you understand very correctly that I do

[73] "Zur Interpretation des Johannesevangeliums," *ThLZ*, LXXXVII (1962), 8. Bultmann is here reviewing David Earl Holwerda's dissertation at the Free University at Amsterdam, *The Holy Spirit and Eschatology in the Gospel of John* (Kampen: Kok, 1959). He answers the analogous criticism of Käsemann similarly: "Can one then deny that the consciousness of belonging to the people, to the new eschatological covenant, determines the self-understanding of each individual?" Bultmann, "Ist die Apokalyptik die Mutter der christlichen Theologie? Eine Auseinandersetzung mit Ernst Käsemann," *Apophoreta* (Haenchen-*Festschrift, Zeitschrift für die neutestamentliche Wissenschaft, Beiheft* 30, 1964), p. 65. In a further "Answer to Ernst Käsemann" Bultmann says: "To this (criticism) is to be said first of all that I do indeed distinguish existentialistic interpretation from objectifying (interpretation), but that I do not separate the one from the other. I would have thought I had emphasized often enough, over against the misunderstanding of existentialistic interpretation as subjectivistic, that existentialistic interpretation cannot be separated from the objectifying view of the historical phenomena." *Glauben und Verstehen* (Tübingen: J.C.B. Mohr [Paul Siebeck], IV, 1965), p. 192. Pannenberg's position would be to the effect that contrary to his intention Bultmann's position involves subjectivism.

not wish to free the message from history (and not from the church, either). Rather the relationship between history (as world history) and the event of revelation is a dialectical one, that is to say, the Christian faith asserts the paradox that a purely historical event is, at one and the same time, an eschatological event. With this assertion we include the statement that the event of revelation must at the same time be proclaimed as an historical event. Otherwise we could surrender the paradox. The Christ event must, therefore, to use your words, be proclaimed as a 'hidden mystery' that happens in this empirical-historical world and its history. It is just this dialectic or paradox that Professor von Campenhausen does not appear to have fully grasped. Otherwise he could not characterize the resurrection of Jesus as an event that breaks through the created order and causality of the world right in the middle of its historical continuity, as an event 'in which the old world with its laws really comes to an end'—in other words, as a miracle. The end of the old world through the eschatological event, as that which continually comes to pass through proclamation and in faith, is open only to faith, and is for every other view (therefore, also for historical science) hidden. In the place of this dialectic, von Campenhausen puts the miraculous rupturing of the reality of this world."[74]

Thus the situation in which Pannenberg's theology emerges is not simply that of history having been eliminated in favor of existentialism by Bultmann, but rather that of different versions of the Christian understanding of history and hence different implications for the structuring of theology. Pannenberg does not regard man's historicness as a universal ontological reality, but rather as an acquired trait of Western man,

[74] Quoted by Gilbert E. Bowen, "Toward Understanding Bultmann," *McCormick Quarterly*, XVII (1964), 26–39, pp. 34 f. Cf. also Bultmann's "Answer to Ernst Käsemann": "Do I advocate a dualism when I distinguish between the church as institution and as eschatological event. . . ? No! For it is of course clear to me that there is no such thing as an eschatological event in history without corporeality. But in this case it is I who speak of dialectic. The relation between the church as institution and as eschatological event is a dialectic (relation)." *GuV*, IV, 198.

the effect on him of Biblical history.[75] Hence it cannot function for him as an all-embracing category as it does for Bultmann. Instead Pannenberg speaks directly of "history" as "reality in its totality."[76] What Pannenberg is seeking to do is to carry through in a way somewhat analogous to Whitehead the replacement of static ontological categories by those for which history provides the model. "The historic process as such has become the bearer of meaning."[77] It is not, however, his purpose to produce a Christian narration of history, what he calls a "total conception of history," i.e., "a conception of the whole course of history in terms of revelational history,"[78] which would indeed, as Kierkegaard argued, limit both the freedom of God and man and the contingency of history;[79] rather he wishes to achieve a "total view of reality as history directed by promises toward fulfillment."[80]

Pannenberg traces the development of this understanding of reality as history from ancient Israel to the present. In the course of Israelite history the fulfillment is progressively extended out into the future toward the end of history, so that the whole historical process takes on the directional character inherent in the prophetic vision and finds therein its unity. The completion of this development is found in Jewish apocalypticism, which is in turn the context in terms of which

[75] *KuD*, V (1959), 232 [*Essays on Old Testament Hermeneutics*, pp. 332 f.].

[76] *Ibid.*, p. 222; Eng. tr., p. 319.

[77] *Ibid.*, p. 219; note 2; Eng. tr., pp. 315 f.

[78] *Ibid.*, p. 235; Eng. tr. omits at p. 333.

[79] *Ibid.*, pp. 234 f.; Eng. tr. omits at p. 333.

[80] *Ibid.*, p. 237; Eng. tr., p. 335. Although such formulations indicate the direction, they are an exploratory effort to break new ground and hence at times fall short of the intention and are subject to immanent criticism in terms of intention. The defining of history as coterminous with reality leaves unclarified what reality is to be attributed to the end of history when God is fully revealed, and suggests a dualism inherent in the timeless reality after history's end, if that is more than a limiting concept for Pannenberg. The reality of such a position as is able to look back upon ended history is emphasized subsequently by such statements as the following: "The revelation grounded by the course of history can be an event only at its end, i.e., after the totality of occurrences run their course, which in turn receive their ultimate light only from the end." So in the "Postscript" to the 2nd ed., of *Offenbarung als Geschichte*, p. 142, note 25.

primitive Christianity is to be understood.[81] Hence Christianity is seen carrying on the Biblical understanding of reality as history through the development of Western civilization, until, with the Enlightenment, man replaced God as the agent held to be at work in history. This elimination of God from historiography has as its outcome theology's failure to maintain

---

[81] In apocalypticism, "end-of-history eschatology has merely replaced the prophets' within-history eschatology," *KuD*, V (1959), 223; Eng. tr., p. 321. This is the reverse interpretation of apocalypticism from that, e.g., of Gerhard von Rad. *Theologie des Alten Testaments; Die Theologie der prophetischen überlieferungen Israels* (Munich: Christian Kaiser Verlag, 1960), II, pp. 314–321, which is largely followed by Jürgen Moltmann, *Theologie der Hoffnung,* pp. 120–124, and would imply that apocalyptic thinking is "history-less" (Moltmann, p. 121). "This contradictory impression is due to the fact that in prophetic eschatology the horizon of promise both in its breadth and in its depth reaches the limits of what we can designate cosmic finitude. But when the historic horizon of the historic hopes has in its development reached these *eschata,* then one is confronted with the possibility of forsaking the historic location of one's perspective and of reading the historic course of the world backwards from the end one envisions, as if universal history is a *universum,* a predetermined historic cosmos. Ancient cosmological speculations about numbers are introduced in order to establish the order of the periods of world history in a way that corresponds to the order of space. The world kingdoms are fixed. The *eschaton* becomes fate. Then, in the place of election that directs one to hope and obey, there emerges—providence, which determines events. In the place of promise, in which one hopes in spite of what appears as the only hope, there emerges—the end drama. In the place of the eschaton that God calls forth in his freedom, there emerges—the finale of history that comes to be by the passage of time. In the place of God's faithfulness in which one trusts for the fulfillment of the promised future in God's freedom, there emerges—the plan of God that is fixed from the beginning of time and is unveiled successively by history. A historic theology becomes a theology of history and a historic eschatology becomes an eschatological view of history. Just as in the *Heilsgeschichte* theology of the 18th Century, there lurks in apocalypticism a noticeable deism of the distant God. On the other side one should not overlook the fact that there is always an element of exhortation in the speculative apocalypses. It is the exhortation to persevere in the faith of the just. He who holds out to the end will be blessed. But faith and unbelief, good and evil, election and reprobation, the righteous and the unrighteous, are fixed, and one remains what one is. This in turn corresponds completely to the setting of apocalypticism in the life of the withdrawn conventicle." *Ibid.,* pp. 121 f. Cf. similarly Gerhard Sauter, *Zukunft und Hoffnung: Das Problem der Zukunft in der gegenwärtigen theologischen und philosophischen Diskussion* (Zürich/Stuttgart: Zwingli Verlag, 1965), esp. the section on "Revelation and History," pp. 239–251 of the chapter on "Apocalypticism and Eschatology."

the historical basis of its faith. Pannenberg's objective, in the light of this analysis, is to create a situation in which faith can rest on historically proven fact. This is not simply a matter of proving objective facts, to which the Christian attributes a significance not shared by the historian as such. "If the really decisive thing, the revelatory and saving significance of what happened to Jesus of Nazareth, can be seen only by faith and is on principle inaccessible to rational research into what happened, then it is impossible to see how the historicity of pure facts is to protect faith against the suspicion of resting on illusion and arbitrariness."[82] Luther's insistence upon the clarity of the word of Scripture is applied to the clarity of history as bearing within itself its nature as revelation.[83]

The meaning of historical occurrence can ultimately be grasped only in terms of the total sweep of history, just as individual units of research are carried on in terms of a working hypothesis concerning their relation to an overarching concept. This universal scope may not however be permitted to weaken the recognition of the contingency of history. Hence the universality may not be conceived in terms of an evolutionary or morphological pattern to which history conforms. The tension one senses in retaining both values can be overcome by identifying a common base for universality and contingency. This cannot be man, "since [man's] spirit always exists only as an individual and for the individual."[84] Hence a transcendent ground in God is to be inferred by rational argumentation,[85] as an *a posteriori* confirmation of

---

[82] *KuD*, V (1959), 275.

[83] *Ibid.*, pp. 275 f. In criticism of this interpretation of Luther's emphasis on the clarity of Scripture, cf. Lothar Steiger, "Offenbarungsgeschichte und theologische Vernunft. Zur Theologie W. Pannenbergs," *ZThK*, LIX (1962), 113.

[84] *Ibid.*, p. 284.

[85] Hans-Georg Geyer, "Geschichte als theologisches Problem. Bemerkungen zu W. Pannenbergs Geschichtstheologie," *EvTh*, XXII (1962), 92–104, esp. pp. 96 f. criticizes Pannenberg here to the effect that his position is "a postulate of historical reason," a "transcendental deduction of the concept of history." Pannenberg replies in his "Postscript" to the second edition of *Offenbarung als Geschichte*, p. 138, note 15, that Geyer

the Old Testament understanding of history. His freedom is the source of contingency, his faithfulness the source of continuity; the latter is visible to man only in retrospect, not in terms of a plan for the future. Hence only at the end of history will the total wholeness of contingent history be apparent. This position is identified with the Israelite-Christian view of God and history, which is thus the condition of the possibility of comprehending the unity and contingency of history.[86]

The historiographical execution of this program must take account of the fact that the meaning of universal history cannot be derived from a small segment of history, but only from the total sweep of history visible only at the end of history. Yet the role of Jesus' resurrection as the proleptic anticipation of that end of history to some extent removes it from the category of just a particular and makes of it the key for attaining a universal grasp of history before the end comes. Thus the historical proof of the resurrection can serve as a materially decisive model for Pannenberg's procedure, as an alternative to Bultmann's access to the resurrection in the existential encounter with the historic witness of the church.

Pannenberg takes his point of departure in a critical scrutiny of a basic principle of historical method, the use of analogy: comparison with what is already known provides a touchstone for evaluating the probability that a reported thing actually occurred and for establishing its specific contours. Pannenberg argues that at times an ideological element in-

---

"fails to note that it is not only a matter of rational construction, but also of the presuppositions, in terms of the history of the transmission of traditions, for modern thought about history." Jürgen Moltmann, *Theologie der Hoffnung*, p. 68, note 98, questions whether Pannenberg's procedure of inferring a doctrine of God from history, which Moltmann sees as parallel to the Greek procedure of inferring a first principle from the cosmos, is appropriate to the Biblical understanding of history.

[86] Pannenberg, *ibid.*, p. 287. Cf. Geyer, *ibid.*, p. 98: "For the logical construction of that mode [sc. of retrospectively connecting events into a broader context], the claim of a transcendent ground is a superfluous axiom, to the extent that the categories of the unity of history and the individuality of the historical suffice as presuppositions."

tervenes, in that we assume an overarching similarity of all phenomena, which in effect limits the freedom of history. Troeltsch had argued for the "principle similarity of all historical occurrence, which to be sure is not identity, but rather leaves all necessary room for differences, but for the rest presupposes in each case a kernel of common similarity, on the basis of which the differences are to be understood and tested."[87]

For Pannenberg, comparison is for the sake of establishing that which is individual and distinctive about the phenomenon under consideration. Hence such comparison may not be used to obscure that which is distinctive, by classifying it as just another instance of a given category. The result of this corrective is that the lack of historical analogy loses any decisive role in determining the historicity of an event. "If analogies that have been found are used in this way in awareness of the limit of their validity, they hardly can serve *in Troeltsch's way* as the criterion for the reality of an event affirmed by the tradition. The fact that a reported event breaks the analogy of what is otherwise customary or frequently attested is not in itself sufficient grounds to contest its factuality."[88] Thus Pannenberg thinks he could overcome "the main argument against the historicity of the resurrection of Jesus."[89] The common denial that the resurrection is *historisch* "rests on remarkably weak grounds."[90] The argument from analogy can be used to indicate nonhistoricity only indirectly, in terms of finding formal analogies, i.e., "if in historical sources positive analogies to unreal forms of transmission (such as myths, but also legends) or [to unreal] phenomena of consciousness (such as visions) can be identified."[91] By arguing there are

[87] *Gesammelte Schriften*, II, 732, cited by Pannenberg, *KuD*, V (1959), 264.
[88] *KuD*, V (1959), 266.
[89] *Ibid.*, note 22.
[90] *Ibid.*
[91] *Ibid.*, 267 f. For Pannenberg's subsequent adjustment of his position with regard to the appearances as visions, cf. *Grundzüge der Christologie*, pp. 88–93, and below, p. 38.

not such formal analogies for Jesus' resurrection, Pannenberg proposes to make room for it as an "event without analogy," as von Campenhausen argues,[92] without making it necessary to affirm it to be a miracle, as Bultmann found to be the case with von Campenhausen's position.[93]

We can to some extent trace the way this proof of the resurrection has been subsequently carried out. In a public debate with Herbert Braun on February 19, 1965, Pannenberg presented a series of theses about Jesus' resurrection that point the direction of a "theological historiography" that would provide the basis for a historical argument for the resurrection. He again identified as the major hindrance the ideological element in historiography that uses analogy to argue that the dead do not rise: "The contesting of the historicity of Jesus' resurrection is based *primarily* on general ideological considerations. In generalizing the experience that, as far as we can see, the dead remain dead, the possibility of a dead person becoming alive again, however it may take place, is precluded *a priori*."[94] (Thesis 8.) Then the condi-

[92] *McCormick Quarterly,* XXVII (1964), 34. In his programmatic essay Pannenberg is arguing in defense of von Campenhausen's approach to Jesus' resurrection.

[93] Pannenberg for his part rejects the concept of miracle as being in tension with the concept of creation. "If God were not the creator, then his will could be carried through in the world only through naked miracles, by eliminating all other forces affecting history. But his will is not done in this way at the expense of human activity, but is actualized precisely through the experiences, planning and action of men, in spite of and within their sinful distortion. Theological historiography, by laying hold of God's activity in such directness, i.e., by searching for relationships among occurrences, in concrete immanent circumstances (to be sure without interpreting away what is novel and more or less without analogy in events), witnesses to God as creator of the world," *KuD,* V (1959), 288. In Pannenberg's opinion it would in any case be difficult to argue that an occurrence is to be regarded as miraculous in the common connotation of the term as referring to a breaking of the laws of nature. For with appeal to modern physics he argues: we do not know all the laws of nature; natural law controls only an aspect of events; the validity of natural law is itself contingent. Since the natural scientist can make no definitive judgment, the decision as to whether an unusual event occurred is left to the historian. *Grundzüge der Christologie,* pp. 95 f. Thus the miraculous as a functional category is eliminated from consideration.

[94] The average reader probably takes this to be what is involved in

tions that would have to be met to be able legitimately to classify the resurrection as an instance of a nonhistorical narrative or experience are so sharply defined as not only to place the burden of proof upon those who would deny its historicity but also to suggest that such a proof is not likely to succeed. Thesis 9 reads: "The traditions of Jesus' resurrection would be subject to evaluation as unhistorical if:

"a) the Easter traditions were demonstrable as *literarily secondary constructions* in analogy to common comparative religious models not only in details, but also in their kernel,

"b) the *Easter appearances* were to correspond *completely* to the model of self-produced *hallucinations* (owing to organic peculiarities or medicines),

"c) the tradition of the *empty tomb* of Jesus were to be evaluated as a *late* (Hellenistic) *legend*."

It is not an evaluation of the synoptic tradition that provides the basis of Pannenberg's argument for the empty tomb. His argument on this point is the historical rather than literary consideration that the church in Jerusalem would have had

---

Bultmann's position, since his emphasis has in fact been directed toward rejecting any historical description or proof of the resurrection and toward presenting instead its kerygmatic meaning as providing the Christian interpretation of the cross. Hence his talk of the Lord Jesus being encountered in the kerygma has perhaps been taken as more figurative than he really intends. Cf. the following statement in the discussion with von Campenhausen, *McCormick Quarterly*, XXVII (1964), p. 37: "You are correct that 'the all-embracing effectiveness of the preaching of Christ is brought into question in so far as it does not give as its basis the real Christ event and as its goal the living fellowship with Christ.' We agree also 'that eternal life through the presence and future of Christ has a concrete eschatological dimension even beyond death.' And I agree when you characterize the hope as a real hope for a final victory over death and the fulfillment of the gift of fellowship and the new existence out of grace alone. This is no mythological speculation. I would only characterize a hope in this way that pictures objectively the new existence 'out of grace alone,' and that would be the case if one understood the new existence in eternal life as a once-for-all possession. But can it ever be anything other than a gift that continually retains its character as a gift? . . . In the new existence there is no more opposition [of "the old 'I,'" as "in earthly life, life in time"] (continual temptation). The distinctions end in the new existence, in eternity. Is that mythological speculation? I think not, even as surely as we must refuse every visualization."

to reach clarity about the grave very early and hence can be safely assumed to have assured itself of its emptiness. "Even if the report we have of the finding of Jesus' grave should turn out to be a late legend conceived first in the Hellenistic church, the weight of the arguments presented [for this historical consideration] would remain intact."[95] Thus the proof of c) would not in fact disprove the empty tomb, which in any case is not a primary factor for Pannenberg in the argument for the resurrection.

With regard to condition a), which has in its background the question whether the appearances can be classified as instances of "unreal forms of transmission," such as myth or legend, Pannenberg points out the "penetrating material difference" between eschatological resurrection and revival of persons who return to normal earthly life and presumably will die again.[96] Some have affirmed on the basis of this distinction that only the latter of these conceptions was characteristic of apocalypticism and that Paul's concept of resurrection as transformation was his distinctive departure from apocalypticism. Pannenberg rejects this view, affirming that "Paul did not arrive at his view of the resurrection as transformation first under the impression of his encounter with the resurrected Jesus. The view of the differentness of the resurrection life as imperishableness, in distinction to the present perishable body, has Jewish parallels."[97] Thus, he is concerned to identify in a more than external way the Easter expectation with forms of expectation provided by Jewish apocalypticism.[98] "The fact that the completely other reality that was experienced in these appearances could be understood as the encounter with one risen from the dead can only be explained on the presupposition of a particular form of apocalyptic ex-

[95] *Grundzüge der Christologie*, p. 99.
[96] *Ibid.*, p. 73.
[97] *Ibid.*, p. 77.
[98] Pannenberg follows Gerhard Kittel in affirming there is "hardly the slightest trace" of the cults of dying and rising gods in first-century Palestine. *Ibid.*, p. 88.

pectation of the resurrection of the dead.''[99] This might seem
to suggest that the reality experienced at Easter was not in
itself a resurrection, but that "resurrection" was simply one
of the languages in which it was interpreted.[100] And indeed
Pannenberg can speak of "resurrection" or "rising" from the
dead as a metaphor built upon the concept of rising from
sleep. "Resurrection" can hence be called a "picture," a "par-
able," of the reality intended. "The intended reality and the
way it is spoken about are essentially different. . . . Rather
there is involved a parabolic way of speaking of an event that
is still hidden from us in its true essence."[101]

At this point a person who, in distinction from Pannenberg, regards resurrection language as mythological, could
think of demythologizing as a way of expressing this essence
more comprehensibly than is possible in the language of apocalypticism. Or one might take the language in which the
essence comes to expression somewhat more seriously than

[99] *Ibid.*, p. 89 f.
[100] Willi Marxsen, *Die Auferstehung Jesu als historisches und als theologisches Problem* (Gerd Mohn: Gütersloher Verlagshaus, 1964; 2nd ed.
1965), follows through this alternative in discussion with Ulrich Wilckens.
Rather than describing the original experiences of the disciples as "appearances of the Resurrected" (cf. Pannenberg, *ibid.*, p. 87), Marxsen
thinks it is more accurate to describe them as experiences of recognizing
Jesus, and hence as "appearances of the Crucified" (p. 16). He points
out that Paul, in describing his Damascus road experience, does not
speak of an appearance of the Resurrected, but rather of "Jesus our Lord"
(1 Cor. 9:1), "God's Son" (Gal. 1:15). It was then an inference, an
interpretation, a way of bringing to expression the encounter with Jesus
alive, when reflection as to how it was that he was encountered as alive
led to the use of the apocalyptic language of resurrection. And Marxsen
argues it was not the only such language. When appearances are interpreted as the commissioning of the disciples, resurrection language is
lacking in early traditions, not only in Paul, but Matt. 28:16–20 and
John 20:19–23, although the merging of the two interpretations and their
language does take place (Acts 10:40–42). From this role of resurrection
language as only one of alternate interpretations of the appearances
Marxsen concludes that "in the case of the resurrection one cannot in a
real sense speak of a datum," but rather of an interpretation of the datum
that the event of God that was taking place in the public ministry of
Jesus, "which was *really* over with his death, began anew with the experience of seeing him" (p. 33). To refer to resurrection as itself the
event is a "forbidden historicizing of an interpretation" (p. 34).
[101] *Ibid.*, p. 70.

does Bultmann by regarding the whole as a language event in which the language is involved in the event, but can in turn give way to other language, as the point scored in the original language event is translated into new situations and thought forms. This would move in the direction of the hermeneutical theology of Gerhard Ebeling, who says on this point: "Both Jesus' assurance, becoming audible after his death, and faith's concurrence that enters in upon that assurance, came to expression as Jesus' resurrection, since it is Jesus' life becoming revealed—to be sure by borrowing apocalyptic conceptualizations, and yet as the arrival of the eschaton already, which breaks down the essence of apocalypticism."[102] Yet Pannenberg maintains that this statement regards apocalypticism as "just any means of expression among others," and rejects it with the assertion "that this significance of the event, even if it 'breaks down' the apocalyptic expectation, could be expressed only in the language of the apocalyptic tradition and hence remains related to the apocalyptic horizon of expectations precisely in its uniqueness."[103] Apparently Pannenberg means by this that Easter remains related to apocalypticism in a sense that goes beyond the truism that a historical occurrence cannot escape from its original context; rather the implication is that the Easter event may not be translated completely out of apocalyptic categories by theology today. "Though apocalyptic portrayals of the end of the world may be false in many details, yet their main lines, the expectation of a resurrection of the dead in connection with the end of

---

[102] *Theologie und Verkündigung (Hermeneutische Untersuchungen zur Theologie, 1; Tübingen: J.C.B. Mohr [Paul Siebeck], 1962), p. 91, cited by Pannenberg, Grundzüge der Christologie, pp. 93 f. Willi Marxsen, ibid., pp. 25 f., develops Ebeling's position by referring to the Easter message as "the carrying on of Jesus' subject matter," "set in motion by the experience of seeing him," for which the source Q is an instance. Incidentally, Q, like the Gospel of Thomas, lacks resurrection language (except in an Old Testament quotation, Lk. 7:22). He presents this as an alternative to Wilckens' view, Offenbarung als Geschichte, pp. 58–63, to the effect that Jesus' ministry was in need of God's ratification by the resurrection, which for Marxsen would make of the earthly Jesus "only a prelude," "the precursor of the Resurrected" (pp. 31 f.).

[103] *Grundzüge der Christologie*, p. 93 f., n. 94.

the world and the final judgment, remain true also for us."[104]

Pannenberg holds that resurrection is an "absolute metaphor." "It is metaphorical, and indeed in the sense of the 'absolute metaphor' that is not more or less interchangeable with other pictures and cannot be reduced to a rational kernel different from it, but is itself the only appropriate expression for a certain situation."[105] To some extent this is meant in the sense that metaphorical language is as near to reality as we can get, so that the metaphor is not to be transcended by rational conceptualization. In part the inescapability of metaphorical language seems to imply a literal reality that is not usually implied in the concept of metaphorical language. Anthropological considerations of man's need to hope in an afterlife, which can today be conceived only in psychosomatic terms of the union of body and soul,[106] provide the argument for this literal apocalyptic ingredient in resurrection faith, which Pannenberg hence refers to as "an anthropologically interpreted apocalyptic expectation."[107] Thus the recognition that the Easter event conforms in its essence or kernel to a comparative religious model, the Jewish apocalyptic view, rather than implying nonhistoricity at the literal level, becomes part of an argument for retaining the main lines of the apocalyptic picture."[108]

[104] *Ibid.*, pp. 78 f.

[105] *Ibid.*, p. 189.

[106] *Ibid.*, pp. 79 ff. To this Johannes Wirsching, "Ein neues theologisches System? Randbemerkungen zur Theologie W. Pannenbergs," *Deutsches Pfarrerblatt,* LXIV (1964), 607, poses critically the rhetorical question: "The resurrection reasonable because it fits men's longing?"

[107] *Ibid.*, p. 104.

[108] An alternate position to that of the Pannenberg circle has been presented by Willi Marxsen, who argues that since "resurrection" is an interpretation derived from reflection on the fact of Jesus' appearances, we should work back through this interpretive process to come to grips with what was being interpreted and then seek to say in our language what that which was being interpreted means in our language today: "Since God resurrected Jesus, and since Jesus consequently is the Resurrected, then he did not remain in death. So he is the Living One. Hence his 'subject matter' is not ended with his death. Therefore what he brought is not simply past and lost to the past, but *is also valid today still.* Hence when I say Jesus has been raised, then this conviction those people

With regard to the form of experience that would suggest nonhistoricity, Pannenberg speaks in Thesis 9 b) of hallucinations rather than visions, since subsequent to his negative evaluation of visions in "Redemptive Event and History" Hans Grass had convinced him the resurrection appearances were, in form, visions.[109] Hence the term "vision" is now taken to say "something about the subjective way of experiencing, but not something about the reality of the occurrence experienced in this form."[110] Visions lacking "extra-subjective" reality are hence designated "hallucinations"; but such nonobjective phenomena "only rarely" occur.[111] "Especially in the area of

---

gained by means of reflection is quite literally *un*interesting so long as I do not say *at the same time:* He is the Resurrected because he, identical with the Earthly One, also still *comes* today with the same (old) claim. But if I say that, then I must clearly realize that I do not absolutely need to appropriate the concept 'the Resurrected,' but that I must indeed of necessity speak of 'the Living One.' And that is actually more, for to refer to him as 'the Resurrected' only gives him a designation, in a conceptualization provided by the history of religion, and this by moving onesidedly from the return of the Crucified to life to just this conceptualization given in the historical context." Marxsen, *ibid.,* p. 27. Thus Marxsen would understand the Easter kerygma to the effect that the "event of God" in the public ministry of Jesus has begun to happen again in the living Christ.

109 *Ibid.,* p. 90, citing Hans Grass, *Ostergeschehen und Osterberichte* (Göttingen: Vandenhoeck und Ruprecht, 1956; 2nd ed., 1962), p. 229.

110 *Grundzüge der Christologie,* pp. 91 f. In effect the indirect historical argument about an alleged incident's historicity, in terms of formal analogy to kinds of narration or experience, seems to be evolving into a more direct argument in terms of positive historical analogy. In a letter Pannenberg clarifies his position as follows: "Does not the formation of our concepts of myth, legend, and vision [sc. insofar as they imply nonhistoricity] rest precisely on *positive analogies,* in that we experience in the present that in the creation of legends today things are claimed that never happened (whereas instead something else happened). Hence where we find positive analogies in old traditions, we regard them likewise as legendary and are skeptical of their claims with regard to their having happened." Thus the argument against historicity would seem to rest less in the classification of a reported incident within certain narrational or psychological categories than upon the close similarities of the reported incident to a modern incident known to be nonhistorical. When such is lacking, as would often be the case, no argument from analogy would function.

111 *Ibid.* Contrast the rejection of such considerations by Karl Barth, *Die Auferstehung der Toten* (Munich: Christian Kaiser Verlag, 1924),

the history of religions, where it is always exceptional occurrences that are recounted, the psychiatric concept of vision [i.e., hallucination] cannot at all be postulated in cases where there are no more exact indications for that fact in the tradition."[112] Thus the possibility of proving the resurrection appearances to be hallucinations becomes very remote, and their conformity to the form of visions no longer weighs against their historicity.

The outcome of this remarkable *tour de force* is the claim of a proof of the historicity of the resurrection, which Pannenberg carefully formulates as follows: "In this sense then the resurrection of Jesus is to be designated as a historical event: If the origin of primitive Christianity that, quite apart from other traditions, is traced back also by Paul to appearances of the resurrected Jesus, is, in spite of all critical testing of the tradition, intelligible only if one regards it in the light of the eschatological hope of a resurrection from the dead, then that which is so designated is a historical event, even though we do not know anything more specific about it. Hence an event is to be maintained to have happened historically that can only

---

p. 78 [*The Resurrection of the Dead*, tr. by H. J. Stenning (Westwood, N.J.: Fleming H. Revell Co., 1933), pp. 137 f.]. "May it not be described as simple tactlessness, to make of 'He appeared,' or what takes its place in the Gospels (appearances of angels and subsequently personal meetings with Jesus), with the liberals, so-called visions (with the extraordinarily profound distinction between 'objective' and 'subjective' visions), or, with the 'positives,' equally banal 'historical facts,' respecting which one can refer to the 'sources' for support, as in the case of all other facts, with only the distinction that what happens here is marvellous beyond comparison and that one is constantly exposed to the danger of running into the arms either of the Scylla of a gross mythology or the Charybdis of a coarse or refined spiritualism—quite apart from the bad historical conscience which we would develop, and which might suddenly drive us once more to the liberal friends of visions! As if this 'positive' manner of asserting the resurrection of Jesus were not in fact the secret denial of the very thing we would fain assert, the resurrection as the deed *of God*, which no eye has seen nor ear heard, which has entered no human heart, neither outwardly nor inwardly, neither subjectively nor objectively, neither mystically nor spiritualistically nor flatly historically, but as a historic divine fact, which as such is only to be grasped in the category of revelation and in none other."

[112] *Grundzüge der Christologie,* p. 93.

be expressed in the language of the eschatological expectation."[113]

This materially decisive instance of the relation of historiography to theology is the model for the general approach to the perennial problem of "faith and history." On this issue the alternative Bultmannian position is shared not only by Barthians, but also by such conservative Lutherans as Paul Althaus and Walter Künneth, namely that the resurrection is not historically demonstrable.[114] Bultmann comes to this position from the following considerations: For modern historiography, as for modern science in general, the "God hypothesis" is not necessary (Laplace).[115] Bultmann has no theological reason to contest this situation of modern science, since for him God, understood in terms of the theology of the cross, is known only paradoxically or dialectically. The meaning of history is furthermore not scientifically ascertainable, but is experienced by the person open to history in his confrontation with it in current events, as a possibility for his own living.[116] Thus Bultmann's position involves a dialectic relation between the objective establishment of facts and of their traditional interpretation, on the one hand, and the existential encounter with current events or with the present witness to past events, on the other.

Pannenberg concedes there is "something correct" about the

[113] Ibid., p. 95.

[114] Cf., e.g., the reservation in the otherwise favorable reception of Pannenberg's programmatic essay by Ulrich Kühn, "Das Problem der zureichenden dogmatischen Begründung der christlichen Auferstehungshoffnung," KuD, IX (1963), 16, with regard to "a few daring formulations about the verifiableness of the historic saving action of God."

[115] Kerygma und Mythos, VI, 1, p. 20; ZThK, LX (1963), 337 [JThC, II (1965), 85].

[116] Cf. Kerygma und Mythos, VI, 1, p. 22: "Being future is the reality in which man stands. This becomes clear in the history of mankind in that the historic meaning of an event always becomes intelligible only in terms of its future. The future belongs essentially to the event. Only from the end of history is consequently the meaning of historic occurrence finally intelligible. But since such a view from the end is impossible for human eyes, a philosophy that seeks to understand the meaning of history is not possible. One can speak of the meaning of history only as the meaning of the moment that has meaning as the moment of decision."

view behind the denial of the historical verifiability of Easter, to the effect that "the reality of the new aeon of course could not be perceived with the eyes of the old aeon; the historian has to judge in terms of the rules of the old aeon and hence can say nothing of the resurrection of the dead."[117] Yet to this view Pannenberg adds: "Since the life of the Resurrected has to do with the reality of a new creation, the Resurrected is indeed not perceptible as an object among others in this world. For that reason he could be experienced only by means of the exceptional kind of experience, the vision, and could be designated only in a symbolic language. But in this way he nonetheless made himself known in our reality, at a quite definite time, in a limited number of events, to certain specific persons. Hence these events are also to be affirmed or contested as historical events, as occurrences that actually took place at a quite fixed time in the past. If we were to give up the concept of a historical event, then it would no longer be possible to maintain that the resurrection of Jesus or the appearances of the resurrected Jesus really took place in our world at a given time. There is no valid ground to claim the resurrection of Jesus as an event that really took place if it is not as such to be maintained to be historical."[118]

From these historically verifiable facts man can gain knowledge of God, if such facts are not seen in isolation but in a context of traditions that speak of God in an "understandable way." "*Then* it is true that in an event—not equally in every event!—God is *recognized again*, to be sure in a new way, in modified form; and only in this context and in this sense would one 'infer' God from an event—to the extent that all recognition implies the logical structure of an inference."[119]

[117] *Grundzüge der Christologie*, p. 96.
[118] *Ibid.*
[119] Quotation is from a letter of clarification from Pannenberg. He apparently does not accept the distinction made, e.g., by Marxsen, *ibid.*, p. 12: "The fact that in encountering Jesus during his lifetime one encountered God remains hidden to historical knowledge. Historical knowledge (i.e., historical exegesis) can always take note only of the claim of the witness to have encountered God in Jesus." Pannenberg has not yet

It is in this sense that revelation can be seen as history, once criticism of the presuppositions of historical method has produced a theological historiography, that is to say, a historiography maintained by theologians to be valid for all history. Systematic theology would provide a Christian view of history as a model or working hypothesis in terms of which the Christian historian would do his detailed research, with its conclusions in turn filling in and modifying that picture. Lest this remain a ghetto separating off the Christian historian from his secular colleague, Pannenberg would argue that the Christian working hypothesis is more adequate than that implicit in secular historiography. Thus the dualism of a sacred and a profane historiography would be overcome in theory by denying the validity of secular historiography at those points where the two diverge.

### III. The Debate in Old Testament Scholarship

If a constitutive ingredient of the position here under discussion is the theological role it attributes to historical research, then one would expect that the issues can be presented in historical terms. This is especially true in the case of Old Testament research, where the school found its initial point of departure. One may compare the way in which Bultmannian theology can be debated in terms of New Testament research as well as in terms of contemporary theology. Indeed when Pannenberg was described[120] as having a "system" for which his colleagues in the historical disciplines only provided "preliminary studies," he clearly rejected such an "honor." "Rather the first impulse came from Rolf Rendtorff, who brought the

---

made fully clear the step from the historical observation that an event occurred in a context in which people believed in God and his action to the theological knowledge by the historian that their belief is true, and the differentiation of such knowledge brought by the historian to the specific occurrence from the view, rejected by Pannenberg, that a theological understanding of the event is limited to the believer.

[120] Lothar Steiger, "Offenbarungsgeschichte und theologische Vernunft. Zur Theologie W. Pannenbergs," *ZThK*, LIX (1962), 90 f.

problem of revelation into relation with Zimmerli's studies on the 'word about [God] demonstrating [himself]' (*Erweiswort*) and characterized this 'word of demonstration' as the most important contribution of the Old Testament to this question."[121] For Pannenberg's insight to the effect that contemporary theology means by revelation primarily the revealing of God himself[122] would seem to put in question not only a theology anthropologically oriented, but also one oriented to an understanding of history. It was Zimmerli's research on the "word of demonstration" that made it possible to interpret Old Testament history as a revelation about God himself.

Zimmerli's basic discovery came within the context of preliminary studies for a commentary on, of all things, Ezekiel, which he himself approached in Barthian terms of a theology of the word of God. His inaugural address as a Professor in Göttingen in 1951 had been on "The Word of God in Ezekiel,"[123] where Ezekiel's "call to genuine decision in the here and now" is God's word of promise answering man's word of despair or is a reactualizing of God's word given by an earlier prophet in terms of the new situation of the exile.[124] And the first major breakthrough in Zimmerli's form critical study of Ezekiel[125] seemed to point in the same direction: He discov-

---

[121] "Postscript" to *Offenbarung als Geschichte*, 2nd ed., p. 132.

[122] Pannenberg, *ibid.*, laid before his group this factor in contemporary theology as still in need of adequate "grounding." Cf. his "Introduction" to *Offenbarung als Geschichte*, pp. 7–20.

[123] Cf. "Das Gotteswort des Ezechiel," *ZThK*, XLVIII (1951), 249–262, reprinted in *Gottes Offenbarung: Gesammelte Aufsätze zum Alten Testament* (*Theologische Bucherei*, 19; Munich: Christian Kaiser Verlag, 1961), pp. 133–147. The title of Zimmerli's collected essays, "God's Revelation," is due to the inclusion of the same essays Rendtorff builds upon, which according to Zimmerli "inquire how God, according to the Old Testament witness, steps forward from his mystery and how human knowing is able to encounter him as he steps forward" (Preface, p. 8). Thus the volume is intended to present thematically his alternative to Rendtorff, which his article " 'Offenbarung' im Alten Testament," *EvTh*, XXII (1962), 15–31, presents more in a form conditioned by the debate. For this reason (according to the Preface) the latter essay is omitted from the collected essays.

[124] *Gottes Offenbarung*, pp. 143 ff.

[125] "Ich bin Jahwe," *Geschichte und Altes Testament, Albrecht Alt zum 70. Geburtstag dargebracht* (*Beiträge zur historischen Theologie*, 16;

ered a "self-presentation formula," in which the deity introduces himself: "I am Yahweh." Although this formula was subsequently expanded with predications about Yahweh (". . . thy God," ". . . who brought thee out of the land of Egypt," etc.), the form critical analysis suggested to him that the brief form is prior, in that the formula is not intended to make predications about the god, but rather to present him.[126] We have to do with "the full, personal presentness of Yahweh in his word."[127] The very fact that Yahweh is described as raising his hand, i.e., taking an oath, as he gives his name, indicates that he is giving his word. "This revelation of Yahweh's name is a revealing of God that happens to certain men, binds him to them, [so that he] remains true to them for the sake of his oath."[128]

Thus far Zimmerli's research could well have led him, e.g., in the direction of Ebeling's "word event," a term which in fact occurs in Zimmerli's writing.[129] Yet growing reserve about the Bultmannian alternative[130] and further research on Ezekiel led gradually into a somewhat different emphasis: God is faithful to his word by carrying out what he promises in history. Thus the history that God brings forth is the carrying out of the revelation of God's person that took place in revealing his name. History is seen not as an end in itself, leading to an "understanding of history," but rather as revealing God,

---

Tübingen: J.C.B. Mohr [Paul Siebeck] Verlag, 1953), pp. 179–209, reprinted in *Gottes Offenbarung*, pp. 11–40.

[126] *Gottes Offenbarung*, p. 14.

[127] *Ibid.*, p. 17.

[128] *Ibid.*, p. 21.

[129] *Ibid.*, p. 110. Cf. also, p. 86: "Old Testament faith is of the opinion that in such a report of Yahweh's deed a full re-actualization happens, in which complete, not just secondary, knowledge can be attained."

[130] Zimmerli on occasion presents his position in rejection of terms that, though vague and anonymous, do point to Bultmann, or, more precisely, to the prevalent misunderstanding of his position. *Ibid.*, p. 80: knowledge of God is not derived "from the analysis of man and the world's being"; p. 108: "all the prerequisites for knowing Yahweh do not lie in man and a pre-understanding to be found in him"; p. 109: "knowledge of God cannot be won by means of an analysis of the world's being and of its causer's being or an analysis of man's existence, nor can it be won by means of clarifying the world with a myth."

and the focus of this revelation tends to shift from God giving his word to the history vindicating that word. "Yahweh's history with Israel is the place where the truth of his revelatory word is knowable in that it is carried out."[131]

Zimmerli works out this position in analyzing a larger formula in which the "self-presentation formula" is quoted: ". . . and they are to know that 'I am Yahweh.' "[132] This larger formula he calls the "cognition formula." It stands normally at the end of a prediction about God's action in history, through which the self-revelation in his name is vindicated. The addition of the "cognition formula" to the prophet's prediction turns the prediction about history into a "pointer to Yahweh's historic self-demonstration in his action, to be known by man."[133] This whole "prophetic word about God demonstrating himself" is a *Gattung* of prophetic speech that Zimmerli designates the "word of demonstration,"[134] i.e., the prophetic "word" to the effect that Yahweh will "demonstrate" himself to be God through historical occurrences that will take place. The basic instance of a "word of demonstration" is the prophet's speech in 1 Kings 20:28: "And a man of God came near and said to the king of Israel, Thus says Yahweh, Because the Syrians have said, Yahweh is a god of the hills but he is not a god of the valleys, therefore I will give all this great multitude into your hand, and you shall know that 'I am Yahweh.' " Thus the "self-presentation formula," originally located in the priestly "service of the word" at a cultic shrine or in the temple, is embedded in the "cognition formula" that turns a prophet's prediction about history into a "word of

---

[131] *Ibid.*, p. 22.

[132] *Erkenntnis Gottes nach dem Buche Ezekiel. Eine theologische Studie* (*Abhandlungen zur Theologie des Alten und Neuen Testaments*, 27; Zürich: Zwingli Verlag, 1954), reprinted in *Gottes Offenbarung*, pp. 41–119.

[133] "Das Wort des göttlichen Selbsterweises (Erweiswort), eine prophetische Gattung," *Mélanges Bibliques rédigés en l'Honneur de André Robert* (*Travaux de l'Institut Catholique de Paris*, 4; Paris: Bloud et Gay, 1957), pp. 154–164, reprinted in *Gottes Offenbarung*, pp. 120–132, quotation from p. 124.

[134] *Gottes Offenbarung*, p. 121.

demonstration of God," which is carried by the prophet out into the midst of life, there to vindicate its power in calling forth history.

Zimmerli understands his form critical research, i.e., his detection of the "self-presentation formula," the "cognition formula," and the "word of demonstration," in terms of a coordination of word and history. "The prophetic word of demonstration, where (with but few exceptions, in Ezekiel) the pure formula of self-presentation, 'I am Yahweh,' is used, is formulated in view of this occurrence in the worship service and understands itself as inwardly coordinated to it, even when it is spoken far from the shrine in the midst of battle (1 Kings 20). The truth of 'I am Yahweh' proclaimed back there in the congregation—the prophetic word now says— shows itself out here in the midst of the historic event, under the promissory word of the prophet (prophecy)."[135] Yet when the prophet's word points to "the historic proof for the truth of the claim that lives at the center in the worship service," i.e., "shows the truth and majesty of 'I am Yahweh,' "[136] then the role of the original proclamation "I am Yahweh" as full self-revelation might seem to some extent to be put in question. This relativizing of the word seems especially apparent when "the circle of people to whom the showing is to be visible cannot be limited to those directly addressed in the prophetic saying, but reaches far beyond,"[137] e.g., "all the trees of the field" (Ez. 17:24), "all flesh" (20:48), "all the inhabitants of Egypt" (29:6), "the nations" (36:23, 36; 37:28; 39:7, 23).[138] Here the structure of revelation seems to have shifted, contrary to Zimmerli's own intention, from a vindication of God's revelatory word by history into a revelation simply through historical occurrence itself.

It is in light of this research on Ezekiel and the "word of demonstration" that Rolf Rendtorff seeks to carry through the

---

135 *Ibid.,* p. 126.
136 *Ibid.,* pp. 127 f.
137 *Ibid.,* p. 128.
138 *Ibid.,* p. 131.

thesis that, for the Old Testament, God reveals himself primarily in history.[139] His positive presentation concerning revelation through history is prefaced with an analysis of such other Old Testament alternatives as might suggest revelation is to be separated from history. The Old Testament word that is most literally translatable as "revelation" can be safely ignored, since it is not a specifically theological term but is used primarily in nontheological contexts. In these cases even the Septuagint translation, *apokalyptein*, means simply "uncover."[140] Another verb, meaning "be seen," "appear," was originally used with cult etiologies, to legitimize a shrine as a place where a god was seen; but this verb is increasingly separated from such shrines and associated with promise and narration, i.e., it is historicized.[141]

[139] "Die Offenbarungsvorstellungen im Alten Israel," *Offenbarung als Geschichte*, pp. 21–41. Cf. the report and comment on Rendtorff by Arnold Gamper, S.J., "Offenbarung in Geschichte," *ZKTh*, LXXXVI (1964), 186: "One can establish as the final outcome that knowledge of God is possible only on the basis of his historical action. (Is Zimmerli here correctly understood?)"

[140] Zimmerli in his reply, " 'Offenbarung' im Alten Testament," *EvTh*, XXII (1962), 15–31, insists, p. 16, that such a formulation as Is. 22:14, "Uncovered is Yahweh Sabaoth in my ears," followed by an announcement of judgment in the form of an oath, is "not unimportant for determining the Old Testament's formulation of revelation." "The word of warning pressing forward to the occurrence, a word echoing in the ears of the prophet, is here said to be the place where God becomes revealed." Arnold Gamper, S.J., "Offenbarung in Geschichte," *ZKTh*, LXXXVI (1964), 185, maintains that the secular and religious meanings are not as readily separable as Rendtorff would seem to assume.

[141] Zimmerli, *ibid.*, pp. 16 f., casts this development more in the direction of the shift from sight to audition. "As the really significant element there emerges the promissory announcement in word that points to coming occurrence. A further movement, e.g., away from word to pure occurrence, in which the word of promise in turn is devalued as something insignificant and preliminary, cannot be found in what has been treated thus far. A splitting of the word of promise and the occurrence it announces is in any case not suggested here." Similarly Günter Klein, "Offenbarung als Geschichte? Marginalien zu einem theologischen Programm," *Monatsschrift für Pastoraltheologie* (abbreviated *MPTh*), LI (1962), 68, argues that this development points to word rather than directly to history, in that the announcing of future deed is itself word, and in that Rendtorff himself, *Offenbarung als Geschichte*, p. 27, asserts that attention is "not directed to a certain deed of the past," but rather assurance for the future is "attained from the *tradition* of Yahweh's sav-

Another Old Testament concept that might come in question, the appearance of God's "glory," was originally located in the heavenly temple or its earthly equivalent (Is. 6:3), but was also historicized (Ps. 97:6; Is. 40:5). Yet the priestly tradition does not share this location of the appearance of God's glory in historical occurrences, but rather regards the glory as "an entity of precise spatial dimensions, that comes down from heaven from time to time and in which Yahweh himself is present,"[142] either in connection with the cult,[143] or related to history—yet with a difference. "In distinction from the non-priestly tradition, 'seeing God's glory' does not here mean seeing his show of power directly; the glory appears rather in order to proclaim the imminent show of Yahweh's power."[144] This priestly understanding of God's glory as his appearance inaugurating[145] the cult or proclaiming what he is going to do is analogous to Zimmerli's understanding of the priestly "self-presentation formula" as God's self-revelation, or his emphasis on the revelatory role of the word even in the "word of demonstration" pointing to history. Yet Rendtorff regards the other view of God's glory, that it appears in "the obvious carrying out of his power" in the sight of "all flesh"

ing acts" (italics by Klein), which is again word. (Rendtorff, however, also points to individual acts of the past, such as the Exodus.)

[142] Rendtorff, *Offenbarung als Geschichte,* p. 29.

[143] *Ibid.,* pp. 30 f. To be sure, even here Rendtorff discovers "an expressly historic function" of the glory, in that it institutes and thus legitimizes the cult. But is this not simply an instance of the original cultic etiological use of the term that was characteristic of its Canaanite origins?

[144] *Ibid.,* p. 30. It is unclear why Rendtorff adds: "Here the priestly alteration is especially evident. The glory has received such dignity that it remains in the background as the initiator of events, veiled in cloud." Is not this concept of God's glory rather a direct development of the original cultic context (cf. p. 29, where the "clouds" in Ps. 97:2 are so understood), and more in agreement with the other aspect of the priestly use of the concept, in that the appearance limited to a cultic place becomes an appearance "only before the eyes of Israel" (p. 31)?

[145] Rendtorff, *ibid.,* p. 30, seems to regard the role of God's glory in the cultic sense as "completed" once the cult is established, and rejects the view that there is "a self-revelation of God in the cult" (p. 32). Although the Priestly Document, to which Rendtorff here has reference, may not refer to God's glory continuing in the temple while the cult is in operation, this view would seem to be presupposed in priestly circles by Ezekiel.

(Is. 40:5) in history,[146] as the normative Old Testament position.

When Rendtorff then turns to Zimmerli's formulae, his presentation rapidly falls into the pattern of a criticism. Zimmerli had regarded "I am Yahweh" as a "formula of self-presentation," especially needed in the context of its polytheistic origin. "One previously unnamed comes forward out of his unknownness by making himself knowable and namable with his own name."[147] Rendtorff points out that this does not fit the *locus classicus* in the Old Testament, Ex. 3:6, in that here God introduces himself to Moses as the God *known* to his fathers. "Obviously the reference back to the previous history of God with the fathers is the decisive element" in the formula, and it is coupled with a promise of events to come.[148] Hence Rendtorff argues that the brief version of the formula, consisting only of "I am Yahweh," is not the original form, as Zimmerli had assumed, but "a reduction of the expression to a formulation of extreme pregnancy."[149] To this Zimmerli replies that the short form occurs in prophetic oracles of the ninth century (1 Kings 20:13, 28) and probably in the usage of the Jahwist, so that the argument of historical priority may be contested.[150] This form critical debate is an instance of the theological debate as to whether God's revelation is primarily in his word, with God being present[151] and thus revealing him-

[146] *Ibid.*, p. 29. Zimmerli in his reply, *EvTh*, XXII (1962), 18, speaks rather of the "distinctive duplication" of God's glory in nature and history on the one hand and in the "verbal encounter" on the other and emphasizes that the latter is "something quite different from a merely human flow of words." In his "Postscript" to the 2nd ed. of *Offenbarung als Geschichte*, p. 132, Pannenberg refers to history as "a reality going beyond mere words." Thus the divergence is to a considerable extent over the meaning of the concept "word."

[147] Zimmerli, *Gottes Offenbarung*, p. 11, cited by Rendtorff, *Offenbarung als Geschichte*, p. 33.

[148] Rendtorff, *ibid.*, p. 33. Zimmerli does not think that this "logical contradiction" that "seems to result," alters the nature of the formula as one of self-presentation, *EvTh*, XXII (1962), 20. E.g., in *Gottes Offenbarung*, p. 25, he says: "God presents himself as one already known by referring to what is already known or what has already happened."

[149] *Ibid.*, p. 34.

[150] Zimmerli, *EvTh*, XXII (1962), 20.

[151] Zimmerli, *ibid.*, emphasizes against Rendtorff that the formula pre-

self in the proclamation of the self-presentation formula, or whether the revelation is primarily in history, to which the formula "I am Yahweh who . . ."[152] refers. Hence it is not surprising that at this point Pannenberg intervenes in the Old Testament debate to argue that since the early instances of the self-presentation formula to which Zimmerli appeals are all embedded in the cognition formula, they are to be regarded as abbreviations of the longer historical form of the self-presentation formula called for by Pannenberg's position.[153]

Rendtorff focuses attention positively on one aspect of Zimmerli's presentation as "above all important": "The revelation of Yahweh is here not understood as if it were visible [only] to a certain group of people or as if there were special presup-

---

sents (makes present) rather than represents (describes) God. In *Gottes Offenbarung*, p. 15, Zimmerli speaks of the "dissolution" of the formula of self-presentation "where the predication about the name Yahweh is put as an emphasized predicate before the whole formula of self-presentation and the name Yahweh is degraded to an attribute of the subject: 'Holy am I, Yahweh your God.' " Cf., also, p. 30. It is indicative of the different approaches that Rendtorff, *Offenbarung als Geschichte*, p. 33, and *EvTh*, XXII (1962), 628, states in criticism of Zimmerli that in some instances (e.g., Gen. 26:24) the name Yahweh does not occur, even though such an exception cannot here be attributed to the Elohist, whereas Zimmerli, *EvTh*, XXII (1962), 21, can appeal to the complete absence of a divine name in the "predicate" ("I am," Is. 48:12), to show that the formula is intended as one in which God presents himself rather than as one in which he characterizes himself or conveys information. Of course the reduction to "I am" is in form also a "dissolution" of the formula, *Gottes Offenbarung*, p. 30.

152 Rendtorff is contesting the accuracy of Zimmerli's form critical analysis. E.g., he says of the use in sacral law, where the formula follows the legislation: "An understanding of the formula as one of 'self-presentation' is in any case excluded," *Offenbarung als Geschichte*, p. 35. In *EvTh*, XXII (1962), 628 f., he argues that the reference to history is constitutive of the formula as formula; in the royal psalms a predication in the third person ("Yahweh is king") seems to be the basic form. He does not accept Zimmerli's criticism that he had reduced the self-presentation formula to a neuter predication, since the formula in his view is insisting it is "Yahweh and no other who is spoken about," *EvTh*, XXII (1962), 628, note 16. Perhaps by "neuter" Zimmerli had meant to refer to Rendtorff's focus upon something said about a person in distinction from his own focus upon the person presenting himself.

153 *Grundzüge der Christologie*, p. 126, note 29. A somewhat parallel criticism is made by the systematician Jürgen Moltmann, *Theologie der Hoffnung*, pp. 102 f.

positions for knowing it. All nations, 'all flesh,' the ends of the world see what happens, and it is intelligible to them all in its significance as Yahweh showing himself."[154] This emphasis leads Rendtorff to assume momentarily a position which they have subsequently modified[155] when critics sensed it as the direction in which they were moving: the replacement of word with history, rather than an understanding of the two in their unity. "Especially in view of the nations that are to know Yahweh in his action from sunrise to sunset, a tying of revelation to the prophetic word seems to be from the very outset excluded."[156] In response to this Zimmerli comes nearest to an antithetic stance, which in general he has sought to avoid. "Where do these odd inferences come from, which quite obviously are not able to do justice to the Old Testament?"[157]

Rendtorff's idea of God's revelation in history apart from the word may well have come in large part from the Pannenberg group's antithetic relation to the theology of the word of God; but in this instance it would seem to be due as well to Zimmerli's presentation of Ezekiel.[158] In reply to Rendtorff Zimmerli can say that in some instances (e.g., Ez. 25) the nations recognize Yahweh in history because of knowing about him in contacts with Israel. Yet Zimmerli concedes: "But alongside such sayings one may note that Ezekiel in his peculiar use of formulae, using obviously traditional phrases and expanding them greatly and using them in new contexts, supplies little express information as to how the name of Yahweh and his warning prediction come to the nations. That breaks through first in Second Isaiah, yet then with unmistakable clarity."[159] Second Isaiah defines Israel as "my witnesses" to

[154] *Offenbarung als Geschichte,* pp. 38 f.

[155] Especially in Rendtorff's reply to Zimmerli's article "Geschichte und Wort im Alten Testament," *EvTh,* XXII (1962), 621–649, he begins by quoting Zimmerli to the effect that history is not to be separated from the word and saying that he agrees "completely," p. 622. Cf. below, p. 58.

[156] *Offenbarung als Geschichte,* p. 40.

[157] *EvTh,* XXII (1962), 24.

[158] Cf. above, p. 46, at notes 137, 138.

[159] *Ibid.,* p. 24.

the nations (43:10; 44:8). "An isolation of the occurrence effected by Yahweh from the word sent in advance is especially in Second Isaiah an exegetically untenable undertaking."[160] Just as Second Isaiah opens with the word of Yahweh that remains forever (40:8), it concludes with a concept of the word effecting history that Zimmerli appropriates: "It shall not return to me empty, but it shall accomplish that which I purpose, and prosper in the thing for which I sent it" (55:11).

Zimmerli does not simply throw the Old Testament concept of the word over against that of history, but rather seeks to provide a definition of the Old Testament understanding of history in continuity with that of the word. Word is "itself occurrence that moves the world and history"; conversely "occurrence is actualized word, proclamation made good."[161] This means with regard to history: "It does not carry hidden within it a secret meaning that man can figure out by means of his own capacity to interpret. Rather God can make it become a living appeal to man by sending a spokesman who names Yahweh's name upon this event."[162] This view of history is more precisely stated as follows: "This faith understands that the historic rescuing act over which Yahweh's name is proclaimed is an aimed occurrence, which is not intended to be understood in the connection of a historic whole, but rather to be heard today as a call under Yahweh's name, and is to be understood and responded to in reverent and believing obedience."[163] Rendtorff in turn denies one must choose between such alternatives. "Precisely in the prophets it is quite clearly discernible that their retrospective views of history and talk of Yahweh's plan, etc., are intended to pre-

---

[160] *Ibid.*, p. 25. Here Moltmann, *Theologie der Hoffnung*, p. 104, shares Zimmerli's criticism. Cf. also Schweizer, cited above, p. 18 f., and Arnold Gamper, S.J., "Offenbarung in Geschichte," *ZKTh*, LXXXVI (1964), 188. In reply Rendtorff points out, *ibid.*, p. 628, in Zimmerli's words, that Israel witnesses to what God has *done*.

[161] *Ibid.*, p. 25. Rendtorff, *ibid.*, p. 622, accepts Zimmerli's formulation.

[162] *Ibid.*, pp. 28 f.

[163] *Ibid.*, p. 29.

pare their contemporaries to recognize the imminent event as Yahweh's action."[164] Yet there do emerge different judgments as to which is primary for the Old Testament, with Rendtorff finding that prophets interpret all the better the further they have an overview of history—so that degrees of knowledge of God are related to the extent of history in one's vision, and complete knowledge possible only at the end of history—and Zimmerli finding the focal Old Testament emphasis to be that upon the importance of "proclaiming into the very hour," "calling for faith"[165]—so that one would not speak of degrees of knowledge, but rather of whether the word strikes home and produces faith.

In view of Rendtorff's unwillingness to see in "I am Yahweh" a revelation of God in his name, Zimmerli senses "the degeneration of language and hence also of [the understanding of the role of] naming in our time."[166] Pannenberg had indeed in his introduction to *Revelation as History* drawn attention to antiquity's identification of the name with the being, as the context of the Barthian location of the revelation of the person in the disclosure of the name. "But the meaning of announcing the name in Ex. 3 is precisely not that from now on the Israelites know Yahweh's essence completely. The communication of Yahweh's name takes place—as 3:15 expressly says—for the purpose of being able to *call on* Yahweh with this name. An important event—Israel thus received the possibility of communion with Yahweh! But this is not self-reve-

---

[164] *Ibid.*, pp. 622 f., and esp. p. 640.

[165] *Ibid.*, p. 29.

[166] *Ibid.*, p. 23. Zimmerli's own presentation of the role of divine names in *Gottes Offenbarung*, pp. 127 f., could itself have suggested to Rendtorff his position. For Zimmerli had contrasted the non-Israelite concept of name as the deity's power, where discovering the god's name means access to his power (e.g., in the Egyptian myth of Isis and Re), and where the glorification of the god consists in multiplying divine names (e.g., in the case of Marduk), with the Israelite view: "The whole display of the glory of the self-presentation in the name is awaited by Israel from Yahweh's *historic action.*" Rendtorff, *EvTh,* XXII (1962), 643, 648, also points out that the potency of the divine word is a concept current in the Ancient Near East, which would suggest that it is basically a mythological concept and not distinctive of Israel.

lation in the sense of full self-disclosing."[167] Thus the revealing of Yahweh's name is not for Pannenberg itself self-revelation, but is subordinate to the self-revelation to take place in history. When the revealing of God's name is put in the context of a "word of demonstration" of God in history to come (Ex. 6:7), Rendtorff can emphasize the importance of the new event at the burning bush. "Finally the concept of Yahweh showing himself is obviously sensed as inappropriate in general. . . . In Ex. 6:3 one reads: 'I let myself be seen by Abraham, Isaac and Jacob as God Almighty, but did not make myself known to them by my name Yahweh.' Here knowing is set over against seeing, and there can be no doubt but that this takes place quite consciously in the careful terminology of the Priestly Document. Yahweh's being seen is relegated to a preliminary stage. With Moses something new begins: Yahweh gives himself to be known as *himself*."[168] Zimmerli describes this, understandably enough, as a "beautiful observation"[169] on Rendtorff's part. But Rendtorff himself did not understand the priority of God's name in terms of the primacy of the word of God, but rather in terms of history (the "name" pointing ultimately to the Exodus) vs. theophany (which could however include a religious experience manifesting God's hypostatized name,[170] in distinction from historic occurrences from which God's name, i.e., might and deity, can

---

[167] *Offenbarung als Geschichte,* p. 13. Contrast Zimmerli, *Gottes Offenbarung,* p. 17: "the full personal presentness of Yahweh is his word." Similarly Arnold Gamper, S.J., "Offenbarung in Geschichte," *ZKTh,* LXXXVI (1964), 185, expresses his disagreement with Pannenberg's evaluation. Gerhard von Rad, *Theologie des Alten Testaments; Die Theologie der geschichtlichen Überlieferungen Israels* (Munich: Christian Kaiser Verlag, 1957; 2nd ed., 1958), I, 182 [*Old Testament Theology, The Theology of Israel's Historical Traditions,* tr. by D. M. G. Stalker (New York: Harper & Row, 1962), I, 180], interprets the passage as a rejection of a "definition of Yahweh's essence in the sense of a philosophical statement about his being."

[168] *Offenbarung als Geschichte,* p. 25.

[169] *EvTh,* XXII (1962), 17. In *Gottes Offenbarung,* p. 44, the verbs for seeing and knowing had been described as "parallel" and "analogous."

[170] Zimmerli, *Gottes Offenbarung,* p. 34, had called this "theophany." But he refers, p. 40, to the "further development within priestly literature, in which the element of epiphany recedes and the self-presentation formula

be inferred). That is to say, he interprets the passage in line with Pannenberg's value structure.

An emerging focus upon the "history of the transmission of traditions" provides the possibility of transcending the alternative thinking that necessitated the question of the relative priority of prophetic word or historic occurrence. Indeed Rendtorff and Zimmerli seem both to wish to insist upon "event in the context of the history of the transmission of traditions."[171] This seems to function for Rendtorff as the integrating factor pulling together all the various kinds of history that come into question: the past history about which the stories tell, the contemporary history that molds the way the stories are told, and the history of the transmission itself as the central stream in Israel's cultural and intellectual history.[172] Here the model is the period prior to the amphictyony, which in the sense of political history is rather prehistoric, but where the decisive historic occurrences that can be discerned were precisely the development and merging of traditions, which is the basic thing the tribes were "doing" as they came together. "On all sides it becomes clear that the origin and development of traditions is an essential component of Israel's history. Indeed the occurrences really effecting history are often to be found here, occurrences that determine Israel's history over and beyond the fluctuation in political conditions."[173] "Hence with regard

---

is clearly to be located in the worship services oriented to the word," as the reemergence of a basic trait of the Yahweh cult. "Mowinckel's rejection of the *culte de la parole* cannot be maintained as sharply as he did." Cf. also, *Gottes Offenbarung*, p. 26.

[171] *Offenbarung als Geschichte*, p. 40. Rendtorff quotes this formulation later, *EvTh*, XXII (1962), 622, to document his basic agreement with Zimmerli in this regard.

[172] This was first suggested in an essay, "Hermeneutik des Alten Testaments als Frage nach der Geschichte," *ZThK*, LVII (1960), 27–40, on which cf. my essay, "The Historicality of Biblical Language," in *The Old Testament and Christian Faith: A Theological Discussion*, ed. by Bernhard W. Anderson (New York: Harper & Row, 1963), pp. 130 f. Rendtorff has presented a more advanced statement in his essay, "Geschichte und Überlieferung," *Studien zur Theologie der alttestamentlichen Überlieferungen*, ed. by Rolf Rendtorff and Klaus Koch (Neukirchen Kreis Moers: Neukirchener Verlag, 1961), pp. 81–94.

[173] "Geschichte und Überlieferung," p. 88.

to the question as to God's action in Israel's history we will
not rest content with the alternative between what critical historical research works out and the picture of history painted
in the Old Testament. The history of Israel takes place in the
external procedures that are customarily the object of the
critical historical study of history *and* in the many inner procedures in many layers that we summarize in the concept of
tradition. Only the total picture resulting from both shows in
the full sense Israel's history."[174] Rendtorff thus proposes to
overcome the usual compartmentalization within Biblical studies into "History of Israel," "Introduction to the Old Testament," and "Theology of the Old Testament," under the
uniting concept of the "history of the transmission of traditions."[175] And Pannenberg can say that "the history of the
transmission of traditions" is "to be classed in general as the
more profound concept of history."[176]

The understanding of the history of the transmission of
traditions in the school of von Rad should hardly give consola-
tion to the traditionalist, for the frequency of the mutations
of the tradition is clearly emphasized in Volume I of his *Old
Testament Theology* which is devoted to *The Theology of
Israel's Historical Traditions.*[177] When correctly understood,
the method of *Traditionsgeschichte* is as critical as is *Formgeschichte* (whose English translation "form criticism" is quite
appropriate), even though both differ from the antecedent
historical criticism in that the question as to the historicity of
the events narrated in the tradition is for the most part brack-

---

[174] *Ibid.,* pp. 93 f.
[175] *Ibid.,* p. 94.
[176] "Kerygma und Geschichte," *Studien zur Theologie der alttestamentlichen Überlieferungen,* p. 139. Cf. the criticism by Jürgen Moltmann, *Theologie der Hoffnung,* p. 101: "This occurrence of transmission,
by means of which continuity is created in the fluctuations of history,
cannot be taken as itself a deeper concept of history. The procedure of
transmission in which one recalls history and has new historic experiences
is only intelligible from what is transmitted: the promise, and the events'
future it opens up."
[177] *Theologie des Alten Testaments; I, Die Theologie der geschichtlichen Überlieferungen Israels* [*Old Testament Theology, The Theology
of Israel's Historical Traditions,* I].

eted (although there is indirect relevance to this issue). There is, however, something of a divergence of focus between *Traditionsgeschichte* and hermeneutic. In the former case the focus is upon a tradition, and the point being scored in any given narration of that tradition is investigated primarily as an influence in the forming of it. But it is not such a point that is followed up by this method, but rather the course of the given tradition, so that one traces continuity in the material used even where the points being scored stand in extreme discontinuity. The false prophets assuring Ahab victory at Ramoth-gilead (1 Kings 22:10–12) are an instance of the holy war amphictyonic tradition in Israel.[178] Conversely hermeneutic has as its focus what happens when the language is used, the point being scored, so that it tends to be open to finding continuity where there is no continuity of tradition, from which results the problem of "anonymous Christianity."[179] This divergence of emphases can also be seen in the way in which those oriented to hermeneutic emphasize the verbal meaning of tradition, i.e., transmission, that aspect that can best be coordinated with the translational process taking place in the ongoing language event.[180]

[178] Cf. Rendtorff, "Erwägungen zur Frühgeschichte des Prophetentums in Israel," *ZThK*, LIX (1962), 155 f.: "In the context of our inquiry we may not without further ado take our point of departure in the answer that the prophets give, but must initially inquire again as to the tradition lying behind it. Obviously inquiring of Yahweh before an expedition is also rooted already in the tradition of holy war. . . . Obviously the difference between Micaiah the son of Imlah and the other prophets is not in terms of the tradition in which he stands. The contrast is rather in terms of the different evaluations of the war. . . . Of course one may not play down the contrast. The problem of 'false prophets' occurs here for the first time. But the debate is not concerning different forms of prophecy. Rather it receives its acuteness precisely due to the fact that both opposing prophets or groups of prophets are rooted in the same tradition, that of the amphictyony."

[179] Cf., e.g., Heinrich Ott, "Existentiale Interpretation und anonyme Christlichkeit," *Zeit und Geschichte*, (*Festschrift* for Rudolf Bultmann; Tübingen: J.C.B. Mohr [Paul Siebeck], 1964), pp. 367–379.

[180] Hans Georg Gadamer, *Wahrheit und Methode: Grundzüge einer philosophischen Hermeneutik* (Tübingen: J.C.B. Mohr [Paul Siebeck], 1960), p. 275, uses the term *Überlieferungsgeschehen*, the "occurrence of transmission," to make this emphasis (compare Bultmann's shift from *Heilsgeschichte* to *Heilsgeschehen*). Cf. also, p. 355 (cited in *The New*

Rendtorff had completed his essay in *Revelation as History* with an explicit attempt to do justice to the fact that "the word has here an essential share in the occurrence of revelation."[181] Yet it was this brief discussion that had drawn the most criticism. Hence Rendtorff replied with an article, "History and Word in the Old Testament,"[182] which seeks more fully to explicate his position. He begins by pointing out that what he is denying is the necessity for the intervention of a prophet's word for an event to become revelatory, and that his rejection here of the term "word" does not involve a denial of the necessity for tradition.[183] Israelite narrators stood in a tradition, and so the conviction that Yahweh acts in history was "the presupposition on the basis of which it first became possible at all to speak meaningfully of history."[184] What is needed is not an inspired interpreter, such as an apocalyptic seer like Daniel. Instead, the Jewish tradition supplies the interpretation, which is now recognized to be a necessary presupposition. This presupposition is necessary for the nations as well as Israel—as indeed the Bible has functioned as a hermeneutical key within gentile Christianity. Although Rendtorff makes here no allusion to his previous statement, he

---

*Hermeneutic,* p. 75). Gerhard Ebeling, *Theologie und Verkündigung* (*Hermeneutische Untersuchungen zur Theologie,* 1; Tübingen: J.C.B. Mohr [Paul Siebeck], 1962), pp. 14 f. (cited in *The New Hermeneutic,* p. 68), emphasizes the verbal element in the Latin noun *traditio* by setting it off against the term *traditum,* the unambiguous term for the substantial meaning, "what is transmitted." Cf. also, Ebeling's book, *Wort Gottes und Tradition: Studien zu einer Hermeneutik der Konfessionen* (*Kirche und Konfession: Veröffentlichungen des Konfessionskundlichen Instituts des Evangelischen Bundes,* 7; Göttingen: Vandenhoeck und Ruprecht, 1964).

181 *Offenbarung als Geschichte,* p. 40.

182 "Geschichte und Wort im Alten Testament," *EvTh,* XXII (1962), 621–649. It is in the form of a lecture, and hence only in the extended footnotes does he explicitly speak to his critics' points.

183 *Ibid.,* p. 623.

184 *Ibid.,* p. 635. Cf. also, p. 629: It is from the divine instruction and reassurance that "the occurrence is knowable as divine action." In "Geschichte und Überlieferung," p. 90, he says: "If we today seek to know God's action, how are we to establish where he acted if Israel's interpretation may not serve us as a guide line?" Cf. above, note 55.

seems to have given up what he initially regarded as "above
all important," that the nations also know Yahweh from history and hence this knowledge "is not in need of special presuppositions."[185] Even though Zimmerli wishes to speak of this
presupposition in Barthian vocabulary as the word, while
Rendtorff speaks in terms of the history of the transmission of
traditions, the area of disagreement would seem to have nar-
rowed. Indeed Rendtorff moves away from his original restric-
tion of the term "word" to a prophet's proclamation, in which
context he had denied it to be a necessary presupposition, and
concludes by suggesting that the indispensable tradition can be
so designated.[186]

Yet Rendtorff proceeds to draw the concept of tradition into
a more functional relationship with a different concept, that
of the divine plan for history. He draws attention to presentations (such as the histories of David's rise to power and of the
struggle as to his successor, and the story of Joseph) in which
the events are not correlated to a prophet's word,[187] but are

---

[185] *Offenbarung als Geschichte,* pp. 38 f.

[186] *EvTh,* XXII (1962), 623, 649. Günter Klein, "Offenbarung als
Geschichte? Marginalien zu einem theologischen Programm," *MPTh,* LI
(1962), 68–70, argues that the various historical insights of Rendtorff
point to an orientation in terms of word rather than history. The primary
intention of the "cognition formula" is not to convey historical information about what Israel's opponents knew in encountering Israel, e.g., that
Israel's God is the true God. Rather the formula functioned primarily
within the subsequent life of Israel as a word of assurance. With regard
to Old Testament statements about history, the question as to whether
they refer to historical fact in distinction from themselves as an event of
language often remains an open question. (Compare Christian Hartlich
and Walter Sachs, *Der Ursprung des Mythosbegriffes in der modernen
Bibelwissenschaft* [Tübingen: J.C.B. Mohr (Paul Siebeck), 1952], pp. 157
f. Since the context of traditions is indispensable for a new occurrence
to be revelatory, Klein concludes it is these traditions, i.e., word, that
provide the revelatory dimension.

[187] Pannenberg, *KuD,* V (1959), 221, in dependence on von Rad, had
presented the situation differently: "In the beginning stands the promise
to David by the prophet Nathan, the assurance of a continuation of the
Davidic dynasty. Everything reported in what follows stands under the
question: Who will be successor to the throne? How will the promise be
fulfilled? Often it seems as if the promise will go unfulfilled. Finally with
Solomon's enthronement the fulfillment is there." Rendtorff, *EvTh,* XXII
(1962), 633 f., note 27, suggests the reverse: "It is striking that both

understood in their theological meaning simply on the basis
of the tradition. Here the connection between tradition and
contemporary occurrence was mediated by the "insight" "that
in every instance what Yahweh had willed and planned happens." "Attention to Yahweh's plan, which was carried out
in the interrelations of occurrences, could have arisen precisely from the experience with Yahweh's word. If in Israel
one experienced again and again that what had been announced by a word of Yahweh happened, then this could—
one must almost say must—lead to the insight that in every
instance what Yahweh had willed and planned happens. It
was then no great step when in a different spiritual situation
the inference was drawn that one is to speak of Yahweh's action and the realization of his plan even where no word of
Yahweh expressly announcing this action had gone before. In
any case one may not simply set up an antithesis between
these different views."[188]

If thus tradition, by bringing individual instances of divine
guidance together into a divine plan, can replace the prophet's
word as the key to interpreting current events, it becomes
questionable to Rendtorff whether the Old Testament concept
of the word of God (that carried through what it says and
does not return empty, Is. 55:10 f.) is really to be identified
with the individual prophet's word, and not rather with the

---

of the stories about prophets, 2 Sam. 7 and 12, are, to be sure, used in
important positions, but that the authors do not suggest with a single
word that the words of Nathan had had any significance for the course of
the events." Probably Pannenberg has here interpreted the scope of the
narrative better than has Rendtorff, who is seeking to carry through his
thesis of the replacement of prophetic word with the divine plan. Rendtorff himself conceives of the sensitivity for a divine plan as due to the
conviction that prophecy was inevitably fulfilled; thus the same assumption that led to the Davidic historiography can hardly be denied to have
been implicit in the narration itself. Gerhard von Rad, *Theologie des
Alten Testaments*, I, 314 (Eng. tr., p. 316) also draws an inverse inference from that initially characteristic of the Pannenberg circle: Since
in such narratives Yahweh does not intervene in the form of the miraculous but acts only implicitly in all occurrence, his control of history "is
fully hidden to the natural eye."
[188] *EvTh*, XXII (1962), 636.

divine plan.[189] Israelites knew that many specific predictions by prophets went unfulfilled; it was rather "the whole of the prophetic proclamations of doom that fulfilled themselves in Israel's fate."[190] In postexilic prophecy, words directed to specific concrete events "fade more and more into the background and finally disappear completely."[191] Thus both the individual prophet's word and even the individual event are subsumed under a "conception of history,"[192] a development which leads into apocalypticism, in terms of which the New Testament is to be understood.[193]

We may conclude this section on the Old Testament by pointing out how the debate carried on primarily by Rendtorff and Zimmerli, while moving within the dimensions of technical Old Testament research, has at the same time been a debate within contemporary German theology as to the relation of history and word. Both sides maintain they advocate a unity of the two, and tend to reject as misunderstandings such criticisms as suggest they are advocating one at the expense of the other. Yet each side tends to approach this unity from one or the other term, and hence the degree of success attained by each approach is, in terms of an internal criticism, the extent to which each provides a theological conceptualization which does justice to that unity. For clarity's sake one may

[189] *Ibid.*, p. 644.
[190] *Ibid.*, p. 645.
[191] *Ibid.*, p. 645.
[192] *Ibid.*, p. 648.
[193] The argument to the effect that apocalypticism is a positive continuation of the Old Testament view of history (on which cf. also Klaus Koch, "Spätisraelitisches Geschichtsdenken am Beispiel des Buches Daniel," *Historische Zeitschrift* CXCIII [1961], 1–32), and is the presupposition for the New Testament, is provided by Dietrich Rössler, *Gesetz und Geschichte. Untersuchungen zur Theologie der jüdischen Apokalyptik und der pharisäischen Orthodoxie* (*WMANT*, 3; Neukirchen Kreis Moers: Neukirchener Verlag, 1960; 2nd ed., 1962). For a criticism of Rössler, cf. Philipp Vielhauer, in *Neutestamentliche Apokryphen*, 3rd ed. of Edgar Hennecke's standard work, edited by Wilhelm Schneemelcher (Tübingen: J.C.B. Mohr [Paul Siebeck], 1964), II, 416 f. [*New Testament Apocrypha*, tr. by R. McL. Wilson (Philadelphia: Westminster Press, 1964), II, 594 f.] The debate revolves largely around the extent to which the concept of two aeons is constitutive of apocalypticism.

express the diverging emphases in terms of summaries that, while not including all the comprehensive statements from both sides or the potential developments of thought suggested above, yet do indicate the gravitational centers: Rendtorff has tended to locate the revelation primarily in history, in which the word is grounded and which in turn confirms the word so that knowledge of God takes place; or to define history as including the word in the form of the history of the transmission of traditions; or to see the valid claims of the word met in the form of an overarching plan of history. Zimmerli has tended to locate the revelation primarily in the (prophetic) word, which calls forth history and recalls history so that knowledge of God takes place; i.e., the occurrence of the word is itself the decisive historic event.

## IV. THE DEBATE IN CONTEMPORARY THEOLOGY

The discussion of the position of the Pannenberg circle broadened out into a general theological discussion with the appearance of the symposium, *Revelation as History,* consisting of papers presented at their semiannual meeting in October 1960.[194] In his introduction[195] Pannenberg points out that the Enlightenment destroyed the concept of revelation as involving revealed truths, but that Hegel redefined the term as the revelation of God's own person. Pannenberg argues that for this to be a complete revelation it must be God himself who reveals himself, so that it is from his role as complete re-

---

[194] *Offenbarung als Geschichte,* ed. by Wolfhart Pannenberg (*KuD, Beiheft* 1; Göttingen: Vandenhoeck und Ruprecht, 1961; 2nd ed., 1963), with an "Introduction" by Pannenberg, followed by four essays: "Die Offenbarungsvorstellungen im alten Israel" by Rolf Rendtorff, "Das Offenbarungsverständnis in der Geschichte des Urchristentums" by Ulrich Wilckens, "Dogmatische Thesen zur Lehre von der Offenbarung" by Pannenberg, and "Das Offenbarungsproblem im Kirchenbegriff" by Trutz Rendtorff. The second edition includes a "Postscript" by Pannenberg. The journal, *Kerygma und Dogma,* which published the symposium as a special supplement, has its center in Heidelberg, and represents by and large the tradition out of which the Pannenberg circle emerged.

[195] *Ibid.,* pp. 7–20.

vealer of God that the deity of Jesus is to be inferred. Now for
Pannenberg the Bible does not have the concept of a direct
self-revelation of God; e.g., appearances of God in the cult
and in the prophetic word are divine manifestations but do
not reveal God in his essence, except perhaps in the view of
the gnostic fringe of the New Testament (the Gospel of John).
Rather one has "an indirect self-revelation [of God] in the
mirror of his action in history."[196] "Indirect" does not refer
to mediation by some third party. Indeed Pannenberg is concerned to emphasize that a prophet is not needed to add an
interpretation to the event. Rather "indirect" means that the
actual content of the revelatory experience, e.g., history, is
not identical with what the experience is intended to reveal,
namely, God himself, who is rather to be inferred indirectly
from the historical event. Thus revelation is the inferential
insight "that God is such a person as to do this and that."[197]
To be sure this would seem to lead to an infinite number of
revelations, since there are an infinite number of events. Yet
this would be contrary to Pannenberg's concept that revelation, if it is to be the complete revelation of the one God, must
be single. Hence it is only the *whole* of history in its unity and
totality that reveals God, as was first recognized by Hegel,
from whom Pannenberg derives his key term, universal history.

After the approach of this symposium had been carried
through for the Biblical material by Rendtorff and Wilckens,
Pannenberg gives focus to the position with a series of "Dogmatic Theses on the Doctrine of Revelation":[198]

1. God's self-revelation, according to the Biblical witnesses,
   did not take place directly, e.g., as a theophany, but
   rather indirectly, through God's acts in history.

2. The revelation does not take place at the beginning, but
   rather at the end of revelatory history.

3. In distinction to special appearances of the deity, the

[196] *Ibid.*, p. 15.
[197] *Ibid.*, p. 17.
[198] *Ibid.*, pp. 91–114. The theses quoted here stand in italics at the
opening of each subsection commenting upon them.

revelation in history is open to everyone who has eyes to see. It has universal character.

4. The universal revelation of God's deity is not yet actualized in Israel's history, but rather first in what happened to Jesus of Nazareth, in that there the end of all occurrence took place proleptically.

5. The Christ event does not, as an isolated occurrence, reveal the deity of Israel's God, but only to the extent that it is a part of God's history with Israel.

6. The development of non-Jewish concepts of revelation in the gentile Christian churches brings to expression the universality of God's eschatological self-demonstration in what happened to Jesus.

7. The "word" is related to revelation as prediction, guidance and report.

Pannenberg had worked out this position to some extent in terms of a criticism directed against the confessional Lutheran position, according to which God's "manifestation" in history was in need of supplementation by his "inspiration" in prophet, apostle, and Scripture. Hence it is not surprising that the leading contemporary advocate of that tradition, Paul Althaus, would, in spite of all appreciation for the anti-Bultmannian position of Pannenberg, argue that Pannenberg had gone too far in the opposite direction and had "missed" "the genuine nature of revelation."[199] He argues that faith is both knowledge and trust, and that such faith is effected by the work of the Holy Spirit. When Pannenberg says the revelation in history is visible to "uninhibited perception" and attributes its nonacceptance to man's reason being affected by sin, Althaus argues that this is "inadmissible anthropological rationalizing,"[200] since it is inherent in God's nature that his revelation should involve his hiddenness. Yet Althaus simply leaves the act of faith unintelligible.

---

[199] "Offenbarung als Geschichte und Glaube. Bemerkungen zu Wolfhart Pannenbergs Begriff der Offenbarung," *ThLZ*, LXXXVII (1962), 321–330, esp. column 323.

[200] *Ibid.*, cols. 327 f., citing *Offenbarung als Geschichte*, p. 101.

Pannenberg's answer is entitled, "Insight and Faith."[201] He acknowledges that the relation between knowledge of revelation on the one hand and faith and the Holy Spirit on the other is the major problem in his proposal. And he agrees that faith is a gift of God, the only question being whether this is "through the mediation of a demonstrable knowledge of what happened to Jesus and of its significance," or whether the work of the Spirit is "just a subjective reassurance."[202] He also agrees that "faith" can be regarded as the overarching category which includes knowledge (Protestant orthodoxy's *notitia* plus *assensus*) and trust (*fiducia*). But he points out that this broader use of "faith" should not be permitted to obscure the question as to whether knowledge grounds trust or the reverse. He holds that if certainty concerning the contents of faith were grounded in man's decision to believe, then faith would ground itself, which would be "the corruption of the correct understanding of Christian faith."[203] "If [the gospel's] truth does not convince my judgment, then its acknowledgement does indeed become a matter of resolve, and thus we would arrive again at the ruinous consequence that faith grounds itself and thus destroys what is essential to it, which is to hang upon a truth outside itself."[204] And indeed when Althaus adds to the definition of "revelation as history" the phrase, ". . . and faith," one can sense that faith tends to become simply a human disposition blunting the rigor of critical rational reflection, an ideological prejudice one brings to the facts so as to be able to recognize them as revelatory. The Holy Spirit seems then a *deus ex machina,* or, as Pannenberg puts it, an *asylum ignorantiae.*[205]

Pannenberg provides a more adequate focus for a modern interpretation of the work of the Spirit: "The Spirit is not added to the gospel as some supplement. Rather the pro-

[201] "Einsicht und Glaube. Antwort an Paul Althaus," *ThLZ,* LXXXVIII (1963), 81–92.

[202] *Ibid.,* col. 81.

[203] *Ibid.,* cols. 83 f.

[204] *Ibid.,* col. 85.

[205] *Ibid.,* col. 90.

claimed eschatological occurrence and, derived from it, the carrying out of the preaching of the gospel, is itself Spirit-filled. Hence the hearer receives a share in the Spirit in that he receives a share in the subject matter of the Gospel, in that he trusts in what he has heard."[206] The verification of the word takes the form of the verification of the history to which it witnesses. "The question as to whether the gospel that is proclaimed to me is true can only be answered from its content, by pointing to what it reports and the meaning *inherent* in the reported occurrence."[207] This leads to Pannenberg's historical demonstration, which for him includes not only the facts but also their saving meaning for the participants, as well as such nonpositivistic historical facts as the incarnation and resurrection of Jesus.

The only other alternative would seem to be "self-redemption by means of the so-called decision of faith," "frivolity and superstition," "arbitrary faith."[208] It is difficult to see how Althaus' position can be freed from such accusations. Yet the decision of faith can be understood other than as a self-saving work,[209] and as part of a program to free theology from arbi-

[206] *Ibid.,* col. 85, note 6.

[207] *Ibid.,* col. 86.

[208] *Ibid.,* cols. 87 f. Similarly, in the "Postscript" to *Offenbarung als Geschichte,* pp. 144 f. Cf. Georg Muschalek, S.J., "Offenbarung in Geschichte," *ZKTh,* LXXXVI (1964), 194 f.: "It is precisely because faith is effected by the Spirit that here too one must say that this 'contribution' of the will does not remove faith from its objectivity, but instead first fully gains access to it. When that is not recognized, then one of course has the impression that the participation of free decision in faith is to hide or replace its deficient objectivity and thus to make it suspect or unacceptable to the modern objectivistic age. In such a view it does indeed become an arbitrary act, so that one understands how Pannenberg can declare faith so understood to be 'self-salvation.' "

[209] Cf. Bultmann's *Theologie des Neuen Testaments* (3rd ed.; Tübingen: J.C.B. Mohr [Paul Siebeck], 1958), pp. 316 f. [*Theology of the New Testament,* tr. by Kendrick Grobel (New York: Charles Scribner's Sons, 1951), I, 315 f.] "As true obedience, 'faith' is freed from the suspicion of being an accomplishment, a 'work'. . . . As an accomplishment it would not be obedience, since in an accomplishment the will does not surrender but asserts itself: in it, a merely formal renunciation takes place, in that the will lets the content of its accomplishment be dictated by an authority lying outside of itself, but precisely in so doing thinks it has a right to be proud of its accomplishment. 'Faith'—the radical re-

trary decisions.[210] For demythologizing arose as an effort to overcome the impasse that results from the recognition that the mythological, though it is not accessible to historical veri-

---

nunciation of accomplishment, the obedient submission to the God-determined way of salvation, the taking over of the cross of Christ . . . —is the free deed of obedience in which the new self constitutes itself in place of the old. As this sort of decision, it is a deed in the true sense: In a true deed man actualizes his being as himself, while in a 'work' he stands side by side with what he does." Pannenberg's position (communicated in a letter) is that the decision of faith as understood by Bultmann is a work "to the extent that the authority of the word, the kerygma, is not 'demonstrable,' and becomes visible as God's authority only in carrying out the decision of faith itself." He then queries: "Does not the decision of faith here perhaps first make the word's authority into God's authority, or what is to be replied to this?" Something of a reply may be inferred from Bultmann's "Reply to Ernst Käsemann," *GuV*, IV (1965), 192: "There is no such thing as a decision without a cause—only the causes do not, as in nature, work with compelling necessity, but are rather the ingredients of decision."

[210] Cf. Christian Hartlich and Walter Sachs, *Der Ursprung des Mythosbegriffes in der modernen Bibelwissenschaft* (Tübingen: J.C.B. Mohr [Paul Siebeck], 1952), pp. 1, 163. "Every principal application of the concept of myth within exegesis brings with it of necessity a certain structure of problems. [Such an application] must begin with the distinction of the mythical form of conceptualization from that which it really intends—the 'content'; as [this application] is carried through, it confronts one with the problem of mythical clothing and (possible) historical factuality, as well as with the question as to the possible truth content of Biblical myths." "The clearer the insight was gained that for this kind of Biblical statements no preference can be claimed for one over another, from the point of view of the truth of [what they conveyed as] *knowledge*, the more urgent became the question as to whether they have truth and significance in some other sense than that of correspondence with some external objective reality." Cf. my essay, "The Pre-History of Demythologization," *Interpretation*, XX (1966), 65–77. Cf. also, Heinrich Ott, "Existentiale Interpretation und anonyme Christlichkeit," *Zeit und Geschichte. Dankesgabe an Rudolf Bultmann zum 80. Geburtstag* (Tübingen: J.C.B. Mohr [Paul Siebeck], 1964), pp. 367–379, esp. pp. 367–370: "[Statements of faith] are not subject to verification or falsification by means of neutral disinterested observation. But if they can neither be verified nor falsified, then they are obviously statements without meaning, empty claims, a sort of declamation or interjection that need not concern us but floats unrelatedly above the realities that concern and determine us—unless another way to verify them can be found. For Bultmann, existentialistic interpretation is such a way. . . . If existentialist interpretation can show that in faith I attain a really new self-understanding, then it shows thereby that [the new self-understanding] really makes a difference. . . , i.e., that faith is not some irrelevant thing floating above reality. . . . For verification does not mean 'proof,' but rather clarification of where it relates to reality."

fication, yet, as the conveyer of meaning, calls upon us to reach a nonarbitrary position toward it. When the mythologically formulated message is put in the form of an understanding of existence that confronts a person as a possibility for himself, it can become meaningful to him in the light that it sheds on his living. Thus in his concrete living the theoretical problem of pervasive relativism is overcome, though at the level of objective verification that problem remains.[211]

Pannenberg concludes his answer to Althaus with the observation "that God's revelation only comes to its goal when it effects faith and hence is revelation for someone."[212] It is this distinction between a revelation inherent in history on the one hand and that revelation becoming revelation to someone on the other that is in substance the point at which Lothar Steiger introduces his critique of Pannenberg's position.[213] He

[211] Cf. Gunter Klein, *Theologie des Wortes Gottes und die Hypothese der Universalgeschichte* (*Beitrage zur Evangelischen Theologie*, 37; Munich: Christian Kaiser Verlag, 1964), p. 35. Pannenberg's own position is not so far from such a view as the widely diverging emphases and terminologies might lead one to think. For he adds the significant clarification: "This is not intended to maintain that one could attain or maintain such knowledge in actual living without faith. That is a new question. The logic of faith and its psychology are to be distinguished. With regard to the logic of faith, what has been said applies, namely, that as *fiducia* it is grounded by knowledge (*notitia*). In the psychological experience both can be laid hold of in a single act. Trust can also emerge in the expectation that the knowledge already logically presupposed will only later be opened up, an anticipation of the result that is characteristic not only of the conduct of faith, but also of the process of knowledge [in general]: One anticipates conjecturally the result, but must then find this conjecture confirmed, verified. For believing trust to arise, the believer does not always himself have to test the knowledge [such trust] presupposes. That is the particular task of theology. Not every Christian need subject himself to this task. He can trust in the assumption that everything is all right with the ground of his trust. To be sure that presupposes an atmosphere of confidence in the Christian tradition that has more and more been lost in the course of the last centuries, not least of all because of the failure of theology. This atmosphere of confidence in what the pastor has to proclaim, to the extent that it is a matter of knowledge, must be rebuilt anew; and one might think that theology should devote all its strength to this task in full critical openness," *ThLZ*, LXXXVIII (1963), 84 f. Similarly in the "Postscript" to *Offenbarung als Geschichte*, p. 145.

[212] *ThLZ*, LXXXVIII (1963), 90.

[213] "Offenbarungsgeschichte und theologische Vernunft. Zur Theologie W. Pannenbergs," *ZThK*, LIX (1962), 88–113.

senses such a separation of the revelatory history in and of itself on the one hand and man's knowledge or appropriation of it on the other to be inherent in the structure of Pannenberg's programmatic essay, in its division into sections, "The Opening up of Reality as History by Means of the Biblical Revelation of God," and "God's History and Critical Historical Research." He also sees the separation in the sequence of Pannenberg's presentation in *Revelation as History,* where his "Introduction" and first two theses treat of revelatory history with "the problem of knowing and understanding it not yet touched," with the rest of the theses then devoted to that topic of appropriation.[214] Steiger argues that Hegel's problem of some "mediation" between history and the observer of history is not fully recognized; rather the facts are assumed to have some "inherent ontological quality" that "discharges as it were automatically their significance."[215] For Pannenberg, when a person does not recognize that meaning, this is due to his lack of intelligence, i.e., blindness. Steiger concludes: "The Pauline dialectic of wisdom and foolishness loses its eschatological background and is generalized and flattened into the relation of rationality and irrationality."[216]

Steiger's criticism to the effect that for Pannenberg theology becomes, without "difference" (i.e., undialectically), part of the history of ideas is put in terms of a theology of the word: "[For Pannenberg] the facts speak only within the plan. The idealistic problem of revelation does not become Biblical simply by eliminating the mediation of thought. How then is the logic of the revelatory plan mediated? Pannenberg has no concept of the verbal nature of revelation, since he conceives of the facts entering into the conception of a plan of salvation as revelation and hence can make room for the word only as the reflex of these facts. On this level there occurs an invalid polemic against the word as revelation, [in

---

[214] *Ibid.,* p. 93.
[215] *Ibid.,* p. 95.
[216] Steiger, *ibid.,* p. 97. Much the same criticism is made by Ernst Fuchs, *ThLZ,* LXXXVIII (1963), 258 f.

arguing that] 'a revelation in need of supplementation in order to become revealed is not yet revelation.'[217] The word is no 'supplement' to the revelation at all! The word witnesses to the event *as* revelation, by saying and doing what an event is and signifies. This meaning of word has nothing at all to do with the gnostic concept of word as a revelatory discourse.[218] Word is not the illumination of a content that a person could see. In the word it is a matter of the genuine indirectness of revelation, in that the genuine contingency of an occurrence is respected, which by its nature is not unambiguous, but rather is ambiguous."[219] Actually, Pannenberg's own view, though cast in another category, is not as far from Steiger as the latter assumes. For Pannenberg holds that the mediation is provided by the process of transmission as a hermeneutical process.

A more congenial interpretation is that of Johannes Wirsching.[220] He senses that Pannenberg has challenged the current rejection of the concept of "systematic" theology, and finds precisely in this fact the positive significance of Pannenberg's proposal. Although he questions "whether theology may ever appropriate a ready-made thought pattern and its systematism as a *closed* unit," he thinks that a system that recasts the given terminology and is "open" to the future for revision (as he understands Pannenberg's to be) avoids the valid criticisms leveled against theological system-building.[221] And the advantage of systematic theology is that it can move beyond dogmatics, "the church's self-reflection on its own doctrine," to include "debate with Christian and non-Christian attacks,"

---

[217] *Offenbarung als Geschichte,* p. 20.

[218] Steiger here alludes to Pannenberg, *ibid.,* pp. 14, 111.

[219] *ZThK,* LIX (1962), 108 f.

[220] "Ein neues theologisches System? Randbemerkungen zur Theologie W. Pannenbergs," *Deutsches Pfarrerblatt,* LXIV (1964), 601–609. Cf. Wirsching's own book, *Gott in der Geschichte. Studien zur theologiegeschichtlichen und systematischen Grundlegung der Theologie Martin Kählers (Forschungen zur Geschichte und Lehre des Protestantismus, Reihe X, 26;* Munich: Christian Kaiser Verlag, 1963). The congenial reviews cited by Pannenberg in his "Postscript" to *Offenbarung als Geschichte,* p. 134, note 5, were not available to me, since they appeared in newspapers and magazines.

[221] *Deutsches Pfarrerblatt,* p. 602.

as "Polemics, Apologetics, the Philosophy of Religion," as well as to enter upon social action, as "Social Ethics." Thus Wirsching, though a pastor writing for pastors, welcomes the fact that Pannenberg's "system" represents what is "only to a certain extent a 'churchly' theology."[222] The broadening of the horizon to include problems that Dogmatics had tended to define as outside its scope, the desire not simply to witness but also to convince, are emphases that could help mark the difference between faith and superstition.

In an evaluation somewhat different from Steiger's, Wirsching approves of the concept of the Bible that "does not have to be constructed hermeneutically by means of preaching," i.e., that becomes normative by means of the Christ event without "any kind of hermeneutical operation separated from it." The "ontological autonomy" of the event itself "carries its case not only by means of the Biblical witnesses, but in some cases against them" and thus "speaks 'its own language, the language of facts.' "[223] This is appreciated as a return to Luther's emphasis upon the clarity of Scripture without ecclesiastical intervention, which occurs even in Protestantism in the form of "the (neo-Kantian) dominance of questions of understanding."[224] Of course "the theologian, especially the one who works systematically, must show how this self-mediation of the Bible's contents is to be grasped conceptually and is able to illuminate the critical mind as true."[225] It is in this sense that Wirsching understands Pannenberg's analysis of the nature of the history of the transmission of tra-

---

[222] All quotations *ibid.*, p. 601.

[223] *Ibid.*, p. 604. Wirsching quotes Pannenberg, *Offenbarung als Geschichte*, p. 100.

[224] *Ibid.* Of course it hardly fits current German hermeneutic to describe it as an activity "separated" from the Christ event and to say that "only" Pannenberg really "takes seriously" Luther's emphasis on Scripture's clarity (*ibid.*). For this emphasis is the source of Ebeling's positive understanding of language at the basis of his hermeneutic. Cf. his essay, "Word of God and Hermeneutic" in *The New Hermeneutic*, pp. 78–110. Apparently Wirsching sees the new hermeneutic primarily through Pannenberg's essay, "Hermeneutik und Universalgeschichte," *ZThK*, LX (1963), 90–121.

[225] *Ibid.*

ditions in correlation to a study of "historical" reason. The view that the facts interpret themselves fits the contingency of individual occurrences, their nonderivableness from some antecedently known principle. The facts are never so identical with any given interpretation that they could be inferred from —or replaced by—that interpretation, but rather reassert themselves over against it as a new step in the history of the transmission of the traditions. Hence one does not have a pattern that one can project into the future. Continuity is visible actually only in retrospect, and whereas such a restrospective view of history can provide an anticipation for the future, such a prolepsis can be no more than that which is to be verified or corrected by subsequent contingent occurrences themselves.

This congenial interpretation of Pannenberg's intention is also accompanied by critical reservations. Wirsching refers to Pannenberg's system as "estheticism," in the original sense of the term: an "observing relation to reality," *visio intellectualis*.[226] The presupposition of Pannenberg's position is hence a "theoretical" relation to reality, rather than, e.g., one in terms of social action or of endurance, as indeed Pannenberg does distance himself from Ebeling's position by rejecting the ethical problem as the point of departure for theology.[227] Wirsching questions whether Pannenberg's theoretical approach does not actually endanger "the uniqueness of the Biblical witness," in that Pannenberg sees "the 'subsequently' intelligible 'evidentness' of a step-by-step mediation of salvation at work, and notices too little that such an evidentness necessarily endangers the contingency of Biblical universalism. When all is said and done it is comparable to any esthetic ideological universalism, i.e., it is intelligible *also* in terms of

[226] *Ibid.*, p. 606. The term "estheticism" seems poorly chosen, not only because it is not used in the sense one would most readily assume, but also because the "original" meaning is not unambiguously what Wirsching takes it to be. He does not seem to know that etymologically the term derives from a verb for hearing rather than for seeing.

[227] "Die Krise des Ethischen und die Theologie," *ThLZ*, LXXXVII (1962), 7–16.

the history of ideas and not only on the basis of its own distinctive occurrence. It has to involve some kind of logical evidentness. For the claim that it is 'the sole appropriate view' of reality reveals after all a necessity such as can be justified only by rigorous logic."[228]

Furthermore the synthesis of Biblical and non-Biblical reality such as is evident in the fitting of the concept of resurrection to that of psychosomatic wholeness seems to Wirsching not to do justice to the "transforming power" of Christianity. "What then is really 'new' in the witnesses to the resurrection, if the significance inherent in them threatens to become an illustration for a truth that can also be discovered elsewhere?"[229] Wirsching is not willing to accept Pannenberg's view that it is merely "narrow-mindedness" not to assume that "accidental occurrences attain an almost rational transparency."[230] The subjection of the resurrection to "empirical confirmation" seems to put it "on a line with the given status of the world"; instead Pannenberg should have implemented his recognition that "all that is earthly must go through the cross," in terms of a "break, transformation and new creation."[231] Hence Wirsching senses that a reversal could take place. Rather than reason and the historian demonstrating the rationality of the Biblical witness, it could turn out that "Biblical investigations are able only to confirm what historical reason also bears in itself in outline without [the Bible]; in its depths the rationality of the Biblical picture of God comes to such conclusive consciousness that the Bible can only confirm but not contradict."[232] Thus, though his evaluation of Pannenberg's position is more penetrating and positive than some of the other articles treating it, Wirsching shares somewhat the same concern as do they. And in conclusion he expresses a further concern, which is more fully developed by William

[228] Wirsching, *ibid.*, p. 606. He cites *KuD*, V (1959), 287.
[229] *Ibid.*, p. 607.
[230] Wirsching, *ibid.*
[231] *Ibid.*, citing Pannenberg, *KuD*, V (1959), 284, note 66, and 237.
[232] *Ibid.*, p. 609.

Hamilton in the present volume. In view of the emphasis upon *past* history as proleptic anticipation of future *end* of history, is not the *present* denied the significance that it theologically deserves? "Are *its* questions, *its* needs, really picked up and treated seriously?" "Man must be met where he really is!"[233]

The sharpest and most extensive debate has been initiated by Günter Klein. His review article entitled "Revelation as History?"[234] analyzes individually each contribution in the symposium, *Revelation as History*. And this review was answered most fully among the critical articles treated by Pannenberg in his "Postscript" to the second edition of *Revelation as History*. Klein, in turn, presented an address answering Pannenberg at the meeting of "Old Marburgers," in October, 1963. This address was subsequently expanded into a small book entitled *Theology of the Word of God and the Hypothesis of Universal History*, which appeared at the end of 1964.[235] It is this exchange that is now to be investigated.

In his review article, Klein first questions the approach outlined in Pannenberg's introduction to *Revelation as History*.[236] He wonders whether the concept of full divine self-revelation derived from German idealism but absent from the Bible can actually provide the appropriate category for approaching the Bible.[237] It presupposes the model of sight rather than hearing, and hence misses the dialectic of God's call, involving his unexposedness and hence calling forth the decision of faith or faithlessness rather than the theoretical judgment of compre-

---

[233] *Ibid.* Similarly Fuchs, *ThLZ*, LXXXVIII (1963), 259 f.

[234] "Offenbarung als Geschichte? Marginalien zu einem theologischen Programm," *MPTh*, LI (1962), 65–88.

[235] *Theologie des Wortes Gottes und die Hypothese der Universalgeschichte. Zur Auseinandersetzung mit Wolfhart Pannenberg (Beiträge zur evangelischen Theologie*, 37; Munich: Christian Kaiser Verlag, 1964).

[236] Pannenberg, *Offenbarung als Geschichte*, pp. 7–20; Klein, *MPTh*, LI (1962), 65–68.

[237] Pannenberg, in his "Postscript" to *Offenbarung als Geschichte*, p. 142, note 24, replies to a similar criticism by Steiger to the effect that though the term, self-revelation, is not present, the substance is present in the Biblical talk of the final revelation of God's "glory" and in the "word of demonstration." Cf. also Grobel's remarks below, pp. 163–166.

hension or incomprehension. When Pannenberg advocates an "indirect" revelation in history, since God is "initially" not the content of the experience of history, Klein infers that the actual revelation takes place in man's *reflection* about history.

Ulrich Wilckens presents apocalypticism as the factor of continuity in primitive Christianity, from Judaism to Jesus and from Jesus to the church.[238] Jesus' conflict with Judaism is somewhat parallel to the clash within Judaism between "the apocalyptic understanding of the law," which Jesus himself as "eschatological place of salvation" incorporates,[239] and the

---

[238] Wilckens, "Das Offenbarungsverstandnis in der Geschichte des Urchristentums," *Offenbarung als Geschichte,* pp. 42–90; Klein, *ibid.,* pp. 71–77.

[239] Wilckens, *ibid.,* pp. 53 and 58, note 39; Klein, *ibid.,* p. 72. Presupposed is Dietrich Rössler's dissertation, *Gesetz und Geschichte. Untersuchungen zur Theologie der jüdischen Apokalyptik und der pharisäischen Orthodoxie.* Pannenberg replies in his "Postscript" to *Offenbarung als Geschichte,* p. 141, note 22, that Klein had not taken into consideration Wilckens' statement, *ibid.,* p. 58, note 39, that Jesus had a "distinctive eschatology." Cf. Wilckens' remarks in his review of August Strobel's *Die apokalyptische Sendung Jesu,* in *ThLZ,* LXXXIX (1964), 671: "Though it is true and worth emphasizing that Jesus can be correctly described only within the comparative religious horizon of the Jewish apocalyptic tradition, the picture of Jesus' distinctiveness the author works out is unconvincing. . . . The distinctiveness of Jesus does not at all consist merely in his sketching himself so to speak into the given framework of the traditional expectation of the end. Rather it is that, contrary to the soteriological structure of the traditional expectation, he proclaimed final salvation as God's gift to the wicked and hence bound it proleptically to their relationship to him. . . . The explicit opposition of Jesus to the Torah tradition and its advocates is completely ignored by the author. Jesus is not, as the author maintains, simply an apocalypticist with remarkably heightened self-esteem. Most of the exegetes attacked by the author (especially Käsemann!) distance Jesus completely from apocalypticism (clearly incorrectly), primarily in view of this materially decisive opposition to the apocalyptic tradition. To this extent they are at least as basically correct over against the author as he over against them. Hence, it is not so 'simple,' but rather a thorny and at times puzzling historical problem, to understand Jesus (as in fact it must be done!) in the context of Jewish apocalypticism without making him an apocalypticist." Wilckens would apparently free Jesus from the personality traits giving a pejorative overtone to the term "apocalyptist," even though he had initially (*Offenbarung als Geschichte,* p. 53) found in the "apocalyptic visionary" the nearest historical parallel to Jesus, and yet retain for Jesus enough of an apocalyptic ideology for Rössler's antithesis between its view of the law and that of Pharisaism to be applied to Jesus.

Pharisaic view,[240] with Jesus' authority to instigate such a crisis perhaps beings based on some "inspirational visionary experience."[241] Thus a psychic occurrence in Jesus' life, together with an inevitable clash in the history of ideas, is in the case of Jesus the history that indirectly reveals God. Klein maintains, conversely, that it is Jesus' message as revelatory word event to which Jesus appeals for his authority. Since apocalypticism expected history to vindicate its conception, Jesus, in Wilckens' view, performed his miracles and brought things to a head in Jerusalem so that God would demonstrate the validity of his claim in what would happen,[242] whereas Klein understands Jesus as rejecting such signs.[243] Although Jesus expected the apocalyptic end of the world rather than an isolated instance of resurrection, the expectation of some confirmatory apocalyptic event provides for Wilckens the connection with the church's reference to the resurrection as such a confirmation. Wilckens had already presented a detailed argument to the effect that the connection of Paul's conversion with his rejection of the law indicated that he originated from an apocalyptic world of thought.[244] And he had already car-

---

[240] In the context of deriving Paul's ideological background from apocalypticism, Wilckens can also speak of a "Pharisaic apocalypticism," *ZThK*, LVI (1959), 285. Cf. Klein, *ibid.*, p. 72, note 14, and *Theologie des Wortes Gottes und die Hypothese der Universalgeschichte*, p. 25, note 22. Oscar Cullmann, *Heil als Geschichte*, p. 42, accepts W. D. Davies' rejection of a separation of Pharisaism and apocalypticism in his article "Apocalyptic and Pharisaism," *Expository Times*, 1948, pp. 233–237, reprinted in *Christian Origins and Judaism* (Philadelphia: Westminster Press, 1962), pp. 19–30, and affirms that Rössler's thesis is "much too schematic," although adding "in a certain sense it is nonetheless a suggestive work."

[241] Wilckens, *Offenbarung als Geschichte*, p. 54, note 31; Klein *MPTh*, LI (1962), 73.

[242] Wilckens, *ibid.*, pp. 60 f.; Klein, *ibid.*, p. 74.

[243] *Ibid.* Pannenberg, *Grundzüge der Christologie*, pp. 58 f., develops a thesis of Jesus' positive stance toward signs.

[244] "Die Bekehrung des Paulus als religionsgeschichtliches Problem," *ZThK*, LVI (1959), 273–293. But cf. Wolfgang Schrage, " 'Ekklesia' und 'Synagoge.' Zum Ursprung des unchristlichen Kirchenbegriffes," *ZThK*, LX (1963), 178–202, esp. p. 198: "The source of Paul's antithesis to the law is not an apocalyptic system of coordinates that the pre-Christian Paul carried with him and into which he merely needed to sketch the new reality at his conversion; rather the source is the preaching of the

ried this apocalyptic continuity through to the post-apostolic age with a monograph arguing that Luke had succeeded in replacing the imminent expectation that had failed, as well as the *Christus praesens,* understood as an "unmediated encounter with transcendence" of gnostic implications, with a "historically mediated participation in a specific past." This "theological discovery of history as the 'comprehensive horizon of Christian theology' " makes of Luke—rather, than, e.g., the gnosticizing John—"undoubtedly the most important theolologian of the post-apostolic age," and the canonical precursor of the Pannenberg circle.[245]

For the discussion of Lucan theology, Klein refers to Ernst Haenchen, whose commentary on Acts has made him one of the most influential interpreters of Lucan theology today. Haenchen points to the equivalent of the Pauline *Christus praesens* that is to be found in the Lucan concept of the miracle-working "name" of Jesus. "Luke—like all New Testament 'authors'—is aware of this 'transcendence' as the power that really determines everything, and not in the sense that God (one should rather speak of him than of 'transcendence') directs every occurrence and hence lies behind every occurrence. Rather Luke is not afraid to report individual interventions of God in earthly occurrence. . . . One should not confuse the Lucan generation's massive conception of the resurrection with a 'positive evaluation of history.' Luke did not think that the salvation that the parousia 'is expected to bring

---

'Hellenists.' " Similarly, Klein, *ibid.,* p. 75, note 21. Klein's essay "Römer 4 und die Idee der Heilsgeschichte," *EvTh,* XXIII (1963), 424–447, was in substance a criticism of Wilckens' view of Paul. Wilckens replied, "Zu Römer 3, 21–4, 25. Antwort an G. Klein," *EvTh,* XXIV (1964), 586–610, to which Klein in turn replied, "Exegetische Probleme in Römer 3, 21–4, 25. Antwort an U. Wilckens," *EvTh,* XXIV (1964), 676–683. Pannenberg holds that (apart from Jesus) Paul is the central figure of the New Testament.

[245] *Die Missionsreden der Apostelgeschichte: Form- und traditionsgeschichtliche Untersuchungen (Wissenschaftliche Monographien zum Alten und Neuen Testament,* 5; Neukirchen: Neukirchener Verlag, 1961; 2nd ed., 1962), esp. pp. 206 f., 218. Wilckens quotes the opening sentence of Pannenberg's programmatic essay discussed above.

for the elect [is] in no sense different from the salvation that was already completely there in Jesus' earthly life.' Even in Luke's view, there will be, after the parousia, no sick to be healed and no sinners to be converted. Perhaps the massiveness of some Lucan statements arouses a longing for a massive theology in which such uncertain things as a 'direct encounter with transcendence' no longer occur."[246]

Klein's criticism of Pannenberg's theses[247] has its focus in the classification of Jesus' resurrection as history. "In the framework of this conception the Easter event loses of necessity its eschatological character and degenerates into a past phenomenon of the world."[247a] Pannenberg in turn is able to deny this inference,[248] since for him history and apocalypticism do not stand in tension to each other. Hence he disagrees with the Bultmannian view that to call the eschatological event a historical event is paradoxical, and states instead that it is only a proleptic form of expression. His emphasis that Easter should be understood in its apocalyptic setting[249] seems to Klein to reflect an assumption that this setting is distinct (though not separable) from the fact, which can be conceived of in and of itself.[250] Klein argues that this distinguishes the object of faith from the ground of faith, with the latter seeming to be the apocalyptic horizon in which that fact is capable of being

---

[246] *Die Apostelgeschichte* (13th ed., *Meyer-Kommentar;* Göttingen: Vandenhoeck und Ruprecht, 1961), pp. 682–689, esp. pp. 688 f. For the longer quotation Haenchen cites Wilckens, *ibid.,* p. 215; the other allusions refer to quotations cited earlier by Haenchen. The other leading German Lucan specialist, Hans Conzelmann, is somewhat more blunt in rejecting the position of Pannenberg. Cf. his essay, *"Randbemerkungen zur Lage im 'Neuen Testament,'" EvTh,* XXII (1962), 228, note 16. Klein's own contributions to Lucan research have in the background the debate with Pannenberg's position, esp. "Lukas 1, 1–4 als theologisches Programm," *Zeit und Geschichte. Dankesgabe an Rudolf Bultmann zum 80. Geburtstag* (Tübingen: J.C.B. Mohr [Paul Siebeck], pp. 193–216.

[247] Pannenberg, *Offenbarung als Geschichte,* pp. 91–114; Klein *MPTh,* LI (1962), pp. 77–84.

[247a] *Ibid.,* p. 78.

[248] In his "Postscript" to *Offenbarung als Geschichte,* p. 143.

[249] *Ibid.,* p. 140, note 19.

[250] Pannenberg replies, *ibid.,* p. 142, note 23, that Klein "bypasses our view that all occurrence strikes upon some context in the history of the transmission of traditions and can be expressed only in relation to this."

understood as the revelation of God. As to the "ground of faith," Pannenberg refers to it as "knowledge" about the revelatory history. Yet such knowledge is "initially" hindered by "superficiality that in earthly affairs sees nothing at work . . . except human motivations."[251] Klein argues that this not only implies a rejection of current critical historical research, but also that it leaves unanswered the question as to how one moves from "superficiality" to "rationality." Recognition of the way Israel came to believe in God seems simply to be equated with recognition that Israel's God actually is. For descriptive statements cast in the mode of the history of religions are taken to be normative knowledge of God.

Trutz Rendtorff seeks in his essay[252] to overcome the current "emphasis on the *otherness* of the church over against the world," which has as its corollary "the basic distinction between the factual historical church . . . and the church of the word."[253] The historical demonstration that the church stems from Jesus is one with the vindication of the empirical church as the true church. Klein maintains that the distinction current in dialectic theology is not ontological, but hermeneutical, i.e., is intended to make clear that it is only as an act of faith that one can identify the empirical church as the true church. He fears that the identification of the historical demonstration of continuity back to Jesus with the vindication of the empirical church as the true church will lead to an "unconditional submission to institutional churchiness."[254]

Pannenberg begins his reply[255] to Klein by expressing surprise at the "tone" of some of the critical articles. "Who would have suspected that some advocates of the dominant theology of the word would be so uncertain of their position that they would have to avoid any divergent proposal by

[251] *Offenbarung als Geschichte,* pp. 101, 103; Klein, *MPTh,* LI (1962), 81.

[252] "Das Offenbarungsproblem im Kirchenbegriff," *Offenbarung als Geschichte,* pp. 115–131; Klein, *ibid.,* pp. 84–86.

[253] Rendtorff, *ibid.,* p. 116 f.; Klein, *ibid.,* p. 84.

[254] *Ibid.,* p. 86.

[255] "Postscript" to *Offenbarung als Geschichte,* pp. 132–148.

means of crude misrepresentations and worn-out tags?"[256] It
is to a considerable extent true that argumentation by gibe,
innuendo, misunderstanding and inadequate representation
has characterized the debate, which makes it at times difficult
to sift out the points worthy of serious discussion. A considerable portion of Pannenberg's "Postscript" is devoted to
correcting misunderstandings or misrepresentations that have
simply been omitted here from the report of the critical essays.
Yet there do emerge in the "Postscript" the beginning of a
formulation of the Pannenbergian position that both ad-
dresses itself to the main line of the emerging criticism and
understands itself as an alternative to the new hermeneutic
(into which the Bultmannian side of the theology of the word
has in part evolved), rather than primarily as an alternative
to the various branches of the antecedent dialectic theology.

Pannenberg makes clear that he does not reject the concept of the word of God, but only "its isolated and generalized
use as a theological principle."[257] And he denies that the stance
of observing from a distance involves disinterestedness; it can
very well implement deep involvement in what is at stake. But
rather than the historicness of existence being presupposed,
the presupposition is rather "that human life always takes
place already caught up in interconnections of traditions."[258]
It is the history of the transmission of traditions that is "the
unity of event and word (i.e., significance)."[259] The traditional context "mediates" the "original meaning," as well as
"all knowledge about what happened (with regard to its factuality and with regard to its significance)," and to this extent
is a kind of hermeneutic.[260] He recognizes "the historical difference [between Biblical times and today] that is constitutive
for the hermeneutical problem," but maintains "that the problems of hermeneutic have been taken up in the concept of

---

[256] *Ibid.*, p. 134.
[257] *Ibid.*, p. 136, note 11.
[258] *Ibid.*, p. 137.
[259] *Ibid.*
[260] *Ibid.*, p. 138.

universal history as the history of the transmission of traditions, i.e., [hermeneutic] is preserved as one aspect and also
left behind as a whole."[261]

Pannenberg concludes his "Postscript" to *Revelation as
History* with the expression of his hope that future discussion
of his proposal might be more oriented to the material issues
than had been the case thus far.[262] He proposes four questions,
which are then accepted by Klein as the topics for the chapters of his response, *Theology of the Word of God and the
Hypothesis of Universal History.*[263]

1. "The question of an alternative to the theology of the
word."[264] Klein argues that Pannenberg does not in fact get
beyond verbal revelation, since it is only the context of traditions that makes of an event revelation, and traditions are
word—although to be sure a different model for language
than "the happening word" of dialectic theology. The understanding of language as "mere words,"[265] in distinction from
one oriented to the view that language "brings with it what it
says," does call for complementation by history; but Klein argues that this is a deficient understanding of both language and
history. He infers that the Pannenbergian position is obliged
to "devaluate" the Biblical word. In the Old Testament this
takes the form of pointing out that prophecies often go unfulfilled, to which Klein comments that the point of the prophetic word is misunderstood when it is taken primarily as
prediction of future event rather than as present event of com-
fort or judgment.[266] The New Testament kerygma is in Klein's

[261] *Ibid.,* p. 139. The detailed presentation of this thesis, to which
Pannenberg at this point alludes, is to be found in an essay significantly
entitled, "Hermeneutik und Universalgeschichte," *ZThK,* LX (1963),
90–121 ["Hermeneutic and Universal History," *JThC,* IV (1967)].

[262] *Ibid.,* pp. 147 f.

[263] *Theologie des Wortes Gottes und die Hypothese der Universalgeschichte. Zur Auseinandersetzung mit Wolfhart Pannenberg (Beiträge
zur evangelischen Theologie,* 37; Munich: Christian Kaiser Verlag,
1964).

[264] Klein, *ibid.,* pp. 12–21.

[265] Pannenberg, "Postscript" to *Offenbarung als Geschichte,* p. 132,
cited by Klein, *ibid.,* p. 12.

[266] Pannenberg, *ibid.,* pp. 132 f.; Klein, *ibid.,* pp. 13–15. Cf. the

view "devaluated" by arguing as does Pannenberg that since it occurs in various forms it is always "left behind" by Jesus' eschatological history. Klein agrees fully that the kerygma is expressed in varying conceptualizations, but argues that there is continuity in the point coming to expression in them, upon which the attention of exegesis as material criticism should be focused.[267] Here one can sense the divergence of the two approaches, one hearing in Biblical language primarily a reference to fact, the other hearing it in primarily the scoring of a point.

2. "The understanding of the relation between the Old Testament, the New Testament and primitive Christianity itself, in terms of the history of the transmission of traditions."[268] Much as in the case of Bultmann's concept of a changing preunderstanding, Pannenberg in his way realizes that the context of traditions may be broken by what happens in history.[269] Yet Klein fears that the possibility of any real criticism of the traditional understanding is eliminated when criticism is "absorbed" as "only an aspect" in a broader context and when the "original meaning" of the "revelatory events" is said to be "mediated" "through the context of traditions."[270] The contingency of new stages in the transmission of traditions seems to be limited by Pannenberg's presupposition that such "steps" are "meaningful," and this in terms of "the understanding of history tending toward a comprehensive unity of meaning," with the history of the transmission of traditions providing the "continuity" between events.[271] From such statements the conventional model of the organic growth

---

similar criticism of Pannenberg by Gerhard Sauter, *Zukunft und Verheissung*, p. 151, note 5: "For [the Reformers] '*promissio*' is not one 'function' of the word of God among others (for example, as 'prediction,' [cf. Pannenberg's thesis 7]), but rather designates comprehensively the character of the life-giving divine word."

267 *Ibid.*, p. 21.
268 *Ibid.*, pp. 22–37.
269 *Ibid.*, p. 137; Klein, *ibid.*, p. 22.
270 Pannenberg, *ibid.*, pp. 138 f., cited by Klein, *ibid.*
271 Pannenberg, *ibid.*, p. 138, note 16, and p. 133, note 3, cited by Klein, *ibid.*, p. 24.

of tradition seems to Klein to emerge. Events that would eliminate tradition hardly fit into the coordinates of traditions in which history is here cast. And the contingency of events would seem to be endangered by the fact that although they are not subsumed under an *a priori* rational pattern or structure, still the given stage of the tradition at which they occur and in terms of which they must have their meaning does function to predetermine the scope of meaning they can be assumed to have. The predominance of tradition over event is also sensed when Pannenberg says that apart from Christianity, the "problem of Old Testament history" was unsolved "in fact" but not "in principle," from which Klein infers that this leaves the Christ event as only a "stimulant" for a "long since potentially complete solution" inherent in the history of the transmission of traditions.[272]

Of course Klein is here drawing inferences from Pannenberg's approach that Pannenberg himself does not draw. And only in a secondary sense can such inferences, even if validly drawn, seriously challenge a theology that would prefer to reformulate its position than to be compelled to draw them. When, conversely, the right wing all too readily bypasses Pannenberg's comments that the relation to tradition may be that of a rupture, and simply takes satisfaction in the fact that intellectual history, often presented elsewhere in modern times in a strange and threatening way, is here cast into the familiar mold of the transmission of traditions, such an inference, neither necessary nor drawn by Pannenberg himself, cannot be made his responsibility[273]

Klein's basic criticism of Pannenberg's approach in terms of the history of the transmission of traditions takes the form of the argument that such a conceptualization is not fully adequate to the subject matter itself. When Pannenberg empha-

---

[272] Pannenberg, *ibid.,* p. 139; Klein, *ibid.,* p. 25.
[273] On the role Pannenberg's position is playing in German conservative circles, cf. Heinz-Dieter Knigge, "Postbultmannian Hermeneutical Attempts," *Perkins School of Theology Journal,* XVII (1964), 26–37, esp. pp. 26 and 37, note 37.

sizes the "indissoluble connection of the Old Testament and late Israelite tradition on the one hand, and the ministry of Jesus and what happened to him on the other,"[274] Klein can agree with the truth in such a statement and yet senses that it is the converse of that structure which would most adequately fit the break with contemporary Judaism involved in Jesus' ministry and what happened to him. He formulates this criticism in the hermeneutical vocabulary of "the difference between language and the intention that calls forth the expression."[275] The (apocalyptic) form of the message and the message itself seem to him not carefully enough differentiated. Pannenberg argues that since the gospel of Jesus' resurrection arose in the context of Jewish apocalyptic expectations of the final resurrection, there is a "connection between that message and this expectation."[276] Klein argues that, materially speaking, one should only say that there was a connection between the *form* the message took and the apocalyptic expectation, i.e., he disagrees with Pannenberg's inference that we have to do here with "a relation that indeed may not be exchanged for just any other."[277] Pannenberg regards a person's decision about the necessity of the apocalyptic sector of Jewish tradition as determinative for whether the person retains the Old Testament. Klein asks "why then [is there] not a corresponding evaluation of Qumran, average Hellenistic Judaism, Philo, the Therapeutae, gnosticizing Judaism, and Gnosticism influenced by Judaism," "to the extent that they have in some way affected primitive Christianity at one or the other layer of its conceptualizations, as many of them have?"[278]

3. "The proleptic character of Jesus' history and especially

---

[274] Pannenberg, *ibid.*, p. 133, cited by Klein, *ibid.*, p. 24.

[275] *Ibid.*, pp. 28 f.

[276] Pannenberg, *ibid.*, p. 140, cited by Klein, *ibid.*, p. 30.

[277] Pannenberg, *ibid.*, p. 140, note 19; Klein, *ibid.* Klein regards such a view as "repristination," the "canonizing of the apocalyptic tradition," *ibid.*, p. 31.

[278] Pannenberg, *ibid.;* Klein, *ibid.*, p. 34. Cf. conversely with regard to non-Jewish elements in Christian apocalypticism Hans Dieter Betz, "Zum Problem des religionsgeschichtlichen Verständnisses der Apokalyptik," *ZThK,* 63 (1966), pp. 391–409.

of his resurrection, is its significance for the concept of revelation."[279] Klein begins his evaluation by noting Pannenberg's remark that the concept of prolepsis is "all too much like a *deus ex machina*," unless, "on the basis of the prolepsis of the Christ event, the proleptic structure of beings as a whole and especially of intellectual acts becomes intelligible."[280] Klein senses a tension between this proleptic view of reality and the other view to the effect that the meaning of all that is preliminary will not only be revealed but will also be first decided by the final event.[281] "The character of preliminariness, which hence pertains to all that is, is the very opposite of the proleptic quality that is to free the thing characterized by it of preliminariness and attribute to it 'insurpassableness.' By bringing together in his mind the proleptic character of the Christ event with the assumedly analogous nature of the whole of being, but then inexplicably declaring the latter to be preliminary, Pannenberg brings the 'insurpassableness of the Christ event' that he has in view into the greatest of danger, and robs himself of whatever argument could be used against the objection that consequently the significance of the Christ event too will only be revealed and even only decided in the eschaton."[282] Pannenberg emphasizes especially the proleptic nature of intellectual activity. For Klein, this prolepsis of the mind is simply what in hermeneutic is called the hermeneutical circle. If a prolepsis seems more intelligible in this area, it is because a prolepsis of the mind is an anticipation of something that already is, even if not already known, i.e., it is a subjective prolepsis, whereas the kind of prolepsis envisaged for the resurrection of Jesus would be an objective prolepsis, in which something that is not yet comes proleptically to be.[283] Klein argues that Pannenberg has not yet made the

---

[279] Klein, *ibid.*, pp. 38–53.
[280] Pannenberg, *ibid.*, p. 143; cited by Klein, *ibid.*, p. 38.
[281] Pannenberg, *ibid.*, p. 142, note 25; cited by Klein, *ibid.*, p. 39.
[282] Klein, *ibid.*, p. 39, citing Pannenberg, *ibid.*, p. 143.
[283] Klein, *ibid.*, p. 40; cf. Gerhard Sauter, *Zukunft und Verheissung,* p. 266, note 35: "Is there demonstrably a genuine connection between [the proleptic structure of beings in general and that of intellectual ac-

category of objective prolepsis an adequately clear concept for interpreting the resurrection of Jesus in relation to history.

Klein argues that the proleptic understanding of Jesus' resurrection as a special instance of the general future resurrection of the dead robs Jesus' resurrection of any decisive significance as itself achieving anything for mankind. He would prefer to think of Jesus' resurrection, rather than being the prolepsis of a future whose reality is in any case assured within the context of Jewish expectation, as the *basis* for the ultimate status of man, which would then be a "follow-up" of Jesus' resurrection.

4. "The dialectic of faith and knowledge in the light of the proleptic eschatological nature of the revelation in Christ."[284] Of course Klein maintains that to hold God to be the object of man's knowledge prior to the commitment of faith is to think of God as being at man's disposal and hence to make of God a thing of the world. But apart from this criticism characteristic of dialectic theology, Klein argues that there is an internal inconsistency in Pannenberg's insistence that knowledge of God is prior to faith and yet is not uninvolved.[285] The difference between the two positions would seem to be neither one of more or less involvement, nor one

---

tivity]? Hardly, in Pannenberg's terminology thus far. Here the apocalyptic structure of 'proleptic unveiling' (*Offenbarung als Geschichte,* p. 107; cf. also p. 105), and what one could perhaps call the anticipation inherent in all knowledge—and hence for Pannenberg also inherent in faith (*ibid.,* p. 102, note 15, and p. 146)—stand alongside each other without mediation."

[284] Klein, *ibid.,* pp. 54–71.

[285] Klein, *ibid.,* pp. 56 f.; cf. Pannenberg, *ibid.,* p. 136: "Every understanding reader of our work must after all see that precisely what is important for us is that the occurrence happening to men strike home to them. . . . Genuine knowledge takes place after all only where a person is completely 'with it,' so that he lets himself be laid claim upon by the subject matter in the act of knowledge—and indeed to the extent that the nature of the subject matter under consideration is able to lay a claim on man. . . . It is uncontested that a purely theoretical stance toward God and his revelatory action would be inappropriate, but this is true only because here the content of knowledge contains a claim upon the whole of one's life, and hence true knowledge must perceive just this factor of being claimed, which points beyond 'mere' knowledge."

of more or less understanding as one gets involved, but rather of the nature of that understanding. For Klein, the fact that the gospel is "a claim upon the whole of one's life" suggests that a person should understand the orientation of his life to God that he is carrying through in the act of faith when he makes that commitment, so that the act of faith is not arbitrary, but an understanding act. For Pannenberg, one's progressive approach toward demonstrated knowledge of the objective truth of the gospel story, to the effect that it happened and was divine action, implies a response commensurate to knowledge of God, which would be the act of religious commitment. In neither case does one come to the gospel equipped with faith as a special conditioning that makes it easier to respond; in neither case can real understanding fail to involve an implicit call for faith. In Klein's view one might, on understanding what is involved in orienting one's life in the light of the gospel, make a negative decision; in Pannenberg's view faith would more directly result as a consequence of demonstrated knowledge.

Pannenberg's distinction between a necessary logical priority of knowledge to faith but an unnecessary psychological priority seems to Klein to break down, since the necessity for the priority is argued psychologically. Klein describes the dilemma in which he sees Pannenberg as follows: "If preaching is assumed not to be able to say to the hearer that 'you must first make the leap into faith in order to be certain,' then [such preaching] would certainly have destroyed itself when it explains to [the hearer]: Before you make the leap into faith you must be certain—but possibly you will become aware of your certainty only after the leap."[286] In Pannenberg's view, on the other hand, one should reckon with degrees of probability in a progressive demonstration of the truth of the gospel, just as is characteristic of other areas of knowledge. The present state of one's knowledge would be adequate to make the act of faith the reasonable thing to do,

---

[286] Klein, *ibid.,* pp. 58 f.; the first quotation is from Pannenberg, in his explanation of Thesis 3, *ibid.,* p. 101.

in that one's present knowledge would lead one to anticipate an ultimate complete demonstration of the gospel's truth.

Klein argues that Pannenberg's intention to ground faith outside itself, an intention shared by Klein, is not successfully carried through, in that faith is grounded in man's knowledge. "For then the difference between the ground [knowledge] and what is grounded [faith] is no longer interpreted as the externality of the ground, but is rather reduced to the difference between two internal ways of human conduct; and this is no real distinction at all, since the grounding knowledge and the grounded faith are connected by an automatic mechanism, which reveals them to be two aspects of a single principle, namely self-assertion."[287] The doctrine of the Holy Spirit seems on the one hand to have no real place, in that the path to faith is identical with the normal exercise of one's rational faculties. But on the other hand some "qualification" of that process is introduced, inconsistently, when Pannenberg affirms: "The elimination of such prejudices [as are in the common mind] can perhaps never be only a matter of rational argumentation. . . . To that extent some sort of illumination is needed in order that the truth, in itself clear and demonstrable, be also accepted by the individual person."[288] The result seems to Klein to be that faith has no certainty, in that it depends on an intellectual capacity largely absent today; lacking also is any implicit trust in the traditions that might replace such intellectual conviction. Hence the believer's assumption that the resurrection is not a hallucination is after all "a simple act of decision, which [Pannenberg] had otherwise so discredited."[289] Pannenberg however explains that "it is not primarily the 'modern world' that is to be brought to an acknowledgement of the truth of Christian claims with

---

[287] Klein, *ibid.*, p. 66. Georg Muschalek, "Offenbarung in Geschichte," *ZKTh*, LXXXVI (1964), 181, argues that such proven knowledge is not the objective of medieval theology, e.g., of Thomas, but is rather a Cartesian innovation.

[288] Pannenberg, *ThLZ*, LXXXVIII (1963), 89; cited by Klein, *ibid.*, p. 67.

[289] Klein, *ibid.*, p. 69.

regard to history, but rather *the Christians themselves* who must live in an atmosphere of the reliability of the Christian message. There will always be a 'world' that does not find the Christian message convincing. But the question is whether the Christians themselves can be validly convinced of the universal validity of this message—and can also convince, to be sure not 'the modern world,' but indeed individual thinking persons."[290]

The most careful and important criticism to come from one who is also partly appreciative of the direction of Pannenberg's thought is that of Jürgen Moltmann, who was Pannenberg's colleague during the latter's three years on the faculty of the *Kirchliche Hochschule* in Wuppertal. Moltmann's *Theology of Hope*,[291] oriented to God's word of promise, is the most recent systematic theology to emerge from within the tradition of the theology of the word, and thus serves to bring to expression in discussion with Pannenberg not only the diverging formulations, but also the extent to which parallel developments are taking place.

Moltmann presents the Pannenbergian position as modeled after Greek more than Biblical thought. "This theology of universal history obviously presents itself initially as an expansion and surpassing of Greek cosmic theology. In place of the cosmic proof of God that inferred from 'reality as cosmos' a divine *Arche* or First Principle and thus demonstrated a cosmological monotheism, there emerges a theology of history that infers from the unity of 'reality as history' the one God of history, by means of the same inferential procedure. The epistemological method remains the same, only in place of the closed cosmos that becomes theophany in the symmetry and harmony of the eternal return of the same, we have a cosmos open to the future with a teleological orientation. Thus

---

[290] Quotation is from a letter of clarification.
[291] *Theologie der Hoffnung. Untersuchungen zur Begründung und zu den Konsequenzen einer christlichen Eschatologie* (*Beiträge zur evangelischen Theologie*, 38; Munich: Christian Kaiser Verlag, 1964, 2nd and 3rd ed., 1965). Quotation is from the 2nd ed.

'history' becomes the new category for 'reality in its totality.' In place of the metaphysical point of unity for the cosmos we have the eschatological point of direction and unity for history. Just as that metaphysical point of unity made the cosmos recognizable as indirect revelation of God, just so now the end of history makes history recognizable as indirect revelation of God."[292]

This comparison with Greek thought gradually moves into a contrast with the theology of the word, and the criticism implicit in Moltmann's presentation comes to the surface. "In the place of kerygmatic theology that experiences God in the event of the word of address, a theology of history would emerge that perceives God from the 'language of facts.' As in Greek cosmic theology the eternal being of God appears indirectly in the beings and can be inferred from them, just so God's being is here to be recognized in the having-been-ness of history. . . . In going beyond Greek cosmic theology, the basic insight of the Old Testament, that 'history is the occurrence suspended between promise and fulfillment,' which was the point of departure for Pannenberg and Rendtorff, has actually been given up in favor of a universal historical eschatology confirming itself in 'reality as a whole.' Such an eschatology achieves its eschatological character only from the fact that reality is not yet visible as a whole, since it has not yet reached its end. But in this position the Old Testament's God of promise is in danger of becoming a *Theos epiphanēs,* whose epiphany is presented by the whole of reality in its completion. . . . It remains unclear whether the place of a theophany in nature is merely taken over by the theophany in history, as nature open to the future, or whether the fundamentally other condition of the possibility of perceiving reality as history, namely on the basis of promise, is intended. This theology of history opposed to theology of the word remains exposed to Kant's criticism of theological metaphysics so long as it does not itself reflect critically on the condition of the

[292] *Ibid.,* p. 68.

possibility of perceiving reality as history in an eschatologically and theologically qualified sense."[293]

Moltmann does recognize that Pannenberg's understanding of the cosmos as in substance universal history reopens the question of the validity of the cosmological argument for the existence of God, in that Pannenberg argues that the unity of reality requires for its completion the existence of God. And Moltmann favors the hermeneutical inference that texts from the past are not to be made relevant to the present only by identifying their understanding of existence, but that "they are to be read with regard to their historical position and hour, their own historical connection backwards and forwards."[294] Moltmann agrees with Pannenberg's hermeneutical principle: "Only a conception of the course of history actually connecting then with today and its future horizon can provide the all-embracing horizon in which the limited present horizon of the interpreter and the historical horizon of the text are fused."[295] But Moltmann observes: "Since this all-embracing historic connection within history can always be formulated only as a finite, preliminary, and hence surpassable perspective, it remains fragmentary in view of an open future."[296] That is to say, Moltmann finds at this point a missing link for a cosmological argument for the existence of God. "Here is maintained the necessity for bringing 'God' to expression in the whole of reality, and yet at the same time the impossibility is conceded of being able to grasp a still unterminated and hence historic reality as a 'totality.' So it would be better to give up the intentions of a cosmological proof of God. As long as this reality of the world and man in it is not yet 'complete,' and indeed its completeness is historically still at stake, no God can be proven from it. The 'all-embracing historic connection' that connects then with today, the historical hori-

[293] *Ibid.*, pp. 68 f.
[294] *Ibid.*, p. 254.
[295] Pannenberg, "Hermeneutik und Universalgeschichte," *ZThK*, LX (1963), 116, cited by Moltmann, *ibid.*, p. 255.
[296] Moltmann, *ibid.*

zon with the present horizon of the future, is no connection of events related one to the other, but rather a connection of the history of commission and promise. The horizons do not 'fuse' in the question of the connection of occurrences between today and then, but only in the question of the intended future then and today."[297]

Moltmann's presentation of Pannenberg's position moves into a more parallel structuring on the basis of the recognition of a second dimension in the Pannenbergian position, as the orientation of "history" to "the language of facts" is transcended by one in terms of the history of the transmission of traditions. "The understanding of history as the history of the transmission of traditions no longer presents itself as an alternative to kerygmatic theology, as was the case with the expression 'the language of facts,' that after all could only be meant polemically. Rather the attempt is made to pull together what is becoming separated, namely 'word,' word event, interpretation, evaluation, etc., on the one hand, and *'factum,'* facts and their interconnections on the other hand. . . . The modern separation of 'factuality' and 'significance' is thus eliminated in the understanding of history as the history of the transmission of traditions, in a way analogous to that in Gerhard Ebeling's 'theology of the word event.' If [in Ebeling's position] the events are done justice to in conjunction with the word in which they were originally proclaimed, then [in Pannenberg's position] the words and traditions are done justice to in conjunction with the historical occurrences. Yet the decisive question arises as to *how* the Cartesian and Kantian separation of reality from the perceiving of it is overcome. The intention of grasping the real occurrences in the original

---

[297] *Ibid.,* p. 255. Cf. Gerhard Sauter, *Zukunft und Verheissung,* p. 191, note 21: "[The agreement of such a universal-history interest with the intention of historicism] raises the question whether the prolepsis of the eschaton in Jesus' history is not primarily intended to ground anew what Troeltsch called the 'metaphysical faith' in the unity and totality of history. If this is the case, eschatology would again be weakened; for this unity and totality cannot be laid claim to as a hermeneutical principle for understanding past history."

experiential and traditional connection in which they first came to expression can be implemented both hermeneutically as word event and in terms of universal history as event in the totality of historical reality."[298]

Moltmann emphasizes that modern historiography's criticism of the tradition must be done justice by both positions. "Since the Enlightenment the historical criticism of the Christian traditions involves in ever increasing radicality a crisis of the traditions, if indeed one should not speak of a revolutionary break in traditions. Since this crisis and this criticism, 'tradition' is no longer 'a matter of course.' The relation to history as tradition has become a reflective relation and has lost its immediacy. Hence if one wishes to understand 'history as tradition,' a new concept of 'tradition' must be attained that takes up within it historical criticism and its consciousness of crisis with regard to history, without repudiating or nullifying it."[299]

Moltmann directs this criticism primarily to the Pannenbergian proof of the resurrection. "The thesis that this occurrence of Jesus' resurrection must be basically verifiable 'historically' would first have to transform the concept of the historical so that it admits resurrection by God and, in this resurrection, can make the announced end of history knowable. To call Jesus' resurrection historically verifiable presupposes a concept of history that is dominated by the expectation of a general resurrection of the dead as the end and completion of history. Thus there is a circle of understanding between the concept of history and resurrection."[300]

Apart from historiographical concerns, Moltmann has theological questions. He wonders if such an apocalyptic understanding of history suffices to give expression to the Easter

---

[298] *Ibid.*, p. 71. For an illustration of the extent to which the two new conceptualizations can be used in a parallel way in historical research, cf. my essay "Kerygma and History in the New Testament," *The Bible in Modern Scholarship*, ed. by J. Philip Hyatt (Nashville: Abingdon Press, 1965), pp. 114–150.

[299] Moltmann, *ibid.*, p. 72.

[300] *Ibid.*

event. For then the church would look forward less to Jesus than to its own resurrection, "the repetition of what already happened to Jesus, but not the future of the Resurrected." The gospel is not that we will be raised as he was, but that he is the resurrection and the life, "and that hence the believers find their future *in* him and not only *like* him." Moltmann's own position comes to expression in the criticism: "The apocalyptic, universal historical horizon for interpreting the whole of reality is secondary to the promissory and missionary horizon of this transformation of the world."[301]

Moltmann also thinks the apocalyptic understanding of history is responsible for a neglect of the theology of the cross, which is not just an interlude between Jewish apocalypticism and Christian eschatology but rather brands the latter as *eschatologia crucis*. "The contradiction of the cross also runs through the existence, the path and the theological thinking of the church in the world."[302] Moltmann favors the Pannenbergian openness to the world, which he also finds in Barth and Bonhoeffer's call to proclaim Christ's rule in the concrete everydayness of the world. But he questions whether Pannenberg has faced squarely the concrete reality of an eschatology in a world such as ours. "The question remains whether [Pannenberg's] expression about 'verifying the deity of the Biblical God on the totality of our time's experience of reality,' is appropriate. For this task will turn out to be less a confirmation or surpassing than a conflict and a difference. The uncritical use of concepts such as 'historical,' 'history,' 'facts,' 'tradition,' 'reason,' etc., in a theological sense seems to show that the methodological, practical and ideological atheism of modern times is more nearly bypassed than taken seriously. If this atheism, as Hegel and Nietzsche most profoundly understood it, derives from a nihilistic perception of the 'speculative Good Friday,' i.e., 'God is dead,' then theology could actually be advocated only as a theology of resurrection over against this reality, over against this reason, and over against society

[301] *Ibid.*, p. 73.
[302] *Ibid.*

structured in this way—and indeed as an eschatology of resurrection as the future of the Crucified."[303]

Concern for the problem of a ground for hope in the future in a world situation such as ours, a topic put in focus in Germany by the philosopher Ernst Bloch's two-volume work on *The Principle Hope*,[304] together with the absence from Barth's *Church Dogmatics* of the concluding fifth volume on eschatology, may account for the fact that another young theologian in the Barthian tradition, Gerhard Sauter, has published a work rather similar to Moltmann's *Theology of Hope*, entitled *Future and Promise*.[305] And, like Moltmann, Sauter is in this regard rather comparable to Pannenberg himself, yet with many of the same reservations.

Sauter shares Moltmann's view[306] that apocalypticism is hardly a category from which to derive an understanding of history as revelation. " 'History is reality in its totality'—but the apocalypticist means this, in spite of the divine 'world law,' in terms of world history as the history of the world that remains separated from God precisely in its totality. The end of history is the negation of [the world's] negativities: time not only as limited, but especially as corrupt time (cf. Rev. 10:6); and the impotency of the world (4 Ezra 4:26 f.)."[307] Furthermore, Sauter regards the view of Jesus as a prolepsis of the apocalyptic end, though related to apocalypticism's deterministic fixing of history before the beginning of time, as breaking down apocalypticism's understanding of revelation. "Admittedly the apocalyptic structure of revelation as a pre-temporal unveiling of the end has helped

---

[303] *Ibid.*, p. 74.

[304] *Das Prinzip Hoffnung* (Berlin: Aufbau-Verlag, 1954–1959, 2nd ed., 1959), as Volume V of his collected works.

[305] *Zukunft und Verheissung. Das Problem der Zukunft in der gegenwärtigen theologischen und philosophischen Diskussion* (Zürich/Stuttgart: Zwingli Verlag, 1965). The book is a *Habilitationsschrift* presented under the Barthians Ernst Wolf and Otto Weber at the University of Göttingen in 1964. Sauter states, p. 80, that his work was completed prior to seeing Moltmann's book.

[306] Cf. above, p. 21, note 81.

[307] Sauter, *ibid.*, p. 244, note 49, citing Pannenberg, *KuD*, V (1959), 222 [*Essays on Old Testament Hermeneutics*, p. 319].

make 'what happened to Jesus Christ' intelligible as such a 'prolepsis.' Of course this took place at the cost of a re-interpretation of prolepsis, perhaps necessitated by the New Testament. Prolepsis cannot subject itself to the apocalyptic concept of revelation, for it materially breaks through [that concept]."[308] Sauter continues in terms of a quotation from Pannenberg: " 'For Jesus, the relation to the whole of reality is given through . . . the eschatological character of his gos-pel, of his claim, and of what happened to him. For in that [history's] end, which happened in advance in the claim of Jesus and in what happened to him, comes into sight, history for the first time attains its completeness'—not at all! For this relation of sight to event destroys precisely the apocalyptic correlation between 'complete' history and revelation! The 'simultaneity' of completeness and the end remains a teleologi-cal, but not an eschatological axiom."[309]

Sauter is also concerned to emphasize that a total view is inaccessible to finite man. "But the concept of 'universal his-tory' lays claim to a totality of truth itself. The true is the universal! Yet this impulse may be appropriated only in view of the 'not yet' nature of our knowledge and [should] not per-mit completion to be reached ahead of time (1 Cor. 13:9 f., 12)."[310] He recalls Barth's use of the term proleptic to refer to man's presumption ("no proleptic clutching after God's fulness"), to warn against a possible danger or misuse in the understanding of prolepsis. "Anticipatory security, *securitas* as distorted hope, would take from prolepsis what grounds it— namely, its being God's own act. Man lays hold of promised future in proleptic security, even though it be merely that by pointing to the prolepsis of the end of the world he seeks to insure himself of its completeness and thus of the history of the promise. If, as with Pannenberg, 'prolepsis' is to serve as a mobile teleological concept for the whole, this danger must

---

[308] Sauter, *ibid.,* p. 256.
[309] Sauter, *ibid.,* note 12, citing Pannenberg, "Kerygma und Ge-schichte," *Studien zur Theologie der alttestamentlichen Überlieferungen,* p. 139, note 19.
[310] Sauter, *ibid.,* pp. 183 f.

be seen, precisely because it is an eschatologically suitable term."[311]

The juxtaposition of the theology of history and the theology of the word comes to expression in Sauter's discussion of the history of the transmission of traditions, which he prefers to conceive of as the hermeneutical process through which a promise goes, as it is reinterpreted in the light of ongoing events, with the promise providing the basis in terms of which such events retrospectively come together into a course of divine acts that can be called a history. "But can one then simply proceed to speak of historical *continuity?* This question, which prophetic reflection leaves completely open, must be posed over against the total claim of a 'world as history.' For this claim reckons with the continuum of a historical world in its unity and completeness. . . . If it is accurate that in prophecy 'the future saving event is conceived of in analogy to the past [saving event],' then this 'conception' is bound to the recall of the past and, to this extent, to the promissory tradition that helps set up the horizon for understanding. [Yet] is a promise [in fact] such a 'concept,' which, by referring to earlier divine action or at least to old announcements, would serve only to let what is coming be *known?*"[312] Sauter would prefer to regard the promise as the active force calling forth history, rather than simply a commentary on it. Somewhat similarly, Sauter acknowledges the history of the transmission of traditions as a method, but prefers to think of promise rather than the transmission of traditions as what is basic to reality. "The procedure of study, the investigation of prophetic texts for elements of tradition to permit conclusions about a context of tradition, can be confused with [the process in which] these texts themselves came to be. The method with its conclusions takes the place of the object, or at least is identified with it. The history of the transmission of traditions, as a process of eclectic and thus creative interpretation of what is transmitted—as can however be established only retrospec-

---

[311] *Ibid.,* pp. 265 f.
[312] *Ibid.,* pp. 208 f., citing Pannenberg, *ibid.,* p. 136.

tively in terms of its results, but not as it is taking place!—
becomes [in such a view] the continuity presupposed by prophetic eschatology, and indeed by the promise itself. . . .
Hence, in such a concept in terms of the history of the transmission of traditions, 'promise' can hardly 'announce' anything
other than the impetus of a tradition that is so saturated with
contents that it cannot be exhausted by individual (quite
unique and unrepeatable) situations. . . . Yet the interest in
historical continuity as a pervasive 'structure' of the promissory history will have to open itself to the question of whether
it takes note of the mobility of prophetic reflection, which can
project the future quite without the guideline of the past, and
even outside the area of play provided by growing experience.
What has been remains too much in dialogue; it is subjected
to reflection, or left to be forgotten. The breaks, turns, and
new beginnings of the history to be investigated cannot be
pointed out in terms of a given continuity; rather God's faithfulness 'perseveres' in and in spite of all apparent discontinuity of the tradition."[313] Hence Sauter is concerned for the
openness of the future when the latter is projected upon the
history of the transmission of traditions,[314] and prefers to think
of the future in terms of God's promise, with *promissio* a
favorite term of Luther's for designating the word of God.

The theology of Wolfhart Pannenberg is to some extent
already known and discussed in America. He was a visiting
professor at the University of Chicago during the Spring of
1963, and at that time lectured widely in the United States.
*Christianity Today* has welcomed him as the way out of the
"chaos in European theology."[315] And Daniel P. Fuller, Dean

---

[313] Sauter, *ibid.,* pp. 210 f.

[314] *Ibid.,* p. 194.

[315] The second installment in the series under that title, in the issue of
Oct. 9, 1964, p. 19, concludes with a positive section entitled, interest-
ingly enough, "The New Frontiers," which begins: "The formative theology of the foreseeable future is not likely to be Barth's, Brunner's, or
Bultmann's, but rather an alternative to all three. The *Heilsgeschichte*
school is calling for a fuller correlation of revelation and history. The
traditional conservative scholars have long attacked dialectic theology

of Fuller Theological Seminary, has become a stanch sup-
porter of Pannenberg, and especially of his treatment of the
resurrection, although Fuller would want to "adjust his system
slightly" so as to include supernaturalism.[316] American Lu-
theranism, whose traditional conservatism has often made it
more wary of contemporary German theology than its denom-
inational and cultural affinities would otherwise indicate, has
tended to look with approval upon Pannenberg.[317] Furthermore his criticism of modern historical method finds its congenial counterpart in Richard R. Niebuhr's study of *Resurrection and Historical Reason*,[318] so that they have independently arrived at somewhat similar positions. And John B.
Cobb, Jr., has welcomed Pannenberg's radical break with dialectic theology and his concomitant openness to American theological trends that have stood in the Hegelian more than the
Kantian tradition.[319] The forthcoming publication of the Eng-

in even wider dimensions. And a revolt against dialectic theology has
been under way among several followers of Wolfhart Pannenberg of
Mainz. . . ." Cf. in the same issue the article, "Revelation in History," p.
33: "In their insistence on objective historical revelation, traditional conservative scholars are now being joined by *Heilsgeschichte* scholars and the
Pannenberg movement in a fresh probe of the problem of revelation and
history." Similarly, Dec. 4, 1964, pp. 13 f., in the editorial, "Basic Issues
in Modern Theology: Revelation in History." Cf. also the republication
of much of this same material under the editor's name, Carl F. H. Henry,
"European Theology Today," *Faith and Thought: Journal of the Vic-
toria Institute*, XCIV (1965), 9–91.

[316] "A New German Theological Movement," *Scottish Journal of Theology*, XIX (1966), 160–175, esp. p. 175; "The Resurrection of Jesus
and the Historical Method," *Journal of Bible and Religion*, XXXIV
(1966), 18–24. Cf. also Fuller's Basel dissertation, *Easter Faith and
History* (Grand Rapids, Mich.: Wm. B. Eerdmans Publishing Co., 1965),
esp. pp. 176–197, 237 f., 251–253.

[317] The Lutheran journal, *Dialogue,* includes Pannenberg on its editorial board and has published articles by him: "The Crisis of the
Scripture-Principle in Protestant Theology," 11 (1963), 307–313; "Did
Jesus Really Rise from the Dead?" IV (1965), 128–135. Cf. by its editor,
Carl E. Braaten, the "How New Is the New Hermeneutic?" *Theology To-
day*, XXII (1965), in which his polemic against Volume 2 of this series
(on which cf. my reply in the "Critic's Corner," *ibid.,* pp. 277–282) is
matched only by his enthusiasm for the theological position discussed in
Volume 3. Cf. also the article by Robert L. Wilken, "Who is Wolfhart
Pannenberg," *Dialogue,* IV (1965), 140–142.

[318] New York: Charles Scribner's Sons, 1957.

[319] "A New Trio Arises in Europe," reprinted from the *Christian Advo-*

lish translations of Pannenberg's Christology, his booklet on Anthropology, and his collected essays,[320] together with a year as visiting professor at Harvard and Claremont in 1966–67, give added impetus to the discussion of Pannenberg's theology in America. Thus the present volume is only a foretaste of significant things to come.

*cate* of July 2, 1964, in *New Theology No. 2,* ed. by Martin E. Marty and Dean G. Peerman (New York: The Macmillan Company, 1965), pp. 257–263, esp. pp. 261 f.

[320] *Grundzüge der Christologie,* being published by Westminster Press; *Was ist der Mensch? Die Anthropologie der Gegenwart im Lichte der Theologie,* being published by Fortress Press; *Gesammelte Studien zur Grundlegung der Systematischen Theologie* will also appear in translation soon. A booklet of lectures in English concerning the relevance of the kingdom of God for theology will also be published by Westminster Press.

# 2. The Revelation of God in Jesus of Nazareth

## WOLFHART PANNENBERG

*University of Mainz*

### I

The central confession of Christians is that in dealing with Jesus of Nazareth we are dealing with God himself. Therefore we can hope to gain our salvation through Jesus: for salvation, the blessedness which all men are seeking, becomes reality only by fellowship with God. But how can we find God in Jesus? That has become more and more difficult for modern men. We do not find God any longer in the natural world, nor in the history of mankind. Jesus, too, is known only as a human being. He may be an especially noble human being, but today it is very difficult to understand that Jesus could have been more than a mere human being.

The problem is made still more difficult by the fact that we are frequently assured that without Jesus we would not know anything of God. For many people today the concept of God in any form seems to be shaken by atheism. It is widely taken for granted that our view of the world no longer has need of the concept of God. Even the possibility of Christian faith without God, without even using the word God and without any concept of God, has been considered.[1] But the-

---

[1] Cf. Herbert Braun, "Die Problematik einer Theologie des Neuen Testaments," *ZThK, Beiheft* 2 (1961), pp. 1–18 ["The Problem of a New Testament Theology," *The Bultmann School of Biblical Interpretation: New Directions?, JThC,* I (1965), pp. 169–183]. Braun tries to

ology has also taken advantage of atheism by maintaining that one can only speak of God because of Jesus Christ. But then, how can I find God in Jesus? How can I find in him the reality which is my ultimate concern and which makes Jesus more important to me than all other men? Can I perhaps find it only by entrusting myself unreservedly to him? But how am I to do so? Formerly many Christians thought that man's conscience is so overwhelmed by Jesus' ethical majesty that men for that reason can take Jesus' image as a guide and completely trust in him. However, I think we can no longer take this course.[2] Conscience does not everywhere and always have the same standards. The last fifty years have shown how variable the contents of men's consciences may be. Even the most monstrous deeds are done, not with a bad but with a good conscience. There are also points of view from which the ethical majesty in the figure of Jesus appears by no means unsurpassed. On the contrary, from them he appears one-sided, a man who avoided the human tasks in the world. Then is there nothing else left but Jesus' claim that people should follow him? Does this mere demand, whether made by Jesus himself or by the proclamation of the Church, justify in itself our trusting in Jesus and his message? Would not such trust be very gullible?

Did Jesus himself demand the confidence of his hearers in such a way? By no means. He claimed the God of Israel as his authority, a God already known to his hearers. He stood in a tradition that expected the coming of this God, the coming of his reign, and it was just this future which he announced to be near. In Jesus' thinking and message the nearness of God's reign became so overwhelming that by comparison all other tasks and interests of life lost their meaning. From this it follows, to be sure, that Jesus' message and his person became one. Rejection of Jesus, who lived only to announce the reign

---

demythologize the concept of God. He concludes that God is "a certain kind of brotherliness among men," p. 18.

2 For further information see my article, "Die Krise des Ethischen und die Theologie," *ThLZ*, LXXXVII (1962), 7–16.

of God, necessarily meant the rejection of God's nearness itself. And where Jesus himself was accepted, that meant that his message was accepted, too. He became one with his message by the exclusive concern for God's nearness that he demanded of men. For him the only important concern in each man's life was orientation toward the God whose coming was near. Jesus realized that with the acceptance or the rejection of the reign of God as the guiding principle of one's life everything is decided, for better or for worse. By comparison, a man's former life, whether meritorious or laden with sins, was of no interest to him. Therefore, without any further condition, Jesus could pronounce forgiveness of sins upon those who opened themselves to his message of the nearness of God or even upon those who only trusted in him personally. Jesus pregnantly expressed his message by celebrating the eschatological meal with publicans and sinners—in every respect unqualified people. If they accepted table fellowship with him, they had accepted his message in accepting him, for in his own person he was bringing that nearness of God which he proclaimed. In this way they were already participating in that community with God which was an object of hope for the end of days, a hope symbolized by table fellowship (the eschatological banquet).

The starting point of the whole conduct of Jesus as briefly sketched above was the proclamation that the reign of God, which the Jews had been praying for and expecting before the appearance of Jesus, was now near. Thus Jesus did not demand trust in his person without giving reasons for it. Only indirectly did his person come into play, on account of the peculiar exclusiveness of his message, which in turn is connected with the fact that it was concerned with God. His message presupposed not only a knowledge of God, but the expectation of his future reign on earth. Jesus brought hardly anything that was new. He shared the Israelite tradition of his hearers. But by so sharply stressing its essence, which consisted in their relation to God, he clashed with other elements of Israelite tradition, especially with the traditional validity of the Law; this was something new which unleashed many a conflict.

If, then, continuity with Israel's understanding of God and with Israel's eschatological expectation was constitutive for Jesus' message through a shared tradition, and consequently for his claim to authority, then it does not accord with Jesus' conduct when today his bare claim to authority (or the corresponding claim of the Christian proclamation authorized by him) is declared to be the ultimate foundation of faith. One cannot understand Jesus' claim unless one realizes its presuppositions, namely, knowledge of God and the anticipation of the future fulfillment of God's will on earth. Israel's God, it is true, does not reveal himself as he really is until the message of Jesus; nevertheless, a knowledge of him is already presupposed for the understanding of Jesus' message. Before that, the Jews knew their God, and yet did not know him aright; otherwise they would not have rejected Jesus. Only through Jesus does it become clear what the God of Israel really is and means. And yet this final understanding presupposes a knowledge of this God prior to it and also a hope for God's presence. To believe in Jesus' claim when one shares these presuppositions of his is obviously something quite different from cleaving to him without them. With his unrestricted message Jesus did apparently also awaken and accept the trust of gentiles. But that is somewhat different from the summons to faith made by the proclamation. This summons of Jesus was addressed to the Jews only.

Now the Jewish presuppositions are not directly our own. We do not stand in the continuity of Israel's tradition, except through Jesus. Our problem is how to come to Jesus, and afterward perhaps through him to Israel too. For non-Jews the uniqueness of Israel in comparison with the other religions is by no means simply a matter of fact. At first they will take Israel's God simply as one among many other deities found in the history of religions. The real meaning of Israel's God will be realized by non-Jews only in connection with the importance of the history of religions as a whole and with the general phenomena of religious experience. If these mean nothing to us, the God of Israel cannot be of any importance to us, and even Jesus then hardly can be for us what he was for his age. But if we are convinced that human religious experiences and ideas are not merely fantastic images, but that they deal with a reality *sui generis*—in whatever queer and inadequate way this divine reality may have been understood by the different religions—if we are aware of something "behind" these, of something that we have to consider seriously, then also the God of Israel attains the status of a reality for us. Then it becomes relevant to ask wherein may consist his peculiarity, as distinguished from other deities of other religions. Even this peculiarity, however, must be understood against the background of the general phenomena of religious experience and in connection with the history of religions, especially those of the Ancient Near East.

This way of thinking is indispensable for the non-Jew, but it stands by no means in unbridgeable opposition to the way in which the Jews themselves, and thus Jesus too, were thinking about Israel's God. That the religion of Israel cannot be taken all by itself, but has to be seen in its religious environment, is not a consideration altogether exterior to it. The religion of Israel did not fall straight from heaven as a pure revelation.[3] On the contrary, the beginnings of Israel and precisely that of the Israelite conception of God were closely interwoven with the Ancient Near Eastern religions and their history. We know today that the Biblical concept of God grew up out of some seven different roots: Yahweh, the Kenite pilgrim's god, from whom the god of the Exodus was probably originally distinct, was at first only one of these seven roots. Only in Palestine was he fused with the three paternal gods, the God of Abraham, the God of Isaac, and the God of Jacob. These paternal gods had probably earlier been fused with a special form of the pansemitic El as god of heaven,

---

[3] Cf. Klaus Koch, "Der Tod des Religionsstifters. Erwägungen über das Verhältnis Israels zur Geschichte der altorientalischen Religionen," *KuD*, VIII (1962), 100–123. On what follows here, see esp. pp. 105 ff.

and thus came to be connected with each other. There is something peculiar about these origins, but that is true in some way of each religious phenomenon. The peculiarity of Israel's religion within the Ancient Near East and then within the whole history of religion has become more and more distinctive within the course of its own history. But even in the Persian and Hellenistic periods the peculiarity of Israel was still taking shape in constant interaction with the religious environment. The growth of Israel's religion cannot be imagined without certain presuppositions which Israel had in common with its neighbors. Without those influences, which were still alive though changed by assimilation, neither the development of Israelite traditions nor the message of Jesus, as far as it is based on these special traditions, is conceivable.

The non-Jew, if he has not yet as a matter of course taken over the Old Testament along with the Christian tradition but rather has yet to assure himself of the Christian tradition itself, must make the general history of religions his starting point for understanding the peculiarity of Israel. The question as to the truth which is to be accorded religious phenomena in general makes possible the question about the truth of religious transformations and peculiarities. These latter are by no means to be reduced to a notion of religion-in-general. Such a conception, however, is indispensable for every preliminary approach to a specific religion. But such an abstract notion must not only be modified, but also be sublimated by penetrating into the specific historical structure of that religion. In so doing the decisive question is whether the historical transformations and peculiarities are judged to be essential (over against a notion of religion-in-general) or whether they are regarded as something merely secondary.

From a notion of religion-in-general to the understanding of the truth of a single, individual religious message—this, actually, was the course the Hellenistic world took in accepting Jesus' message and its Jewish heritage. And here, too, the particular individuality of the Christian proclamation, and not some general notion of god, had to be taken as essential for true knowledge of the Christian God. The inquiry of Greek philosophers into the true structure of the divine, into its very nature in contrast to the man-made conceptions of their traditional religions, had given Hellenistic man access to all foreign religious traditions. Thus the originally philosophical question concerning the truly divine, penetrating the common consciousness of the Hellenistic age, provided the presupposition for the early Christian mission to the gentiles. In this it corresponded to the function of the Old Testament concept of God in the message of Jesus. As a matter of fact, then as now, it was indispensable that the hearer have the conviction corresponding to the presupposition of the Israelite conception of God, that a single God is the author of the world and of all reality if the message of Jesus is to encounter any understanding at all among gentiles or his claim be meaningfully heard. This presupposition, however, can be made still more precise. It was probably not until the Hellenistic age that Greek thinking arrived at this level. Then it became widely acknowledged that the one God is not known in his essence to everyone, but unknown. Hence men need a revelation of him in order through union with him to be redeemed from transitoriness and to participate in his imperishable life. Only in such a mental climate could Jesus' message of God's future reign and of the apocalyptic expectation, which he shared, of a corresponding transformation of the righteous to an imperishable life, be understood by non-Jews, or at least be translated into their own world of thought.

It is true, however, that the gentile presuppositions cannot simply be equated with the Jewish ones involved in Jesus' message, whose place they took in the Hellenistic Christian proclamation. Jesus himself and his message emerged from the Jewish tradition, and, as we have already seen, compared with that tradition he taught nothing that was completely new. His message was new only insofar as it so radically stressed the central content of the Jewish faith (that is, hope in the God of Israel himself), that everything else seemed no longer to be of any importance—even the traditional Law, which hitherto

had been considered the criterion for salvation. In this respect
Jesus' message also implied a transformation of the Jewish
heritage, even of the hitherto prevailing Jewish understanding
of God, although at this very point Jesus' roots are firmly in
the tradition. The traditional anticipation of the coming reign
of God became with Jesus the only decisive point. Thus the
traditional understanding of God as the author and guarantor
of the law was changing into the concept of a sin-forgiving
Father who through the message of Jesus has turned toward
men in unconditional love. This transformation occurred, however, not as an innovation, but precisely because Jesus took the
expectation of the coming reign with utter seriousness.

In comparison with this, it was an encounter between two
quite different positions when the early Christian message
came into contact with the philosophical conception of the
true God. Therefore the Hellenistic conception of God was
obliged to undergo a transformation not inherent to its nature.
The Jewish tradition had been transformed from within by
the appearance of Jesus. The non-Jewish conception of the
one unknown God, however, was taken over and transformed
from *without* by the Biblical heritage as shaped in the message and history of Jesus. And yet it remains true, as we mentioned above, that no real violence was done to the Hellenistic
conception of God; rather, it found a deeper fulfillment. In
the proclamation of the Christian mission it was possible for a
Hellenistic man to recognize in a surprising and unforeseen
shape that God about whose true nature he had been inquiring. Such acknowledgment of the God of the Bible as the true
God had been only exceptionally possible before Christ. In
spite of all the Jewish propaganda the Jewish religion of law,
conserving as it often did many elements of inner-Jewish tradition which had long been obsolete, was never really able to
convince Hellenistic men that (as Philo, for example, claimed)
it was the only true worship of the one true God. In this respect the Epistle to the Ephesians very well characterizes the
religious-historical process of the expansion of the Christian

faith in the Hellenistic world: by the cross of Jesus Christ the
Law as the middle wall of partition that separated the Jews
from the gentiles is broken down (Eph. 2:13 ff.). Not until
he was presented in the form of the Christian message did the
Biblical God convince the gentile world of his claim to be the
one true God.

## II

We have thus far concluded that Jesus' claim to authority
did not arise by itself, or in isolation, as the basis for faith in
God's revelation in Jesus Christ, because Jesus' message itself
presupposed that his Jewish audience had a knowledge of
God. We noted that on the part of the gentile hearers of the
early Church's missionary message, the philosophers' search for
the true God (in contrast to the gods of the state) was a presupposition that to a considerable extent corresponded with
what could be presupposed in a Jewish audience. However,
neither Jesus' message nor the early Christian proclamation
was content simply to rest with these presuppositions. They
were *only* presuppositions, though of varying value. The presupposed Jewish knowledge of God was recast by the appearance of Jesus. Only then for the first time was the God of the
Jews revealing himself as the God he really is. And the Greeks'
quest for God was revised and corrected when it found its
answer in Christianity.[4] This answer was not to be found in
the direction which the inquiry had taken, but was one which
transformed the seeker himself. Not until then did he realize
for whom he had been inquiring. Hence one obviously cannot
maintain that in the Christian message the gentiles were confronted with the same God they actually had had before, as
the Jews were. The gentiles had had this God—otherwise
than was the case with the Jews—at most in the form of a

[4] Cf. my article, "Die Aufnahme des philosophischen Gottesbegriffs als
dogmatisches Problem der frühchristlichen Theologie," *Zeitschrift für
Kirchengeschichte,* LXX (1959), 1–45, esp. pp. 12 ff.

question that was open toward him. This quest for God, which man can never completely lose, was in the pagan world darkened by many a perversion. Men exchanged the Creator for the creatures (Rom. 1:18 ff.). And they falsely regarded the quest for God as a key to obtaining an answer by the philosophical procedure of inference from the world, or from man, to the true God. The Jews, however, already had the true God, though they had not yet recognized who and what this God really is.

But now, to what extent is it the case that through Jesus it became apparent who and what the God of Israel really is? Are we now after all thrown back again upon the mere claim which Jesus raised? If this were the case, all the traditional continuity between Jesus and the Jews would have been of little use, because the most important thing would still have been the inescapable "decision" of those who listened to him, as to whether or not they were willing to accept the new understanding of God proclaimed by Jesus. And in this respect the situation of the non-Jew would be quite analogous to that of the Jew.

To examine this, let us consider once again the circumstances in which the original audience heard Jesus' message. Were they called to a decision regarding what was *new* in Jesus' message? Certainly this cannot be denied. Jesus summoned his hearers to turn, heart and soul, toward God's near future, toward his near reign. He made the final salvation of each man depend upon accepting or refusing that appeal. That means, of course, that Jesus claimed that he himself as the proclaimer of the nearness of God meant the parting of the ways for two kinds of mind. But to understand that appeal, two points should be noted.

First, Jesus did not make this appeal for decision unveiledly for himself, but only indirectly. He made it primarily for his eschatological message of God's near reign. This message, however, did not offer anything completely new. It only stressed, as we have recognized, the main content of the Israel-

ite tradition as being alone decisive, namely, the pre-eminence
of the Israelite God over all other powers and interests and,
closely connected with this, the hope for future realization of
God's will on earth. Thus Jesus' claim to authority is not
founded upon his merely subjective assertion, but grows out
of a message that had all its roots in the Israelite tradition.
His claim gets its cutting edge from the fact that, measured
against the God of eschatological hope and his imminent coming, the detailed regulations of the traditional law and the
cultic traditions of Israel come to be of no consequence. In
the name of the sole honor of Israel's God, Jesus was able to
disregard Israelite traditions which had hitherto been thought
inviolable.

To justify this attitude Jesus could claim in addition—this
is our second remark—the ultimacy of the coming reign itself.
That was a consistent development out of Jesus' basic message. No one can fail to see the conflict that was caused in
Jesus' hearers. They suddenly had to choose between God and
the law, which had hitherto belonged together. By the fact
that in Jesus' person the Jewish tradition entered into conflict
with itself, his own appearance involved an ambiguity which
could be solved only by an act in which the God of Israel
himself would confirm the message of Jesus. The whole activity of Jesus was in need of such divine confirmation. Only by
anticipating it could his Jewish audience trust in him. Hence
the claim of Jesus was not an isolated and arbitrary one. It
belongs together with a specific past and a specific future.
Only by understanding its roots in Israel's tradition and anticipating its future confirmation by God himself could the Israelite audience of Jesus respond to his claim.

The connection between the different elements in Jesus'
ministry will become clearer as we consider the background
of apocalyptic thought behind Jesus. Nothing but the specific
line of apocalyptic tradition which lies behind Jesus made his
opposition to traditional law a historical possibility. "Only
where interest in God is not directed toward the Torah but

rather to history and its End, can polemics arise against the
rabbinical understanding of law, as happened in Jesus' case."[5]
This was connected with the tradition of proleptic revelation,
which came out of old Israelite prophecy and which was
shared by Jesus and the whole apocalyptic tradition. Such
circles had become accustomed to claim God's own authority
for proleptically granted announcement of God's future. "The
necessary condition for the possibility of claiming special authority, as Jesus did, against the all-embracing authority of
the rabbinic Torah existed solely where the coming of the
final decisive action of God was taught as an actual knowledge
which even now proleptically has eschatological validity above
and beyond the written Torah."[6]

To be sure, Jesus was not an apocalyptic seer nor a col-
lector of apocalyptic traditions. He did not provide a symbolic
presentation of the course of history up to its coming End.
More plausibly one may think of Jesus in connection with an
apocalyptically colored prophecy. The call for repentance with
which, like John the Baptist, he came forth is an old element
of prophetic tradition. But unlike the prophets of ancient Israel
Jesus made no special predictions. The content of his message
was the general eschatological expectation of God's reign, but
this was to be expected in the near future. And owing to the
exclusiveness claimed for this message because it was God
himself who was involved, the ministry of Jesus was already
the dawn of the reign of God announced by him. Evidently
Jesus himself knew that he differed in this respect from the
prophetic traditions which lay behind him, and even upon the
Baptist he bestowed an exceptional position by calling him
the last of the prophets (Matt. 11:9–13). Nevertheless, the
ministry of Jesus shared with prophecy the character of an
anticipation, but not only as in prophecy and apocalyptic in

[5] Ulrich Wilckens, "Das Offenbarungsverständnis in der Geschichte des
Urchristentums," *Offenbarung als Geschichte* (2nd ed., *KuD, Beiheft* 1;
Göttingen: Vandenhoeck und Ruprecht, 1963), pp. 53 f.
[6] *Ibid.*, p. 54.

the sense of a mere pre-*cognition,* but, so to say, as a pre-*realization* of the future, as its proleptic dawning.

Admittedly it was only within the horizon of the expectation directed toward the future coming of God's reign that it could be recognized what it was that was dawning in the ministry of Jesus. Thus the future and the presence of the reign are intertwined in the ministry of Jesus. But the future remains future. There is no "realized eschatology," as if the future had faded out. The presence of God's reign in Jesus was founded, as we have seen, only in the exclusiveness in Jesus' pointing to the *future* of God. The immediacy of God which is so distinguishing for Jesus' message and so characteristic of the everyday language of his parables, is rooted in the eschatological nearness of God. Only in the light of the End is the close proximity of the Creator to his creation revealed and hence the true nature of his creation. The present reality of the reign of God, thus mediated by the exclusiveness of Jesus' eschatological message, is to be considered a proleptic reality. Nevertheless, even as anticipation the ministry of Jesus referred in its very essence to the complete coming of the reign of God—the fulfillment of his expectation of the near End.

Jesus' claim to authority could not but raise the question of the announced future both among his disciples and among his adversaries. But decision about Jesus' call could not be postponed, it had to be made immediately. Yet if the fulfillment of Jesus' anticipation failed to appear, then the basis of his message was retroactively destroyed. Even if one judges skeptically the "consistent eschatology" of Albert Schweitzer in regard to the importance of the "delay of the parousia" for early Christianity and for the further history of the church, it is scarcely possible to ignore the fact that the imminence of God's reign, even in the sense of temporal nearness, was constitutive for Jesus' expectation and for his ministry as a whole. After a lapse of two thousand years no one can claim Jesus as authoritative without wrestling with this problem.

But now to all appearances Jesus' expectation of the near End was not fulfilled—at any rate *not* in the way Jesus and his contemporaries understood it: neither as the beginning of a series of final events of cosmic dimension nor within Jesus' own generation. This fact cannot and may not be lightly dismissed. It was only in the light of the urgent proximity of the last judgment and of possible final salvation by the dawning of God's reign that all sorrows and cares of the world became for Jesus so peculiarly unimportant. There would be no escape from judging Jesus a dreamer, though perhaps a very noble man, as Karl Jaspers does,[7] were it not for the Easter message which makes us reckon with the historical reality of the event there reported.[8]

But how does the resurrection of Jesus justify his expectation of God's reign as very near? Well, the early Christian message of the resurrection of Jesus intended to say that the expected general resuscitation of the dead at the End had already occurred in Jesus' case. Thus Jesus' expectation of the speedy realization of the eschatological reality did not simply fail. It was fulfilled, and thus confirmed, though only in his own person. Now I frankly admit there is some difficulty in this, for the resurrection of the dead was generally thought of as the ultimate destiny of all mankind to be shared by all the righteous and not separately by any individual. Within the apocalyptic literature the eschatological resurrection of a single man is a quite unknown notion. Therefore the resurrection of Jesus was to be spoken of in close connection at least with the destiny of all mankind. The general human destiny has occurred in Jesus—if he *really was* resurrected from the dead.

Now, precisely because the resurrection of a single man was

---

[7] Cf. Karl Jaspers, *Die grossen Philosophen* (Munich: Piper, 1957), I, pp. 186–228 [*The Great Philosophers*, ed. by Hannah Arendt, trans. by Ralph Mannheim (New York: Harcourt, Brace, and World, 1962), pp. 74–97].

[8] To a considerable extent I share Richard R. Niebuhr's point of view, *Resurrection and Historical Reason* (New York: Charles Scribner's Sons, 1957), though I think that historical certainty will not be reached on any theory of memory, whether individual or collective, but only by critical reconstruction.

quite unfamiliar to the apocalyptic tradition, we must suppose that a special event underlay the apostolic Easter message, an event that caused so decisive a change in the traditional expectation of the End. Evidently something had happened to the witnesses of the appearances of the Risen One for which their language had no other word than that used to characterize the eschatological expectation, i.e., resurrection from the dead. This expression is a metaphor. It suggests the idea of being awakened and arising from sleep. Hence Jewish traditions often join mention of the future resurrection of the dead with the metaphorical description of death as sleep. It is important to notice this metaphorical meaning of our talk about the resurrection, though of course not of the thing itself. The metaphorical character of our speaking about resurrection means that we do not know what sort of reality corresponds to that word. It surpasses our imagination, because we live on this side of death. Speaking and thinking about a life on the other side of death is possible only in images of hope and is legitimate only on the condition that we be aware that that new "life" must be completely different from all we now know as life. So we do not really know even yet what happened to Jesus then nor what kind of reality the Risen One may have in relation to our present life. Only metaphorically can we speak of this. The most that we can really *know* is whether or not Easter witnesses were confronted by a reality which we too can comprehend only in terms of that parabolic word of eschatological expectation: resurrection from the dead.

Apparently early Christianity only gradually realized that the resurrection of Jesus was not yet the beginning of the general End. On the contrary the earliest opinion seems to have been general, that the final events would continue to follow quickly one after another. The description of Jesus as the firstborn from the dead (Col. 1:18; Rev. 1:5; cf. also 1 Cor. 15:20; Rom. 8:29; Acts 3:15) still indicates the originally close connection between encounter with the reality of the resurrected Lord and the expectation that the final events for everybody would soon follow. Characteristic of the immediate expectation of the earliest community is the cry *"maranatha"* during the celebration of the Lord's Supper, summoning the Lord to his ultimate advent, and further the recognition that the resurrected Lord himself is the Son of Man, the future judge. Only in the course of time did the Christian community realize, because of the "delay" of Jesus' parousia, that his resurrection had to be understood as a single event. To be sure, it was not completely apart from the general destiny of all mankind, in that it was an exceptional anticipation of the general End of history. Nevertheless, this delay did not cause any such crisis in Christian faith as has been ascribed to it, because the resurrection of Jesus assured Christians of their own future salvation, whenever it might arrive or however long it might delay.

Without the resurrection of Jesus his message would have turned out to be a fanatical audacity. But in a certain sense, as we have now seen, the resurrection did justify Jesus' expectation of the near End. It was in him himself that it was fulfilled. Admittedly, this happened otherwise than Jesus and his disciples probably had imagined the announced future. But it is true of every "fulfillment" that it only rarely corresponds exactly to the announcement prior to it. Nevertheless, in view of the resurrection of Jesus and the eschatological quality of that event, we cannot be satisfied with the simple judgment that Jesus' expectation of the near End remained unfulfilled. The eschatological resurrection of the dead became an event in Jesus' own case, and thus the God whose nearness Jesus had proclaimed declared himself for him.

Jesus had made the claim that by the attitude taken toward his message and thus toward his person, each man's final fate in the coming judgment is already decided. This claim is supported by the realization of eschatological salvation in his own resurrection from the dead. But as his claim was founded in the exclusive decision which Jesus demanded for the near reign of God, the confirmation of his claim means also the confirmation of the expectation of the near End which underlies it. Briefly: just as in Jesus' demand of his hearers to devote themselves completely to the coming reign of God this reign was already present, so through the raising up of Jesus, and through the certainty that Jesus as the Risen One lives and will die no more, eschatological salvation is certain and to this extent near to those who are joined to him. By the resurrection of Jesus, God himself and his salvation are near to the world for all time to come—no matter how long the world endures.

Thus the transformation of the apocalyptic hope caused by the history of Jesus tends toward the idea of incarnation. But it was only in the Hellenistic world that the eschatological nearness of God revealed in Jesus could find expression independent of the temporal distance remaining until the End.

How, then, did it become clear in the ministry of Jesus who the God of Israel really is? In the first place, by the fact that in the message of Jesus no subjective assertions about the God of Israel were made, but all importance was given to this God, as he had been understood by the prophetic tradition up to the time of Jesus and to the coming of his reign. The change in the understanding of God which we recognize in the message of Jesus resulted precisely from this concentration on the God of Israel and on his future reign. This is the offer of salvation without any reserve to sinners and publicans, if only they respond to the message of the imminent God and welcome him who proclaims this message. This is his unconditional blessing for all those whose special situation leaves them no other hope than God's future. Thus Israel's God was revealed as a Father who gives his love unconditionally to men. And God's love became the only criterion for human behavior. In the second place, this clarification of the Israelite understanding of God took place in Jesus' own claim to have ultimate significance, for it was *he* who was proclaiming God's eschatological future. And this claim was confirmed when in the resurrection of Jesus the End of all occurrence proleptically took place. So the ultimate reality, in accord with Jesus' claim, is already present in the midst of time.

## III

God's revelation in Jesus of Nazareth is not a single and isolated event of supernatural origin, but, as we have seen, has a relation to an already presupposed, though provisional, knowledge of the God whose true reality is first revealed by Jesus. Revelation, as Richard Niebuhr said, is "revolution in religious knowledge."[9] Revelation is not the starting point, but the end of a long path, which began with still indistinct and inadequate notions of God. It is not true that the revelation, the self-disclosure of God, falls from heaven ready-made. Nor must it be the starting point of all knowledge of God, as if one could not otherwise know anything about him. There is rather, speaking metaphorically, a veiled God in the beginning, and only in the end is the veil taken away, i.e., the re-vel-atio takes place. Men could not endure a nonmediated confrontation with the actuality of God. To do so they would have to be something other than creatures who seek their way by orientation to finite things. Men can approach God only through the world of finitude. Through the veil of the finite, men become aware of the infinite God. Therefore their perspective is always one-sided and distorted. But at the end of the veiled way revelation from God can occur, the self-unveiling of the God already provisionally known through all the obscurities of the veiling. The self-unveiling of God, however, is salvation to mankind because only in God's proximity, in community with God, does human existence find its fulfillment.

That knowledge of God is made possible on a path guided by God himself—by a history—was already known to Israel. In the Old Testament tradition we find over and over again the idea that the basic acts of Yahweh in history were intended to make known to Israel the divinity of Yahweh. Originally this idea was probably connected with the exodus from Egypt; at least it already is in the Yahwistic source. In the

---

[9] H. Richard Niebuhr, *The Meaning of Revelation* (New York: The Macmillan Company, 1964), p. 183.

prophecies of the early monarchy we find this idea expressed in the summons to battle in the holy war. They shall know the divinity of Yahweh by the victory given to Israel (1 Kings 20:13, 28). Among the prophets of the exile Deutero-Isaiah and especially Ezekiel proclaimed that the purpose of the heavy sentence which Israel had undergone and of the new deeds of God predicted as future salvation was to make Yahweh's divinity known.[10]

But much more extensively than in the "cognition formula" that occurs in these texts, the whole Israelite tradition was convinced that it was the will of Yahweh that his divinity should be made known by his historical acts. Of course this presupposes a preliminary knowledge derived in some other way. So it is in the appearance of Yahweh to the patriarchs and Moses and in the divulging of his name to Moses. It is evident, however, that these early theophanies and even the announcement of Yahweh's name were not understood as providing ultimate knowledge of God. It is precisely in reporting the announcement of Yahweh's name to Moses (Ex. 6:7) that the Priestly Document speaks of knowledge of Yahweh as a thing of the future. At the same time it relegates the theophanies (the appearance of Yahweh) to an earlier, inferior stage in the knowledge of God. With Moses a new stage begins: Yahweh makes himself known as himself by his actions.[11] I have characterized this way of revelation as indirect over against the direct concreteness of theophany.[12] This indirect revelation of Yahweh granted by his actions appears in the Priestly Document as a higher stage of knowledge over against the direct manifestation in the theophanies. These manifestations had communicated only a preliminary acquaintance with Yahweh which was to be elucidated and transformed by the experiences that Israel was to have with Yahweh in the course of its history.

Those events which were to reveal the divinity of God were

[10] Rolf Rendtorff, "Die Offenbarungsvorstellungen im Alten Israel," *Offenbarung als Geschichte,* pp. 35 ff.

[11] *Ibid.,* p. 25.

[12] Cf. the introduction to *Offenbarung als Geschichte,* p. 16.

often preceded by prophetic announcements, making the future events discernible as acts of Yahweh because they had been announced in his name. Deutero-Isaiah and the Deuteronomist based a whole theology of the word of God upon this. One may well wonder whether the knowledge of Yahweh's divinity is not due to the word spoken in his name rather than to the events which were announced by this word, since the latter can be conceived as mere effects of the word.[13] But first, that is not right because those words about the future are finally proven to be Yahweh's words only by their coming to pass (1 Kings 22:28; Deut. 18:9–22; Jer. 28:6–9).[14] Furthermore, only very few of them occurred exactly according to the prediction. Time and again the course of events surpassed the words, giving them new meaning and a new reference. Under these circumstances one can hardly conceive the events as mere effects of the prophetic word. Of course the opposite is also true: the actual reality of any particular present was again and again outstripped by prophetic words that turned Israel's eyes to the future. Hence one has to reckon with an intertwining both of prophetic words and of events. The event cannot be understood as an unessential appendage to the word. The future was each time opened up by the word of the prophets announcing Yahweh's action. Thus the future event became recognizable as Yahweh's act, but on the other hand there was very seldom an exact realization of the prophe-

---

[13] In this vein Walter Zimmerli writes, "The occurrence is word made reality, a proclamation (like a promissory note) redeemed." " 'Offenbarung' im Alten Testament. Ein Gespräch mit R. Rendtorff," *EvTh*, XXII (1962), 15–31, esp. p. 25. While he recognizes that "the actual history, when it comes, may fall short of what was announced," p. 31, he significantly does not mention that the events may also surpass the words of announcement. Jürgen Moltmann, likewise, speaks of God's revelation in "the history-generating word of election, vocation, justification, and commissioning," without discussing the problem involved in the fact that the event itself may surpass the announcement of it. "Exegese und Eschatologie der Geschichte," *ibid.*, pp. 31–66, esp. p. 58.

[14] Cf. Rolf Rendtorff, "Geschichte und Wort im Alten Testament," *EvTh*, XXII (1962), 621–49, esp. pp. 630 f. In *Theologie der Hoffnung* (Munich: Christian Kaiser Verlag, 1964), pp. 99 ff., Moltmann discusses the problem and, while sticking to the superiority of the word, comes close to my own position.

cies. Their "fulfillment" gave a new sense to them. The Israelites themselves became aware of Yahweh's freedom over
against the words proclaimed by the prophets[15] without, however, harmonizing this awareness with the presupposed Ancient Near Eastern idea of the powerful and effective word of
the divinity.

In the older texts of the Old Testament, insofar as they
expressly cite knowledge of Yahweh as the purpose of the occurrence, specific, single events are involved, e.g., the miraculous deeds of Moses in the Yahwist Document (Ex. 7:17;
8:20–22; 9:14) or victory in a holy war (1 Kings 20). In
the same way the "cognition formula" was used in the Exodus
tradition for the miraculous passage through the Sea of Reeds.
But already the conception of the Yahwist Document as a
whole implies that Yahweh's divinity is recognized through
the whole history which extends from the promise to the patriarchs to the fulfillment in the occupation of the land in Palestine. Several centuries later Deuteronomy expressly formulated
it: "And because he loved your fathers and chose their de-
scendants after them, and brought you out of Egypt with his
own presence, by his great power, driving out before you nations greater and mightier than yourselves, to bring you in,
to give you their land for an inheritance, as at this day; *know
therefore* this day, and lay it to your heart, *that the Lord is
God* in heaven above and on the earth beneath; there is no
other. Therefore you shall keep his statutes and his command-
ments . . ." (4:37–40). Here it was no longer a single event,
but a whole connected history that Yahweh had promised and
that was accomplished according to this promise, which provided the basis for Israel's life in Palestine. In this history the
divinity of Yahweh was proven to Israel to be true.

During the early kingdom Israel could look back upon
God's revealing acts, as if his revealing activity in its main
points had been completed. But this changed with the prophecies of woe in the later period of the kings and especially with
the predicted end of the Israelite states. The eyes of Israel

[15] *Ibid.*, p. 643.

were turned again toward the future. From this future the Israelites expected a new and final salvation and with its arrival also the final demonstration of Yahweh's divinity to all nations. Hosea and Isaiah already had recognized Yahweh's plan of history as extending from the beginnings of Israel, through the present in the activities of the Ancient Near Eastern world powers that Israel's God was directing, and on into a distant future. Then, in the age of the Babylonian exile the fulfillment of future salvation seemed quite near at hand. Later on, salvation was again placed by the apocalyptics in the distance beyond the present, but now at a determinate distance at the end of a series of world kingdoms succeeding each other. At the same time apocalypticism took on the otherworldly aspects of eschatological hope. In those prophetic circles which were the starting point of the apocalyptic movement,[16] the whole history of Israel and of the world into the far future was understood for the first time as a continuing totality of divine activity realizing a plan which had been decided at the beginning of creation. Accordingly, God's final revelation, the revelation of his glory,[17] together with the glorification of the righteous, was now hoped for as the End of all occurrence. Thus in 2 Baruch the author, a disciple of Jeremiah, prays for the coming of the final age: "And now quickly show thy glory and do not defer what has been promised by thee" (21:25).

Since knowledge of God's divinity was no longer expected from single events but from one final occurrence which would gather together all earlier, single events into one single history, this ultimate knowledge had to be placed at the end of all history. Only when all occurrence is ended can the divinity of God be known on the basis of the connection of history. So one may say that only the last, the eschatological, event which binds history into a whole brings about final knowledge of

---

[16] For the connection between old Israelite prophecy and the apocalyptic teaching about the series of world powers, cf. Klaus Koch, "Spätisraelitisches Geschichtsdenken am Beispiel des Buches Daniel," *Historische Zeitschrift,* 193/1 (1961), 1–32, esp. pp. 27 and 28 ff.

[17] Rolf Rendtorff, *Offenbarung als Geschichte,* pp. 28 ff., 93 ff.

God. Likewise, earlier events in the course of history and the meaning of present suffering will be revealed in their proper significance only in the light of the eschaton.[18]

The Israelite idea of knowledge of God brought about by a history wrought by God for this express purpose is the closest parallel in Biblical thought to the modern sense of the word "revelation": God's self-disclosure, his making himself known. As is common knowledge, the other terms which are usually rendered by our word "revelation," or "reveal," do not mean *self*-revelation in either Testament.[19] But with respect to the term "know," it is expressly said that God makes *himself* known through his deeds, and in content the same thing is meant when it is said that his deeds make his *glory* known.

The notion of God's self-revelation, as understood in the Old Testament as indirect revelation through the events which are wrought by God, corresponds remarkably with the way the knowledge of God opened up by Jesus is presented. On the one hand there is always a preliminary acquaintance with God which precedes the final knowledge of him brought by Jesus. This is what resulted also from the Old Testament understanding of the way leading to more precise knowledge of God. On the other hand Jesus is the final revelation of God to the extent that his ministry and his history have eschatological character. His ministry had eschatological character because he announced the coming of God's reign as the beginning of the End, and therefore he understood men's attitude toward his message to be a predeciding of the final judgment. In spite of the nonappearance of the general and final catastrophe which Jesus had expected, his own fate also has eschatological character because his message was confirmed by God's

---

[18] One of the many contradictions in which Günter Klein sees my thought entangled is my conception that revelation occurs at the End of history but also in the whole course of history ("Offenbarung als Geschichte? Marginalien zu einem theologischen Programm," *MPTh*, LI [1962], 65–88, esp. pp. 79 ff.). What he fails to see is that it is precisely by its *End* that the total course of history is gathered into a whole.

[19] For the New Testament, cf. Hannelies Schulte, *Der Begriff der Offenbarung im Neuen Testament* (Munich: Christian Kaiser Verlag, 1949), p. 42.

raising him from the dead, an act in which the general eschatological hope took place in him. In Jesus' ministry and in
his fate, i.e., in his person, the final revelation of God's divinity
at the end of all ages occurs already in advance insofar as the
history of Jesus has the character of ultimacy in the midst of
our perishing time. Furthermore, God's revelation in Jesus has
the same indirect character which we observed in the Old
Testament. What is decisive is not the isolated fact that Jesus
announced the imminence of God's reign, but that in this announcement and in the course of Jesus' life up to his resurrection the reign of God *became* present reality.

Although the idea of God's self-revelation through the history wrought by him, and ultimately by the End of all history,
corresponds to the tradition in which Jesus and primitive
Christianity lived, it occurs relatively rarely in the New Testament writings. Thus Paul refers to the cognition of God's glory
in the face of Jesus Christ (2 Cor. 4:6), and in the Gospel
according to John, Jesus, who himself will be glorified by the
Father, accomplishes in advance the eschatological glorification of God and of those who were chosen by him (17 *passim*). That the idea of God's eschatological revelation in Jesus
Christ does not stand explicitly at the center of early Christian
tradition is probably connected with the fact that it developed
mainly through the traditional Christological titles when they
were transformed and applied to Jesus. But the most important of these titles—Son of Man, Messiah, Kyrios, Son of God,
Logos—imply that the eschatological revelation of God is
already anticipated in Jesus. This implication of the Christological titles is becoming important today, because neither
these titles, nor the theology of incarnation as developed in
the following age, nor Jesus' divinity itself has remained a
self-evident truth for us. At any rate the human existence
of Jesus is still self-evident in our century; therefore we must
examine the ministry of Jesus and his fate and ask how God
is revealed in him. Only after having done this can we perhaps
speak in a responsible way of Jesus' divinity itself and so re-
gain an understanding of the concept of incarnation. If Jesus

was the final revelation of God because of the eschatological importance of his appearance and of his resurrection from the dead, then we cannot think of God in any more appropriate way than that suggested by Jesus. And that means that Jesus belongs to the very idea of God and thus, himself, is one with God.

## IV

Jesus of Nazareth is the final revelation of God because the End of history appeared in him. It did so both in his eschatological message and in his resurrection from the dead. However, he can be understood to be God's final revelation only in connection with the whole of history as mediated by the history of Israel. He is God's revelation in the fact that all history receives its due light from him.

But how can it be recognized that Jesus is the revelation of God? We came to the conclusion that the claim to authority of the pre-Easter Jesus does not, taken by itself, constitute a sufficient basis for such recognition, because it already presupposes some preliminary knowledge of God and also requires the confirmation which it received through the resurrection. Jesus' resurrection, however, has its eschatological significance only because it is a proleptic occurrence of the general eschatological salvation expected by the Jews of that time, and hence only in the context of the totality of human history, whose ultimate future it unveiled.

Is this significance of Jesus' history recognizable from within itself? And is such a recognition already a knowledge of the revelation of God in him? Or is some supplementary explanation necessary, an explanation emerging out of faith in Jesus and not derivable from the bare facts of his story?

The distinction just suggested between the facts of Jesus' history and their meaning as revelation, which allegedly only faith can find in them, is widespread. Thus Richard Rothe following Carl Ludwig Nitzsch made his famous distinction between the *manifestation* of God in the external facts of his-

tory and the *inspiration* of the Biblical witnesses who teach us
about the meaning of the facts and whose teaching is absolutely necessary if we are to recognize those facts to be the
manifestation of God.[20] Since that time, under the influence
of positivism and of neo-Kantianism, scholars have come to
distinguish more sharply between the facts on the one hand
and their evaluation or significance on the other hand. Most
radically of all, Rudolf Bultmann carries out this distinction
by relegating the early Christian Easter message totally to the
significance side, describing it as the interpretation of Jesus'
cross.[21] Less violent is the procedure of Paul Althaus, who
hangs on to a historical kernel in the Easter tradition but
maintains, referring expressly to Rothe, that the meaning of
Jesus' history as revelation is only accessible to faith.[22] And
even H. Richard Niebuhr distinguishes between experienced
history and history as investigation, because historical research
evidently knows nothing of any action of God or of a revelation of him in history. Only through the experience of men
themselves living historically, he claims, can God's activity in
history be known.[23]

Such a splitting up of historical consciousness into a detection of facts and an evaluation of them (or into history as
known and history as experienced) is intolerable to Christian
faith, not only because the message of the resurrection of Jesus
and of God's revelation in him necessarily becomes merely
subjective interpretation, but also because it is the reflection
of an outmoded and questionable historical method. It is based
on the futile aim of the positivist historians to ascertain bare

[20] Richard Rothe, "Offenbarung," in *Zur Dogmatik* (*Theologischen
Studien und Kritiken;* F. A. Berthes, 1863), pp. 55 ff.

[21] As Bultmann says in his programmatic essay, "New Testament and
Mythology": ". . . faith in the resurrection is really the same thing as
faith in the saving efficacy of the cross." *Kerygma and Myth* (New York:
Harper & Row, Torchbook Edition, 1961), I, p. 41 [*Kerygma und Mythos*
(Hamburg: Reich und Heidrich Evan. Verlag, 1948), p. 50].

[22] Althaus, "Offenbarung als Geschichte und Glaube. Bemerkungen zu
W. Pannenbergs Begriff der Offenbarung," *ThLZ*, LXXXVII (1962),
321–30, esp. pp. 325 f.

[23] *The Meaning of Revelation*, pp. 59 ff.

facts without meaning in history.[24] Both neo-Kantianism and the philosophy-of-life school have accepted historical positivism as one of their presuppositions and have merely supplemented it by an "evaluating" contemplation or by the interpretation of the facts according to their expressive value. Against this we must reinstate today the original unity of facts and their meaning. Every event, if not artificially taken out of context (out of its historical environment, stretching into the past and the future), brings its own meaning for each particular inquirer, brings it with its context, which of course is always a context of tradition.[25] Admittedly not every event has equal clarity of meaning. This differs from case to case. But, in principle, every event has its original meaning within the context of occurrence and tradition in which it took place and through which it is connected with the present and its historical interest. In spite of our statement that the meaning of an event is inherent to its original context and is not something injected into it by the interpreter, nevertheless that meaning can be determined only in relation to the vantage point of the particular inquirer. The reason for this is that the historical continuum within which an event has meaning also includes the present. But one may not arbitrarily attach whatever meaning one will to a given fact. Only when the original unity of event and meaning is grasped may the question of the historicity of Jesus' resurrection be properly raised again. For the event here in question can only be expressed in the language of apocalyptic expectation by the metaphorical phrase,

[24] For critical discussion of this positivistic understanding of history, see R. G. Collingwood, *The Idea of History* (Oxford: Clarendon Press, 1946).

[25] For further development of these ideas, see my article, "Kerygma und Geschichte," *Studien zur Theologie der Alttestamentlichen Überlieferung,* ed. by Rolf Rendtorff and Klaus Koch (*Festschrift* for Gerhard von Rad; Neukirchen: Neukirchener Verlag, 1961), pp. 129–140. In my criticism of historical positivism and its concept of isolated "facts" I agree with Heinrich Ott, *Die Frage nach dem historischen Jesus und die Ontologie der Geschichte* (*Theologische Studien,* 62; Zurich: EVZ-Verlag, 1960), pp. 12 ff. and 21.

resurrection from the dead, but nevertheless it was experienced as a concrete occurrence from without, not simply as a subjective experience. Therefore, even modern historians must at least examine it as external occurrence. Such an examination cannot be undertaken here. Its result, however, is absolutely fundamental to Christian faith. "If Christ has not been raised, then our preaching is in vain and your faith is in vain" (1 Cor. 15:14).

Whether or not Jesus was raised from the dead is a historical question insofar as it is an inquiry into what did or did not happen at a certain time. Such questions could be answered only by historical arguments unless we had present experiences of the resurrected Jesus from which we could conclude that he did not remain dead. But obviously we have no such experiences. All the talk about Jesus' presence in his congregation is *already* based on the conviction that he was once resurrected from the dead and not on immediate encounter with the risen Jesus. Now let us assume that the historical question concerning the resurrection of Jesus has been decided positively, then the meaning of this event as God's final revelation is not something that must be added to it; rather, this is the original meaning inherent in that event within its own context of history and tradition. The early Christian proclamation only unfolded the inherent meaning of Jesus' history in the language and the conceptualization of the time and the particular hearer. Sometimes it succeeded very well in expressing it, sometimes not. But it did not invent a meaning that was not already there.

Well then, is faith superfluous for the recognition of God's revelation in Jesus Christ? Is such recognition a matter of mere knowing? Such an alternative (faith *or* knowledge) is basically incorrect. One cannot really know of *God's revelation* in Jesus Christ without believing. But faith does not take the place of knowledge. On the contrary, it has its basis in an event which is a matter for knowing and which becomes known to us only by more or less adequate information. To be able to have Christian faith one must at least presuppose that

the message about Jesus Christ is true. This includes primarily
the affirmations that Jesus really proclaimed the coming of
God's reign and that he really rose from the dead. It may very
well be that one cannot always comprehend the truth of this
message, but one must be able to *presuppose* that it is correct,
and that, at least in principle, its truth is intelligible. In the
sense of a logical presupposition (though not always a psychological antecedent), the knowledge of Jesus' history, including
his resurrection from the dead, is the basis of faith.[26] Furthermore, this knowledge has the peculiarity that it leads on to
faith. Knowledge is not a stage beyond faith, but leads into
faith—and the more exact it is, the more certainly it does so.
In order to illustrate this we return to the Old Testament
once more.

Where God had made himself known through his deeds,
no further interpretation was necessary for Israel. At least for
those who lived within the context of Israelite tradition the
events spoke for themselves. "That an event, ambiguous in
itself, should have to be interpreted as Yahweh's deed by a
speaker commissioned by him" is an idea completely foreign
to the Old Testament.[27] For Israel it was a basic presupposition that all history is wrought by Yahweh. The narration of
the succession to David's throne and the story of Joseph found
the activity of Yahweh in the reported events without men-
tioning any preceding prophetic word.[28] Therefore the prophets themselves held the conviction that "their contemporaries
should really be able to recognize the great deed of Yahweh
by themselves."[29] To bring the people *back* to this recognition
was the intention of their mission. The preliminary announcement of the coming events to Israel "was only a concession to
Israel's unbelief."[30] For the future they announced the recog-

[26] This is more extensively developed in my reply to Althaus, "Einsicht
und Glaube," *ThLZ*, LXXXVIII (1963), 81–92.
[27] Rendtorff, "Geschichte und Wort im Alten Testament," p. 631.
[28] *Ibid.*, pp. 633 ff.
[29] *Ibid.*, p. 637.
[30] Gerhard von Rad, *Theologie des Alten Testaments* (Munich: Christian Kaiser Verlag, 1960), II, p. 106; cf. Rendtorff, "Geschichte und
Wort im Alten Testament," *EvTh*, XXII (1962), p. 645.

nition of Yahweh's divinity through his deeds, a knowledge which the people of their time had lost. The future deeds of Yahweh were expected to be so clear and unequivocal that not only Israel, but all peoples, "all flesh," would know the glory of Yahweh through his deeds (Isa. 40:5).[31]

God's demonstration of himself through the ministry and the history of Jesus of Nazareth is that final revelation of God which is to be recognized by all peoples. It is that revelation, but for the time being it is only proleptically so, not yet as the general occurrence of the End for all men. One can understand the history of Jesus only if one understands the future salvation of mankind as having already appeared in and with him and as having been made accessible through him. In the history of Jesus a future was anticipated that has not yet appeared in its general bearing. Therefore those who penetrate into the meaning of Jesus' history will inevitably be led to God's not yet accomplished future, which nevertheless is held to have appeared already in and with Jesus when one speaks of his resurrection from the dead. Hence through knowledge of Jesus' history they are led to faith, to trust in God's future. For this future is meant for all men, though it has so far occurred only in Jesus and will be imparted as salvation only through him—i.e., only to those who are bound up with him. The universal, though not automatically imparted, meaning of the salvation which was accorded to Jesus gives his history its character of promise. He who understands this meaning inherent in the history of Jesus is drawn, by knowing Jesus as the prolepsis of the coming general salvation, into the movement which is faith. This faith lets itself be drawn into God's future, such as it appeared in Jesus. It is this faith—not the preliminary knowledge of Jesus—which unites us with God and imparts salvation. For the believer does not remain alone with himself, but "forsakes" himself when he trusts. But the act of faith or trust presupposes a knowledge of the trustworthiness of the partner. Without such well-founded knowl-

---

[31] Rendtorff, in *Offenbarung als Geschichte,* pp. 38 ff., gives some examples of this. Cf. also pp. 98 ff.

edge faith would be blind gullibility, credulity, or even super-stition.

Christian faith must not be equated with a merely subjec-tive conviction that would allegedly compensate for the un-certainty of our historical knowledge about Jesus. Such a conviction would only be self-delusion. For much too long a time faith has been misunderstood to be subjectivity's fortress into which Christianity could retreat from the attacks of scien-tific knowledge. Such a retreat into pious subjectivity can only lead to destroying any consciousness of the truth of the Chris-tian faith.[32] Faith can breathe freely only when it can be cer-tain, even in the field of scientific research, that its foundation is true. This does not mean that such truth could ever be finally surveyable in a rational way. For the history through which the divinity of God stands revealed to us has an open future still before it. This characteristic gives expression to the personhood of the Biblical God: his dealing is never irrevoca-bly fixed, its conditions are never finally surveyable. He can be known only by trusting him on the basis of the demonstrations of his will and disposition toward us. It is precisely as that kind of God that the God of the Bible is revealed in the history of Jesus.

The fact that God's revelation in Jesus of Nazareth is open toward the future does not contradict the finality of this event. God's final self-demonstration through Jesus—and perhaps one should, as Barth does, use the term revelation only for this *final* self-demonstration of God—is given to us only by way of *anticipation* of the coming general End for all men. Any other finality would do justice neither to the personhood of the Biblical God, nor to the openness and self-transcendence which characterize human nature. The history of Jesus, pre-cisely in the form of mere anticipation, is the final revelation of God.

---

[32] Cf. G. Rohrmoser, "Die theologische Bedeutung von Hegels Aus-einandersetzung mit der Philosophie Kants und dem Prinzip der Sub-jecktivität," *Neue Zeitschrift für Systematische Theologie,* IV (1962), 89–111.

## V

Israelite prophecy had promised for the final age that not only Israel but also the gentiles would recognize Yahweh's exclusive divinity through his future deeds. This promise was fulfilled in Jesus by the fact that through the early Christian mission not only Jews but also gentiles recognized the revelation of the one true God in Jesus. By what sign could the men of the Hellenistic age recognize the God of the Bible, when he encountered them in the message about Christ, to be that true God for whom Hellenistic thinkers were searching? By this: The God of the Bible was both the Creator (Hellenistically, the origin of the All) and the redeemer from the transitoriness which dominates this present world. As he appeared in Jesus, he united both, and stripped off all merely Jewish elements of tradition as well. This fact made it possible for the true God whom the philosophers sought to be known in him, and this in purer and more convincing form than the form available to philosophical thought itself.

The philosophers could think of God only as the origin of the given world, as an inference from it. They could not conceive of him at the same time as the redeemer who helps one out of the transitoriness of the given world. In the Biblical conception of God both functions are tightly connected because he is the God of history. The world is not conceived to be just the given order of things, but is conceived to be a succession of events in which God's omnipotence ever brings about new occurrence. Therefore it is only from its End that the total reality of the world will be complete.[33] But the final age, the End, will bring about the transformation of the given world and bring in the salvation of the righteous. Here *mythos* and *logos,* which for Plato were divorced, are brought to-

---

[33] On the significance of the future, and especially of the eschatological future, for a Biblically grounded understanding of being and truth, see my article, "Was ist Wahrheit?" in *Vom Herrengeheimnis der Wahrheit,* ed. by K. Scharf (*Festschrift* for Heinrich Vogel; Berlin: Lettner-Verlag, 1962), pp. 214–239.

gether and united. Once the world is understood as history, the origin of the All, who is also the End of history, becomes, as that End, the author of a salvation which lifts man above the transitoriness of the present. Thus the God of the Bible, revealed in Jesus as savior of the world, was acknowledged as the true God.

A decisive element in this process was the fact that the conception of reality opened up by the God of the Bible— viz., that reality is *history hastening toward an End*—was raised by apocalypticism to the same universality as lay in the Greek understanding of the cosmos as an ever-stable order. Both views embrace the whole of reality. Only in this way could the God of history come into view as the author of all reality in the domain of Greek thinking, at the same time transforming its understanding of the world. The God of the Bible, as he was revealed through Jesus, was the answer to the open questions of Hellenistic men. And they realized that through him the whole of reality was more deeply unfolding itself than it ever had before. To the present day this is the only criterion of the truth of God's revelation in Jesus of Nazareth: that again and again it subsequently proves itself true as we experience the reality in which we live. As long as the whole of reality can be understood more deeply and more convincingly through Jesus than without him, it proves true in our everyday experience and personal knowledge that in Jesus the creative origin of all reality stands revealed.

Consequently theology may not and must not withdraw from the world to an exclusive supernatural realm accessible only by that suspect "decision" of faith, but must understand Jesus in the context of the world and understand all things from Jesus and to him. Then theology will understand the world as God's world, history as the field of his action, and Jesus as his revelation.

# PART II. American Discussion

## 3. The Meaning of History

MARTIN J. BUSS

*Emory University*

### I. CONCEPTS OF HISTORY AND TIME

As an Old Testament scholar, one may welcome the increasing interest in Old Testament affairs on the part of systematic theologians. This interest is related to a broader movement widely known as the "revival of Biblical theology," which has been in vogue for some time now. In this context the Old Testament has received special attention from those who find support therein for a "historical" emphasis, and who intend by that term an interest in factuality. Pannenberg's work, including the essay in this volume, provides an occasion for examining the justification of such use of the Old Testament.

Rolf Rendtorff has already noted that the word history lacks clear definition.[1] Here lies one of the most fundamental stumbling blocks for appropriate procedure. It may be entirely true that the Old Testament is interested in "history"; but what does that word mean? It is an easy matter to document the ambiguity involved. If one canvasses published works or private opinions for definitions, one will find highly varied conceptions. The phrase "the Old Testament is interested in history" is quite useless until the meaning of the word history is clear.

[1] *ZThK,* LVII (1960), 34 f.

Conceptions of history revolve around several discrete topics. Among the most notable are: the past, time in general, man, factuality, recording, and meaning (in the approximate order of frequency in which these meanings occur at the present time). There is often no obvious or necessary relation between and among these denotations.

With such a great variety of possible conceptions, it is not surprising that a given culture can be seen by one person as the founder of an interest in history and by another as unconcerned about history. Both views can be right—each within its own context of definitions. It is often claimed, for example, that Judaeo-Christianity is responsible for the historical consciousness of the modern Western world. This is only a half-truth, for the Greek tradition plays an equally important role, ultimately more lasting in its influence on the educated classes. Scholarship (as distinguished from faith), including historical scholarship, finds its antecedents more in Athens than in Jerusalem. The Greeks told some outstanding epics (which have a "historical" kernel). Some of them, at least, had a world view of continuous change. It was Aristotle for whom being is equivalent to action.[2]

Some historians use the term "universal history" (especially in Germany); but it is well to recognize at least three different meanings of this expression.[3] One usage emphasizes the study of all of history—the whole West or both East and West. Another usage centers on the elementary patterns of historical development. Only a third—and this is generally rejected by historians—refers to the totality of history seen as a meaningful whole. The last seems to be in accord with Pannenberg's usage;[4] if so, his program has less relation to other work pro-

----

[2] The affinity of the concept of *Heilsgeschichte* to Aristotle's theories is dramatically illustrated by the acceptance of Aristotelian theory by J. S. Marshall, "History in the Aristotelian Vein," *Anglican Theological Review*, XXXII (1950), 245–256.

[3] Cf., e.g., Joseph Vogt, *Wege zum historischen Universum* (Stuttgart: Kohlhammer, 1961). For a cautious attitude toward history, see, e.g., the modern classic, Raymond Aron, *Introduction to the Philosophy of History* (Boston: Beacon Press, 1961), p. 43, and *passim*.

[4] Very specifically developed in *KuD*, V (1959), 280.

ceeding under the title of universal history than it might seem.

The value of definitions depends upon their adequacy to the object or objects in question. Instead of adopting an *a priori* definition of history, therefore, it will be useful to describe the main outlines of different aspects of reality with respect to their temporal character, in order to see how one can recognize in them categories which may somehow be called historical. To conduct such a survey is not easy, for most of present-day theology has isolated itself from other disciplines. Certainly no theologian has even attempted an over-all assessment of the present situation. The closest approach to such a program by a theologian is that of Pannenberg himself; note, for example, his book *Was ist der Mensch?*[5] But even this does not go far enough.

The lowest level of reality known to us is the subatomic world of electrons and other strange particles, which is extremely difficult for the nonspecialist to explore. It has been repeatedly asserted, however, that macrocosmic categories of space and time do not apply here.[6] The phenomenon of antimatter, to which negative time has been attributed, complicates the situation.[7]

The operation of spatiotemporal processes is a little clearer with respect to such aspects as those to which relativity applies. Relativity implies a fully determinate four-dimensional manifold, in which one dimension, which is somewhat different from the other three, is known as *t* (time). This *t*, however, is not something *in* which a process occurs, but it is one aspect of the process. This point deserves underscoring: physical time is *one aspect* of a reality which itself is four-dimensional. The concept of simultaneity in relativity theory is a functional one that refers to the absence of a direct causal effect or informational relation between two events.[8] Time-

[5] Göttingen: Vandenhoeck und Ruprecht, 1962.

[6] Cf., e.g., Ernest Nagel, *The Structure of Science* (New York: Harcourt, Brace & World, 1961), p. 298.

[7] Cf. among others Maurice Duquesne, *Matter and Antimatter* (New York: Harper & Row, 1960), p. 122.

[8] It is not possible in this context to defend or adequately to define the

related events are process-related: to come "after" an event is equivalent to being its effect.

The temporal aspect of the physical world is so relatively unimportant that many theorists prefer to speak of the geometry of the world rather than of its temporal movement. It is true that some data suggest that the world began a limited time ago and has a history; but this whole question depends on the type of measurement one adopts—quite apart from the possibility of other equally cogent theories.[9] In relation to the future, it is now clear that the law of entropy, being statistical, cannot be rigidly applied—for example, an infinite universe would be immune—and that opposite developments must also be expected.

Space time is modified by the emergence of organismic structures. Theoretical biology has by no means reached a coherent general theory of life, but it should be clear that self-projection is a fundamental characteristic of organisms. In this context, "future" is not merely equivalent to "effect," as it is in physical reality, but it becomes a "goal." The emotive quality associated with goal-directedness involves a behavioral pattern which may be described as possessing a low degree of consciousness—if that is a proper term for reactive processes of approach and avoidance, commonly rendered as pleasure and pain. The relationship of an effect-future to goal-directedness remains obscure, but the relation must be analogous to that of other phenomena of transition. The metaphysical question involved may be left open here.

A new emergent arises in the phenomenon of culture, the principal bearer of which is man. Culture is connected with

---

concept of causality; it is used here as in Hans Reichenbach, *The Philosophy of Space and Time,* trans. by Maria Reichenbach and John Freund (New York: Dover Publications, 1958), p. 145.

[9] On the rather arbitrary interchangeability of presentations, cf. Bertrand Russell, *The ABC of Relativity* (London: Allen and Unwin, 1958), p. 136, and *passim.* Adolf Grünbaum, *Philosophical Problems of Space and Time* (New York: Alfred A. Knopf, 1963), pp. 325–329, sharply supports the view that in a sense, nothing happens in unconscious physical reality. This, however, has nothing to do with the concept of eternity, or even with that of a present (against Wolfhart Pannenberg, *Was ist der Mensch?* [Göttingen: Vandenhoeck und Ruprecht, 1962], pp. 52 f.).

selfhood, in the sense that a participant reflects upon himself. Such a person does not engage in uncritical self-projection as does an animal which takes itself for granted and evaluates all other objects in terms of its own self-enhancement; instead, he asks the question of his own being, objectifies the world to some extent,[10] and is grasped by the problem of infinity. Man can march deliberately to his own death and even commit suicide; usually, he hopes for immortality. He can reject himself; he can annihilate himself in a spiritual sense, losing himself in God. It is in this context that God first makes his appearance—not, to be sure, directly as God, but as the symbol "God" ("Gott," "Deus," "Yahweh"), together with other symbols referring to infinity or to realities which man recognizes as beyond his control. Therewith a new set of concepts arises: Beginning and End, which are best described as mythical categories.

These categories possess a quality different from the forms of time that appear on lower levels of reality. "Beginning," for instance, deals frequently with a norm, i.e., with a standard of evaluation to which one is subject. In other words, whereas an animal sizes up good and evil as characteristics of objects outside itself and in terms of whether they support its own self-enhancement, man evaluates himself and asks whether he himself is good in relation to a higher reality. Thus while the emotive power of the organismic future-as-goal is directed outward, the directive action of time as Beginning or End is inward, and thought of as coming from a realm that transcends human power. Beginning and End stand not in a positive, but in a polar (if not opposite) relation to other temporal categories, raising conflicts between self-enhancement (goal) and self-sacrifice (End). Pannenberg's statement that salvation is what "all men are seeking"[11] is insufficiently dif-

---

[10] Max Scheler, *Man's Place in Nature* (Boston: Beacon Press, 1961), pp. 39 f., points out both openness to the world and self-consciousness as human characteristics. Pannenberg one-sidedly emphasizes the world relation, which is relatively secular.

[11] Cf. above, p. 101.

ferentiated at this point; his general outlook, indeed, does not distinguish between the mythical hope for the infinite and the historical exertive will for the finite.[12]

Primitives recognized some of these distinctions in drawing a rather sharp line between mythical and historical periods. Events located in mythical time have gods as their heroes. Events associated with historical time center upon human exploits, supported but not dominated by divine forces. Mythical narratives are sacred, told at festivals and in association with rituals. Historical narratives are told for the glorification of one's clan or family. Often different labels are applied to the two types.[13]

A further difference between myth and history can be observed. Mythical events tend to be perfect and to serve as model archetypes to be appropriated in behavior. Historical time is always imperfect. Part of the equipment of primitive folklore consists of stories dealing with the origins of evil and death. These, too, are in a sense myths, but they deal, not with the mythical reality itself, but with the transition from mythical time to history. The origin of evil is usually blamed on an accident, sometimes on the trickery of the gods or on a culpable error of man.[14] In any case, it is clear to the ancient man that he now lives in a time contaminated with evil, in which he is relatively separated from the divine.

In cultic action, however, man has a chance to reactivate the "original" relation with God, to experience or effect an integration with the universal powers, and sometimes to have communion with the departed. In these instances, he transcends mere history and participates in the eternal and absolute fullness of Being or Life.

In more developed religious structures, however, the situa-

[12] He speaks of man's *unendliches Streben* (unending striving or tendency); *Was ist der Mensch?,* p. 11; cf. also above, p. 113. Such a description has some truth but is not sufficient.

[13] These facts are well known. Some of them are documented in Martin Buss, "The Language of the Divine 'I,' " *Journal of Bible and Religion* (abbreviated *JBR*), XXIX (1961), 106, notes 8, 15, and 16.

[14] On the last point, see the important study by Hans Abrahamsson, *The Origin of Death* (Uppsala, 1951).

tion becomes more complicated. Not only their external arrangement but also their inner structure achieves a greater complexity. For instance, a time of the heroes frequently interposes itself between the time of the gods and the present time, often with an element of high tragedy. More especially, there appears in higher religions a tendency to find evil within man himself instead of locating it in the outside world. Guilt becomes a much more acute problem than in the primitive structure, where evil largely took the form of natural forces that threaten man's existence from without.

It is true, high-god aspects of primitive religions have almost always had a moral character (though this fact may have been exaggerated by some scholars),[15] so that no simple evolutionary scheme is possible. Yet, it is also clear that strikingly similar developments away from primitive religion toward more moral and otherworldly religion occurred almost simultaneously and for the mosts part independently in the East and in the West. The dividing line between these two worlds runs between India and Persia, with mountainous terrain producing a relatively sharp barrier, though mutual relations proceeded through Central Asia or along the sea route. Since the Near East and India form the geographical center of the Afro-Eurasian land mass, it is not surprising that the spearhead of civilization should occur here.[16] From this area, civilizations and religions spread toward the West and toward the East, developing two cultural systems which remained relatively isolated until recent times. Hegel made the error of considering Eastern religions a stage of the divine spirit earlier and less profound than Western faith. Modern study has made it rather clear, instead, that Eastern and Western develop-

[15] Despite probable exaggerations of this point by Wilhelm Schmidt, the remarks by Fritz Graebner, *Das Weltbild der Primitiven* (Munich: E. Reinhardt, 1924), pp. 26, 129, hold up rather well.

[16] Ralph Linton, *The Tree of Culture* (New York: Alfred A. Knopf, 1955), regards India as a part of the Southwest Asia Complex; but many developments took place independently on the basis of similar sociological backgrounds. A geographical symmetry of religions is noted by Arnold Toynbee in *Christianity among the Religions of the World* (New York: Charles Scribner's Sons, 1957), p. 34.

ments parallel each other in some detail. This striking situation should show that God has not acted arbitrarily within history, but that inherent tendencies of development have produced such phenomena as Israelite and Christian faith, comparable respectively to Hinduism and Buddhism. If God acts in history, he must be seen to act within the patterns that inhere in history itself.

The fact that theology has not dealt adequately with these phenomena is one of the signs of its severe isolation from other intellectual disciplines. Pannenberg and his group are now calling for renewed attention to the history and philosophy of religion. One may hope that they will deal adequately with the perspectives which have just been outlined, unless, of course, they find them to be erroneous.

It seems that a major change took place in human development which marked a transition from preliterary man to *homo historicus* who occupies recorded history. The mechanics of the transition can quite easily be seen to be sociological in nature.[17] Record-keeping, made possible by the development of writing, facilitated the development of certain aspects of man's concern for his existence. Complexity of society made possible a more highly differentiated self-consciousness. Man was finding himself in a new way, no longer immersed in the processes of nature.

Under the circumstances, there arose a belief in soteriological events which are assigned to a time distinct from world-creation (the Exodus, Rome's founding, Jesus, a Krishna-incarnation, Gautama Buddha, Mohammed, Quetzalcoatl). Individual religions differ in the ways in which they weave the historical element into their faith. Generally speaking, the more otherworldly religions (Christianity, Buddhism) find the historical center and the person of their "founder" more important than the relatively more thisworldly, and more man-accepting, religions (Hinduism, Israel, Confucianism, Tao-ism). This seems paradoxical, but it shows that man, as an

---

17 Cf. E. A. Burtt, *Man Seeks the Divine* (New York: Harper & Row, 1957), pp. 93 ff.

object of his concern, is a problem to himself; selfhood is most acutely active when one judges the self negatively.

At the same time, antireligious skepticism arose as a formal system, both in the East and in the West. In such a structure, man and his own reason are made the measure of all things, and the gods disappear. It is largely from within this group that critical historiography arose; Herodotus and Thucydides, for instance, were both tinged with skepticism.

## II. BIBLICAL PATTERNS OF HISTORY

To understand Biblical patterns of history it is well to proceed form-critically. The advantage of a form-critical approach is that it does not lead to the formulation of abstract ideas with which one might be asked to agree or disagree intellectually; instead, it reconstructs the functional structure of a nation such as Israel on the basis of the formal patterns of its verbal expression. No claim is made that the following discussion is one that Israelites would have accepted themselves, but only that it is an appropriate description, with the categories matched to the actual use of their language. This is important, because it does not appear possible in any case that agreement between ancient and modern views can be reached. Pannenberg's analysis of the Old Testament is for this reason inadequate, even assuming that his representations are roughly correct.[18] What his analysis does is to state somewhat abstractly, viewpoints which were held more concretely by Old Testament writers (e.g., the Old Testament has no concept of history as such), and to state them in such a way as to be acceptable to his contemporaries. This bridging attempt, however, loses contact with both sides. The only possible approach from the modern situation is to describe the linguistic behavior of Israel as a symbolic system. One may indeed still refer to Israel's view of history, but this is at best a form of shorthand for the structural elements that make up its way of speaking.

---

[18] Cf. above, Pannenberg, pp. 104 ff.

Gerhard von Rad has recognized that Israel's faith is connected with the picture which it has of its history. This picture is identical with what Bultmann would call its self-understanding.[19] The *fact* that Israel has such a view is a matter of historiographic record. The *content* of its view is religious symbol or myth. Its mythical picture of its history and the facts as reconstructed by modern historiography are intertwined because of that structure of man by means of which he has a relation to himself. Man's view of himself and of his position can be described as the content of human history. In the Old Testament, myth and history are especially closely intertwined because God is pictured as battling against man.

The distinction between historical fact and picture of history has been blurred somewhat in the past because the second of these terms has been called *Geschichte,* implying that its content somehow really happened. Such an assumption, however, is unnecessary. It is true, a picture of history does usually include references to events which are also recoverable by historiography—this is particularly true of the more prominent data in the collective memory—but the sociopsychological structure of such a picture is independent of the correctness of the factual references.

In Israel, God was pictured as dealing with and in history. This means that God's enemies are not primarily mythical powers but are human forces, both within and outside of the elect people.[20] Israel's negative view of man can be recognized in the somber tones of the quasi-mythical period before the Flood, in the descriptions of continuing evil and recalcitrance within the patriarchal narratives, and in the accounting of obstinacy and lack of recognition on the part of Egyptians and Israelites in the rest of the Pentateuch. History (human history) is emphasized here, not because it is good but rather

---

[19] The importance of memory for individual self-concepts is well known. It is perhaps even more applicable collectively. E.g., Alfr. Heuss, *Verlust der Geschichte* (Göttingen: Vandenhoeck und Ruprecht, 1959), p. 17.

[20] For more details, see *JBR,* XXIX (1961), 104. Cf. also, Johannes Hempel, *Altes Testament und Geschichte* (Gütersloh: Bertelsmann, 1930), p. 21.

because God has to struggle against it. God is seen as winning the battle, at least partially, and establishing a new normative period,[21] in which God constitutes a people and presents them with fundamental laws. The effect of this is to create a new mythical period against the background of history.

The chaotic dragon that has been slain is human history itself. Yet in the Israelite view history does not end with the Exodus or Mt. Sinai. Human evil again raises its horrible head —if not in the wilderness, at least in the promised land itself. Israelite existence is viewed as a constant deviation from the norm established by Yahweh. A "negative archetype"[22] of its existence becomes a fundamental feature of the form of the stories in which it presents its own past history.

The sacred period itself, running from the time of the Patriarchs to David, becomes the content of cultic celebration. The priestly presentation contains laws and other statements expressed in the form of divine speech. This form arises in the Old Testament whenever the Israelite is challenged to obedience and gratitude and thus to an acknowledgment of authority and the recognition of dependence on a reality greater than himself.

It is thus clear that a sense of guilt and the acknowledgment of a divine authority are closely related. It is, however, one of the paradoxes of guilt that it is canceled in recognition and confession. Thus Israel has a negative form of history;[23] the

[21] Similarly, Brevard S. Childs, *Myth and Reality in the Old Testament* (Naperville, Ill.: Alec R. Allenson, 1960), p. 82. It is "existence-founding" for Israel; Rendtorff and Koch, ed., *Studien zur Theologie der Alttestamentlichen Überlieferungen* (*Festschrift* for Gerhard von Rad; Berlin: Evangelische Verlagenstalt, 1961), p. 89.

[22] Andrew C. Tunyogi, "The Rebellions of Israel," *Journal of Biblical Literature*, LXXXI (1962), 388. From this perspective, one must revise the interpretation of Rolf Rendtorff, *KuD*, VII (1961), 69–78; for J's perspective is not that "myth" is bad and "history" is good, but rather that a divine struggle in history is necessary, because the archetype of man is negative.

[23] The general possibility of a negative history, and its presence in Israel, has been noted already by Hegel, though this crucial aspect of his thought was largely overlooked in the optimism of the nineteenth century. Cf., similarly, Mircea Eliade, *The Myth of the Eternal Return* (New York: Pantheon Books, 1954), pp. 95 ff.; also, Johannes Hempel, *Die*

very negativity of its view transforms the life that holds it, so that it is precisely the redeemed community that confesses its sins and acknowledges that God loved it out of a free will.

The historical period of the Exodus was one of the crucial events which triggered (or supported) the acceptance of a post-Creation normative action of God. This is probably the reason it was chosen as the focal point of Israelite myth. This is a modern historiographic way of putting the matter. For the Israelites, the intervention of God in human existence was important within what we would now call its symbolic framework.

To questions about the past must be joined an analysis of the future. The future activity of God may rightly be termed, with von Rad, eschatological. Von Rad also gives the right reason for designating it thus, namely that the eschatological outlook involves a negative attitude toward existing structures of Israel.[24] This negative element in eschatology, however, has been overlooked by von Rad's students. Pannenberg's friend Rössler has pointed out a close connection between history and apocalyptic.[25] Such an observation, however, does not prove that apocalyptic tradition has a positive attitude toward history. On the contrary, apocalyptic literature clearly implies that history moves progressively downward, until it is over-

---

*Mehrdeutigkeit der Geschichte als Problem der prophetischen Theologie* (Göttingen: Vandenhoeck und Ruprecht, 1936), p. 5. A somewhat negative view has been championed recently by Jean Daniélou, *The Lord of History* (Chicago: Henry Regnery Co., 1958), p. 33, and by the usually rather optimistic Claude Tresmontant, *Biblisches Denken und hellenistische Überlieferung* (Düsseldorf: Patmos, 1956), p. 171. For Heidegger, for whom time was once directed toward death, history is now the realm of "erring"; cf. *Holzwege* (Frankfurt: Klostermann, 1950), p. 310. The negativity of history, however, did not mean a devaluation of history by Hegel. Similarly, for Heidegger the salvation of history comes only with its danger (*Holzwege*, p. 343).

[24] *Theologie des Alten Testaments* (Munich: Christian Kaiser Verlag, 1960), II, p. 129, and *passim*. The fact that von Rad has adjusted the definition of eschatology to fit his understanding of prophecy should not be criticized (as by Fohrer, in *ThR*, XXVIII [1962], 357), but should rather be pointed out as an excellent example of guarding against irrelevant *a priori* definitions.

[25] Dietrich Rössler, *Gesetz und Geschichte* (Neukirchen: Kr. Moers, 1960).

thrown by the Eternal Kingdom.[26] In fact, we have already seen that an emphasis on history is often negative in character. The same situation applies also to prophecy, as distinguished from apocalyptic. The prophet's interest in history—at least this is true for the prophets of doom—is determined by his opposition to it.[27] Insofar as there is a positive expectation, it is utopian.

One important feature of the announcement of doom is that the end is expected very soon. Pannenberg has attempted to justify Jesus' expectation of an imminent End by seeing it partially fulfilled in his resurrection.[28] This suggestion fails to do justice to the phenomenon of a regular correlation between the expectation of an imminent End and a heavily negative attitude toward the present. In view of this correlation, the affirmation of an imminent End can be understood as an expression of intense hope for a better situation.[29] Outside Israel, "messianic" expectations, confident hopes for a new world and its speedy coming, have arisen when primitive cultures crumbled under the impact of more advanced civilizations. Nichiren Buddhism was burdened by a sense of profound evil and a conviction that the last days before the victory of true reality had come. In undisturbed primitive religions only an individual eschatology is needed, since the communal order is seen as sufficiently able to cope with its problems. But some of the great Old Testament prophets saw the Israelite community as existing in a basic contradiction with deity. Thus they announced a hasty End, seizing on international phenomena for confirmation when possible.

The predictions of the prophets are usually not very spe-

---

[26] That in general the Israelite conception of history is one of decline has also been pointed out by W. F. Albright in A. O. Lovejoy and George Boas, *Primitivism and Related Ideas in Antiquity* (Baltimore: Johns Hopkins Press, 1935), p. 429. Cf. also Klaus Koch, *ZThK*, LV (1958), 45.

[27] Cf. also Martin Buber, *Israel and the World* (New York: Schocken Books, 1948), p. 130.

[28] Cf. above, Pannenberg, pp. 113 ff.

[29] Cf. also Carl Becker, *The Heavenly City of the Eighteenth Century Philosophers* (New Haven: Yale University Press, 1932), p. 138.

cific. They speak in rather general, heavily emotion-laden terms about the good or evil that confronts Israel's existence.[30] Such a way of speaking is indeed all that is necessary to provide proper help in decision-making, which is the age-old function of a prophet. Indeed, prophecies must usually be considered conditional, especially when doom is pronounced. Only in some of the extreme prophets is the conviction present that doom cannot be averted and the final denouement is definitely to come. In that case, a true End-expectation is present and the character of decision required is one of inner submission to the coming of God rather than a change of actions through one's will; a "new heart" is needed. This kind of temporal perspective is not equivalent to a (physical) "effect" nor to an (organismic) "goal" of striving, but is the (spiritual) "End" toward which one relates oneself receptively. Israelite religion fuses goal and End in varying ways, a fact well-known to Jewish theologians.[31]

The category of "future," as distinguished from "End," belongs properly in the sphere of wisdom, where 'aharit (outcome, result) appears frequently as the term for the consequences of evil. Klaus Koch has emphasized for the Old Testament the wisdom character of what might otherwise be called retribution, in that the so-called reward is really a consequence of one's action.[32] (In fact, the Pannenberg circle has affinities with wisdom in stressing rationality and objectivity.)[33]

Matter-of-fact historiography in the Old Testament—such

[30] In this respect, the Old Testament prophets scarcely differ from Jesus (against Pannenberg, above, pp. 111 ff.). Cf. Ernst Jenni, *Die politischen Voraussagen der Propheten* (*Abhandlungen zur Theologie des A.T. und N.T.*, 29; Zürich: Zwingli Verlag, 1956), even though his reconstruction is not always convincing. For a more detailed treatment of the whole problem of Israelite prophecy, see Martin Buss, "The Prophets," *Emory University Quarterly*, XVIII (1962), 221–228.

[31] E.g. Martin Buber, *Die chassidische Botschaft* (Heidelberg: Schneider, 1952), pp. 76, 79.

[32] Recently again, now in evident dependence on Pannenberg, in *Vetus Testamentum,* XII (1962), 414 f. While I could largely agree with Koch's original formulation, his present emphasis appears too rationalistic.

[33] A similar emphasis on rationality and objectivity can be found in E. J. Carnell, *The Case for Orthodox Theology* (Philadelphia: Westminster Press, 1959).

as that found in court records—was probably handled by scribes who were members of the wisdom class. It is, in fact, misleading to say that wisdom has no relation to history. Wisdom has indeed little connection with sacred history, but it has many contacts with secular forms of history, which are the most appropriate counterparts to Pannenberg's view of history as a verifiable reality. The narration of the succession to David's throne and the Joseph story (in which Pannenberg rightly sees no prophetic determination[34]) are well-known examples of wisdom-influenced writing.[35] Human narratives (fictional and otherwise, e.g., the memoirs of Nehemiah) abound in the third division of the Hebrew canon. The Deuteronomic school, which is responsible for an elaborate work of history, contains pronounced wisdom elements.

Wisdom perspectives probably also entered into the presentation of Israelite sacred history itself.[36] Pannenberg refers to the phrase "that they may know that I am God" as indicating that Israel expected that Yahweh's actions would be publicly known.[37] There is some truth in this. But it must also be noted that this phrase appears on the lips of Yahweh. It is a part of priestly and prophetic revelation and not primarily—despite the use of the word "to know"—a part of the humanistic knowledge of wisdom, which always puts its dicta into human speech. This "cognition formula" is limited to a very small language circle belonging to the Exilic period,[38] probably reflecting anxiety over Yahweh's power after the downfall of Jerusalem; it is the—perhaps awkward—result of a combination of at least two elements, the sacral self-presentation form and the term "knowledge," which has both priestly and wis-

[34] Cf. above, Pannenberg, p. 129.
[35] Cf. Gerhard von Rad, *Gesammelte Studien zum Alten Testament* (Munich: Christian Kaiser Verlag, 1958), pp. 148–88, 272–80.
[36] The element of rationality in Israel's view of existence has been emphasized by Arthur Weiser, *Glaube und Geschichte im Alten Testament* (Stuttgart:Kohlhammer, 1931), pp. 44–47 (with the exception of prophets, p. 85). Specific traces of wisdom require a separate investigation.
[37] Cf. above, Pannenberg, pp. 119–122.
[38] Ezekiel, Psalms, and I Kings 20. (That the last is exilic is documented in an unpublished dissertation by Max Miller, 1964.)

dom associations and would thus lend itself to a conflation of perspectives.

Despite a certain overlap and fusion, however, Israelite language is careful to represent foundational (priestly) and eschatological (prophetic) language primarily in terms of divine speech, clearly distinguishing these realms from others. Ordinary human events are considered accessible to observation in wisdom. The divine reality or plan is a mystery to be revealed.[39] The only place God speaks in wisdom literature is at the end of the Book of Job (if this work is, indeed, wisdom), where God says simply, "I am greater than you," indicating that human comprehension is limited and cannot fathom the meaning of the ultimate structure of life. Within pure wisdom, only a *via negationis* leads to God, though one treads paths coming from him.

Recognition of the world thus has its place in Israel in connection with the challenges of deity to one's own existence. These two aspects, though often distinguished, are not sharply antithetical; for the Israelite attitude to history was not entirely negative, and positive attitudes toward the world and the self appear not infrequently. It remained for Christians to break more thoroughly with history and to alienate man from himself, from God, and from the world of objects. It is true that for Christians Jesus Christ constitutes the center of history, but as historical event his life culminates in the cross, a symbol of the complete failure of existence.

The resurrection, the center of Christian faith, is an eschatological category. As we have already seen, eschatology is structurally different from human history (as in primitive religion and in Judaism), for it is a mythical or revelational category, and calls for an attitude of receptivity. In Christianity, the possibility of human reason or moral assertions is even more severely limited than in Judaism, at least as regards a positive relevance to faith. So, for instance, the teaching of Jesus rigorously excludes matters of practical wisdom which

39 Cf. Eccles. 3:11, whatever the precise exegesis may be.

had been an enduring concern of the rabbinic tradition.[40] His ethics are fantastically impractical. Such wisdom as continues in the New Testament takes the peculiar form of an eschatological wisdom, which had already made its appearance in Jewish apocalyptic. An adequate discussion of apocalypticism, which has become an important theme for the Pannenberg group (and recently for some others in a similar way[41]) is not possible here. Yet it may be pointed out that the apocalyptic tradition is a form of negative theology. Its wisdom is designed to put man in his place; its attitude toward history is one of decided hostility to national cultures. A close analogue is probably to be found in Buddhism, which too is essentially an otherworldly wisdom, seeking to transcend the present situation and using reason to slay pretensions.

Christianity's major modification of apocalypticism was its belief that the resurrection was already present for faith. Certain forms of Buddhism, similarly, took the step of accepting the presence of *nirvana*. The two religious groups, it is true enough, solved their problems in somewhat different ways, partly because of their differing inheritances from the Old Testament and early Hinduism respectively; but they share many common elements which set them off from their forebears.[42]

Pannenberg begins his essay above with the statement that "in dealing with Jesus of Nazareth we are dealing with God Himself." This looks like a factual statement and is indeed

[40] Cf. Joseph Klausner, *Jesus of Nazareth* (New York: The Macmillan Company, 1925), p. 373, and *passim*, and the listing in Gustaf Dalman, *Jesus-Jeschua* (New York: The Macmillan Company, 1929), pp. 223–36.

[41] E.g., Ernst Käsemann, "Zum Thema der urchristlichen Apokalyptik," *ZThK,* LIX (1962), 257–84, a very different conception of apocalyptic from the one here accepted.

[42] The dividing lines between Hinduism and Buddhism do not precisely match those between Judaism and Christianity, but they come fairly close. *Hinayana* and *bhakti* are perhaps examples of overlap; but the two Western faiths are also not internally homogeneous. (One might compare *Hinayana* with Jesus, though the latter's view is still not quite clarified.) On a comparison of certain Biblical with some Eastern themes, cf. also, Thomas J. J. Altizer, *Oriental Mysticism and Biblical Eschatology* (Philadelphia: Westminster Press, 1961).

taken by Pannenberg as such. But already Luther recognized
that an anticipatory or creative judgment is equivalent to the
doctrine of justification by faith.[43] The preceding analysis has
given us reason to believe that all eschatological declarations
are emotive statements relating to oneself. To believe in the
presence of the End is to believe in the presence of that reality
which one receives receptively, or, in Lutheran terms, it is
equivalent to accepting the forgiveness of sins. Retracing one's
steps, one may say this: If present history is evil and eschatological reality is perfect, then the presence of the End means
the apprehension of the perfect within the imperfect, of true
Being within mere existence. This is the structural meaning
of the sentence "Jesus is the Christ."

It is not necessary to understand such a statement in a factual sense. That would place it in the context of critical objectivity, which has its place in the world of humanistic reason,
of which some traces appeared in Israelite wisdom, more, in
Greek culture, and most of all, in modern scholarship. Humanistic and critical studies, however, have as an axiom that
value decisions and ultimate commitments cannot be determined on the basis of objective data, and they cautiously
avoid such statements as Pannenberg's that "the Jews knew
their God, and yet did not know him aright; otherwise they
would not have rejected Jesus"[44] or, "the Hellenistic conception of God . . . found a deeper fulfillment" in the message
of Jesus.[45] It is true that Pannenberg is trying to change this
modern—and in many ways ancient—convention. But in the
process, he proposes conclusions (such as that of the occurrence of a "real" resurrection) which do not convince most
historians,[46] while at the same time unnecessarily attributing
to ancient man an interest in impartial objectivity. Not only
did Jesus specifically reject signs as a means to faith, but an-

[43] Heidelberg disputation (1518), thesis 28.
[44] Cf. above, Pannenberg, p. 104.
[45] Ibid., p. 108.
[46] On the basis of purely historical considerations, one might give the
story of the empty tomb a maximal 30 per cent probability of occurrence;
it can hardly be made the cornerstone of faith.

cient religious man generally had little concern for facts viewed from an impartial standpoint.

Judaism, of course, rejected Jesus, continuing along a path that follows fairly closely that laid out in the Old Testament.[47] A good case can be made for the Jewish way, since it unites all aspects of life in a coherent whole, while Christianity (when taken earnestly) represents a severe threat to the social order. Christian faith, since it is not closely tied to human life in society, naturally became a missionary religion.[48] It thus spread to the Hellenistic world, just as the similarly individualistic and otherworldly Buddhism became a world religion though unable to maintain itself in its land of origin. In this way Christianity was able to make contact with the Greek religious developments to which Pannenberg has referred.

## III. The Present and the Infinite

One question a reflective person can ask himself is, why does a portion of the world happen to be where it is at the moment? Why does man exist now? The answer is relatively simple. No one would be thinking about existence or worrying about it, if there were not a being that did so think or worry. Man *must* exist in the present. The present necessarily is where one exists and reflects; so there is nothing arbitrary in relating infinite reality to man in the present. In each present moment man can live to the glory of God—a glory that reveals itself in the grace he extends to an existence that is apart from him.

Though Pannenberg emphasizes the infinite element in Christian faith, he vitiates this element by making it appear finite, locating it in time and space. The infinite can be pres-

[47] Christian scholars are often not careful enough to recognize Judaism as a truer descendant of the Old Testament than Christianity. (On this point, see Nietzsche, *Dawn,* Par. 84.) There is a tendency among writers to use "Israel" with a good connotation and "Judaism" with a bad one (Pannenberg's essay in this volume comes close to this usage; cf. above, p. 104). There is no historiographic justification for such a distinction, unless it is of such a kind as might separate first-century Christians from later ones.

[48] Cf. Gust. Mensching, *Die Religion* (Stuttgart: Schwab, 1959), p. 73.

ent in the world at best paradoxically. In some ways, Pannenberg is quite modern. He wants to ascertain the reality of faith on the basis of his own knowledge. Like many other moderns he lacks a vision of the transcendent.[49] He wants to affirm human existence. But can he save his faith, on the basis of a humanistic reason? Hardly. Not only will he remain at the level of probability or possibility—which is constitutive of worldly knowledge[50]—but he must also lose the sense of self-abandon (and with it a self-finding) in God, which is the essence of faith as it confronts what the Old Testament calls a divine word. Even critical study knows that man's deepest moments lie beyond the assertive mode.

The activity of God is important in Biblical religion. But one must make clear what it means to say that "God acts." As Abraham Heschel pointed out some time ago, God reveals not himself but his "pathos."[51] Here one must be more radical than is Pannenberg. Strictly speaking, God does not reveal himself as an entity, even indirectly. God, rather, establishes a situation of grace. God reveals, or better, effects his forgiveness and thus his lordship. The meaning of world history for Christians is that God claims it in love and gains the victory only upon meeting death there.[52] Faith in Christ means that one accepts one's worth as a gift, i.e., without self-pretension. "God" designates the ineffable infinity, of which glimpses appear in an ecstasy and love, known only in self-abandon.[53]

---

[49] Cf. above, Pannenberg, p. 128, in denying that one has convincing experiences of the risen Christ. This is correct in a way, but direct apprehensions of infinity are different from substantive experiences related to an object and are perhaps comparable to the making of important decisions. On the phenomenon, cf. Marghanita Laski, *Ecstasy* (Bloomington: Indiana University Press, 1961).

[50] The fact that all historical knowledge has only a probability of certainty is not an argument against Pannenberg, if he chooses to accept the consequences; one would like to know just what degree of uncertainty he feels. Uncertainty in theology (as distinguished from a faith which is not in the realm of "opinion") is in any case inevitable.

[51] *Die Prophetie* (Berlin: Reiss, 1936).

[52] Cf. the very sensitive discussion by Sigmund Freud, *Moses and Monotheism* (New York: Alfred A. Knopf, 1939), pp. 215 f.

[53] Susan Sontag, a young Jewish literary figure, in a recent lecture perhaps aptly designated this reality as the Transpersonal.

# 4. Revelation and Resurrection

## KENDRICK GROBEL
### Vanderbilt University

## I

In his essay, "The Revelation of God in Jesus of Nazareth," Professor Pannenberg refers to previous work both of his own and of his colleagues, Rolf Rendtorff and Ulrich Wilckens, in *Offenbarung als Geschichte*.[1] On the basis of this work he declares: "The Israelite idea of knowledge of God brought about by a history wrought by God for this express purpose is the closest parallel in Biblical thought to the modern sense of the word revelation: God's self-disclosure, his making himself known. As is common knowledge, the other terms which are usually rendered by our word 'revelation,' or 'reveal,' do not mean *self*-revelation in either Testament. But with respect to the term 'know,' it is expressly said that God makes *himself* known through his deeds, and in content the same thing is meant when it is said that his deeds make his *glory* known."[2] Thus Pannenberg's relation of revelation to history is based upon the Biblical concept of "knowing" God through history.

With regard to "history," neither Testament has a term for it (certainly not that hard-worked word *dbr*, not even in *dbry hymym*, which seems to mean *diarium*, journal), still less for "Hebrew history" or "world history," and least of all for the totality of all happening, "universal history." Pannenberg quite rightly expects his hearers and readers to agree with him that again and again the Bible talks about history (or

---

[1] *KuD, Beiheft* 1; Göttingen:Vandenhoeck und Ruprecht, 1961.
[2] Cf. above, Pannenberg, p. 123.

should we leave out a heavy little word and say merely "talks history"?) without ever naming it or even having a name for it. How many other things the Bible deals with or discusses, yet never names! It has no word for theology, probably for the simple reason that it does not talk *about* God, but *declares him.* (Furthermore, *theologia* was tainted: it meant the theogonic myths of the Oympians and the mystery deities.) It has no word for psychology or anthropology, though it has a lively interest in man and in his mind. It has no word for ethics (if one had been invented out of New Testament material, it very well could have been *peripatēsis!*); and perhaps we do certain Biblical views a great wrong by labeling them "ethical," if ethics is merely the societal residue of the conventionally acceptable *ēthos* or *mos* without any reference to the will of a righteous God! The list could be greatly extended. The Biblical writers felt nowhere nearly so great a need as do we to identify their reflections with word labels, nor even when they did, to make their labels of the very abstract sort used by philosophers in classifying universal knowledge. Consequently, the absence of a given technical term in the Bible does not prevent us from finding its essential subject matter there; nor does its presence guarantee that our employment of it will assure the legitimacy of our deductions from Biblical thought.

All the discussions of revelation in *Offenbarung als Geschichte* are carefully *verklausuliert*—in American: well provided with ifs, ands, and buts. Alternative positions to that of Pannenberg would presumably have to appeal to some Biblical kind of self-revelation distinct from knowledge of God inferred from history. Pannenberg does not find such an alternative view in Scripture. According to him, such a view would have to pass at least three tests: first, it would have to be direct, not indirect; second, it would have to be complete, not partial; and third, it would have to have as its object God himself and not merely something pertaining to God. A fourth condition, that it be expressed by a technical term, revelation, is apparently regarded as a desideratum but not a requirement. If any *one* of his three requirements is missing, Pannenberg can declare that an alternative kind of self-revelation to that through history is not present. Certainly any prospector has the right to decide what he is looking for, but he may in the process let gold or uranium glide by him.

Let us first examine the term revelation more closely. *Apokalyptō* had been in use at least since the fifth century B.C. (Herodotus); *revēlo* is not known to be older than the Augustan period. Since there were already numerous synonyms (*nudo, retego, patefacio,* etc.), it is likely that *revēlo* is simply one more of that large class of words with which Latin enriched its vocabulary by piecemeal translation of Greek words: *apo* = *re, kalyptō* = *velo*.[3] So when we speak of *apokalyptō* we are also speaking of *revēlo* as a satellite and derivative.

It is a bit startling at first to have one's attention called to the fact that the noun *apokalypsis* never occurs with a theological meaning in the Septuagint, and indeed, only once in a book from the Hebrew canon, and that the Hebrew verb *glh* (Greek, *apokalyptein*) also rarely has such a meaning.[4] The surprise rapidly diminishes as one recognizes that a verb which never loses its original meaning, "to lay bare," is appropriate to perception by *touch* or by *sight* but not by *hearing.* The Bible almost never describes the experience of perceiving God in revelation in tactile metaphors.[5] The Bible does indeed speak of *seeing* God and of God's causing himself to be seen (1 Sam. 3:7, 21). Still the Greek Bible never calls the visually described encounter with God a *theōria,* nor does it ever speak of an attempt to make a mental *theōria* to fit the God of Israel and the church. It is probably true that Biblical man more frequently, or at least more characteristically, speaks of

[3] The derivatives of *revēlo* seem to be almost entirely ecclesiastical, having arisen out of the churchly need for translation.

[4] These rare exceptions, e.g., 1 Sam. 2:27; 3:7, 21; Isa. 40:5, are really weightier than is implied in Rendtorff's remark (*Offenbarung als Geschichte,* p. 23) that this term is "the worst one conceivable" to take as a point of departure.

[5] A possible exception is in Acts 17:27. But even here psēlaphaō must not mean "touch" but "grope after." If touch were meant, the verbs would need to be reversed—not "touch" and then "find," as the text reads, but "find" and then "touch."

*hearing* God than of seeing him, although I can offer no sta-
tistics. It would seem the obvious thing, then, to turn from
visual to auditory description in the search for a quasi-tech-
nical term for God's self-communication or for man's reception thereof. Except when one is dazzled by a new discovery
(e.g., that history, even raw, uninterpreted history, may be
revelation) it ought to remain clear, and does to most, that
"word" or "speech" is the noun we are seeking, and "speak"
and "hear" the verbal pair. These remain, I contend, both the
basic technical *terms* for God's self-communication and the
basic Biblical *conceptions* of it.

Why should the Bible so un-Hellenically favor the ear over
the eye in attempting to describe the ultimately indescribable
perception of the God who communicates? Hans Jonas wrote
a little article, written entirely from the Greek point of view,
which by antithesis suggests some interesting answers. He
called it "The Nobility of Sight."[6] Sight gives a simultaneous,
instantaneous sweep of a vast field; whereas hearing, like the
other senses, can only give a temporal sequence of sensations,
can only communicate successive acts of the environment. In
the light of this distinction noted by Jonas, we can see that if
the Bible were primarily interested in the being and nature of
God, visual terms would be more appropriate. But since it is
more interested in God who emerges, says *Fiat!,* and with-
draws until his next good time, then hearing seems appropriate. Again, Jonas notes that sound can give, and the ear
receive, only dynamic, never static, reality. Even though the
God of the Bible is conceived as abiding from everlasting to
everlasting and as enduring ever the same (Ps. 102:24 ff.),
rather than as existing in some timeless eternity, even to ask
whether he is basically conceived as static or dynamic immediately illumines why hearing is more appropriate than sight.
Again, Jonas holds that hearing is at a disadvantage compared with sight because the hearer "is entirely dependent on

---

6 *Philosophy and Phenomenological Research,* XIV (1954), 507–19,
reprinted in *The Phenomenon of Life* (New York: Harper & Row, 1966),
pp. 135–56.

something happening *outside his control.* All he can contribute to the situation is a state of attentive readiness for sounds to occur."[7] His ears have no eyelids for shutting out, nor can his ears go roaming like peering eyeballs to gather in. He who sees may be lord of all he can survey, but he who hears is at the mercy of a reality which surrounds him and chooses to make a sound or keep still. The Paul who says parenthetically "for we walk by faith, not by sight" (2 Cor. 5:7), is very close to saying "we walk by ear, not by eye," insofar as faith is, for him, *hypakoē* (obedience), and *hypakoē* is a qualified kind of *akoē,* hearing. Finally Jonas states, "*things* are not by their own nature audible as they are visible."[8] But is this true of persons? Does an environmental entity come to life as a *person* to me until it becomes vocal, until it enters into the give-and-take of speech? Probably not. The personhood of God is probably the ultimate anthropomorphism of the Bible, and perhaps an irreducible one. It is probably as helpless a human metaphor as the "posterior of God" (Ex. 33:23), which was all that even Moses was allowed to see; but we should be ready for the possible demonstration that by the personhood of God the Bible only means to say that God is at least a person, or that his reality lies unknowably further out along the line that for us characterizes a person. At any rate Biblical men described God's encounter with them in terms of the way a person is perceived: as speaking God to hearing man—the greatest and most frequent Biblical analogy of the personhood of God. Jonas' article proved the "nobility of sight" over all the senses for the philosopher. It should be supplemented by a companion essay, which he could very well write himself, on the "Blessedness of Hearing" for the man of faith.[9]

[7] *Ibid.,* 509 (italics mine).

[8] *Ibid.,* p. 514.

[9] [Cf. Jonas, "Heidegger and Theology," *The Journal of Metaphysics,* XIII (1964), 207–33, esp. pp. 207–9, reprinted in *The Phenomenon of Life,* pp. 235–61, esp. pp. 236–38. Quotation is from the first publication: A telling symbol of what happened to the Biblical word through him [sc. Philo] and his successors is unwittingly supplied by an allegory which he evolves from an etymology of the name "Israel." (Heidegger was not

## II

We return to Pannenberg's three tests for the recognition of the kind of revelation that would support an alternative to his own position, an alternative he thinks is not to be found in Scripture.

1. *It would have to be direct, not indirect.* Where there is need of revelation or disclosure, there is a veil, or closure, some kind of barrier between the two parties involved. The recipient party may *describe* the barrier either as an attribute of the one to be revealed or as an attribute of himself. In the former case the Other is hidden, "clouds and thick darkness are round about him" (Ps. 97:2), he is mute, deaf, withdrawn, unapproachable, inscrutable. In the latter case the nonrecipient who is longing to become recipient describes himself as in the dark, blind, deaf, lost, stumbling, athirst, brutish in understanding. Whichever way the barrier is projected by the mind—upon the donor or upon the recipient—it symbolizes, so or so, the one barrier that must be pierced if communication and communion are to take place.

If the need for disclosure arises solely from the inadequacy

the first to underpin philosophical propositions by masterful etymologizing.) The name is taken to mean "He who sees God," and Jacob's acquiring this name is said to represent the God-seeker's progress from the stage of hearing to that of seeing, made possible by the miraculous conversion of ears into eyes. The allegory falls into the general pattern of Philo's views on "knowing God." These rest on the Platonic supposition that the most genuine relation to being is intuition, beholding. This eminence of sight, when extended into the religious sphere, determines also the highest and most authentic relation to God—and with it also to the *word* of God. To this Philo indeed assigns a nature which makes vision, i.e., intellectual contemplation, and not audition, its genuine criterion. Referring to the phrase in Exodus, "All the people saw the voice" (20:18), he comments: "Highly significant, for human voice is to be heard, but God's voice is in truth to be seen. Why? Because that which God speaks is not words but works, which the eye discriminates better than the ear" (*De Decalogo,* VII, 47). "Works," finished realities, are what God "speaks," i.e., what he, either by his being or by his acting, puts before our eyes. And the finished or perfected is objectively present and can only be looked at; it presents itself in its *eidos.* But Biblically understood, the word of God is primarily call and command, and commands are not looked at but heard—and obeyed or disobeyed. Eds.]

of the human senses, all of them, then the disclosure can only be indirect, mediate, i.e., through a medium that can affect the sense(s) of someone. For Pannenberg, if I understand him rightly, history, and history alone (or the acts that constitute history), plays the role of this mediate disclosure. The acts of God in history! Good! But when is an event in history *eo ipso* an act of God? Only the insurance companies seem to know that—and most theologians would flatly reject their system of classification. Is it not the old problem of *Wunder* vs. *Mirakel* all over again? All the members of a crowd may equally witness a *Wunder* in all its multiambiguity. Some will react to it in mere astonishment. Some will superstitiously see it as *Mirakel,* as God intervening in the causal nexus. Others will see it, or feel it, as a wondrous deed wherein God works in and behind normal occurrence without *Mirakel.* Yet all had witnessed the same event! All had received the same sensory data. Hence the piercing of the barrier should have been for *all* or for *none*—unless the recognition of an act of God here was neither solely, nor even basically, a matter of sense, but was instead a product of a higher function of the mind than perception, viz., that combining power we call thought. The brute fact, the external event, was *there*—no one in the crowd denies it—and to some that brute fact was the vehicle of revelation; but *how* the individual took it, experienced it, understood it, assimilated it into his own being, did not come *from* the fact but was brought *to* it. I am uneasy about calling the source of that "how," thought, for it suggests something too rational, too conscious, too calculating. I am speaking of what the Bible calls *lb* or *kardia* (heart) with all their comfortable blurriness of outline. Particularly I mean to include the will, which these Biblical terms include but "thought" does not. To experience an act of God in an event of the world, be it ever so extraordinary or ever so commonplace, requires a willingness *so* to see, requires a preconditioned will *so* to understand. If I did not suspect that it would be tautologous, I might also say that the source of that "how" is *pistis* in Paul's sense, but is not *pistis* precisely Paul's name for that way of experiencing reality? I could also use the pompous phrase *testimonium internum Spiritus sancti*—but is that not also just a label for the experience in which the divine has leaped the barrier? Are these not simply stammering human attempts to say that the indirect disclosure must always be helped out by a direct disclosure?

2. *Revelation would have to be complete, not partial.* The question seems to me to be whether revelation has degrees: whether God after making himself *revealed* can become *more revealed* and finally *most revealed.* Is not the all-important thing that the barrier *is pierced through* from the only side from which it can be breached? Not the *size* of the breach is important but the *fact* of it. God has reached through and touched man, has spoken to his inner ear, has uncovered to his inner eye a new dimension of reality. More-or-less seems irrelevant here. Oh, the revelation can be impeded—it usually is. Its competitors for attention can be so clamorous that it can be drowned out. The recipient can be hampered by fear, convention, superstition, resistance, or by sheer obtuseness. An apparent plus of revelation will come at a moment when the impeding factors are at a minimum. On the recipient's side that will mean that revelation has become more effective. But is it more *complete?* The content and extent of a concrete revelation are determined by him who reveals, not by him who receives. But any revelation at all *is revelation*—to which we had better refrain from adding the adjective "complete," for two reasons: first, revelation is a qualitative, not a quantitative, matter; and second, God's "beyond-ness" to all we can say or think, though not transcendence in any naïve spatial sense, is utter beyond-ness to all human understanding. He is always beyond his latest, his most nearly "complete" revelation—and hence revelation can never be complete.

Pannenberg himself seems to sense the inadequacy of the "complete" terminology when he comes to speak of the eschatological revelation that takes place proleptically in Jesus. For here he no longer speaks of "full self-disclosure"[10] or

10 *Offenbarung als Geschichte,* p. 13.

"complete self-disclosure";[11] rather the revelation in Jesus is "final,"[12] ultimate, definitive, valid to the end. The choice of "final" was certainly facilitated by the fact that Pannenberg was thinking, quite properly, in eschatological terms. Is it reading too much into this shift to think that it means Pannenberg has recognized a certain self-contradiction in "complete revelation," perhaps even a suggestion of blasphemy?

3. *Revelation would have to have as its object God himself,* not merely something pertaining to God—it would have to be *self*-disclosure. Pannenberg quotes Hannelies Schulte as saying, "Nowhere in the New Testament do the Greek words which we translate as 'reveal' have God as their object pure and simple."[13] To which Pannenberg adds interpretatively: "It is always 'something' or 'someone' that God reveals, never downright 'himself.' "[14] Grammatically that seems to be true. Neither *apokalyptō* nor *phaneroō* occurs in the New Testament with God as subject and *heauton* as object. With the terminology that *we* have made technical the New Testament never says just that. But can Ignatius be accused of falsifying the gist of the New Testament message when he speaks of "God . . . who manifested himself (*phanerōsas heauton*) through Jesus Christ his son?"[15] Certainly the Gospel of John often says something very similar to this in its own terms, especially in chapters 1 and 17.

Let us return to the interpersonal analogy which so pervades Biblical passages about revelation or disclosure. What is it that one human person reveals of himself to another? Only the most self-conscious of men *says* that it is his "self" he reveals or that it is the "self" of the other that is revealed to him. Rather, what one recognizes as revealed is kindness or cruelty, goodwill or spite, genuineness or sham, depth or shallowness. These are all nouns, grammatically; but in the person-to-person situation, do they not really function as adjec-

---

[11] *Ibid.*, p. 17.
[12] *Ibid.*, pp. 103 ff., and above, p. 125. The German term is *endgültig*.
[13] *Ibid.*, p. 12.
[14] *Ibid.*
[15] Ignatius, *Magn.* 8:2.

tives or verbs? They are similar to adjectives in pointing to
the elusive substantive they modify, the other person. His
name and image may be known; but what is *he* really like?
They resemble verbs in pointing back along many radii to
the unknown or enigmatic subject at the center who activates
these verbs; that subject is given nonvisual "color" by the
verbs in which he lurks. *Is* he what he *does?* No, he is the doer
of his doing. But his doing reveals the doer. However seldom
our self-consciousness lets us say so, we are nevertheless constantly revealing ourselves, though ostensibly and consciously
it is almost always something else, not ourselves, that we are
manifesting. Nevertheless, the reception of such revelation always involves interpretation, usually not conscious but existential; and it always involves the risk of self-commitment to the
other. Nor is the revelation ever complete, even though the
other is at the moment completely *in* his self-revelation, for
persons are temporal and can only be known from time to
time by a person who is, himself, also temporal. Must we not
say that a person *can* only reveal himself by revealing something other than himself, something *about* himself, *pertaining*
to himself, issuing *from* himself, but not identical with himself?

Without prejudging the ultimate appropriateness of the interpersonal analogy for God-to-man disclosure, the fact is that
the Biblical writers hold tenaciously to it. Following their lead
in regarding it as at least a meaningful analogy, let us note
*what things* God is said from time to time to reveal.

*a.* God reveals, makes known, his will. No one can ignore
the great bulk of Scripture devoted to the will of God,
whether as Torah, as the prophets' protest, as the Sermon on
the Mount, as Christian parenesis, or, by and large, as eschatology. Certainly God's will is not God—or *is* it? When
we are talking of a human person, do we ever get much
closer to the central mystery of his person than when we speak
of his will, his intention, his demands, the goal he strives for?
Far be it from me to hack the human self into multiple psychological parts! But from a given angle of view and in given

situations a self *is* a will and wholly will. When a man reveals his will, there, if ever, he reveals himself. Do the Biblical writers mean it otherwise when they speak of the will of God?

*b*. God reveals life. "He brought life and incorruption to light through the gospel" (2 Tim. 1:10); the gospel itself brings the choice between death and life (2 Cor. 2:16). God is not life, but he is the "living God" and the "life-giving God"; when he reveals life he is not revealing something external to himself.

*c*. God reveals love, not love in general but his own love. "In this the love of God was made manifest [surely the resolution of that passive into the active would be: in this *God* manifested his love] among us, that God sent his only Son into the world, that we might live through him" (1 John 4:9). Here the very content of the revelation is God's love—but love is never a "what," a "something"; it is always a "how" of the subject, it is the subject with his will, his intent, focused in a particular way. Indeed, here the preceding clause in the text says it in so many words: "God *is* love"—where his love is revealed, he himself is revealed.

*d*. God reveals his Son (Gal. 1:16), and the Gospel of John is one continuous paraphrase of how the Son reveals the Father—in revealing him God reveals himself. One could go on to point out that God revealed righteousness (Rom. 1:17) and wrath (Rom. 1:18), faith itself (Gal. 3:23) and "placed in us [a circumlocution for "effectively revealed"] the word of reconciliation" (2 Cor. 5:19). These few examples must suffice in support of the contention that in and behind whatever else he may be revealing, God is disclosing himself.

So far several pages have been devoted to reflections upon Pannenberg's insistence that the Bible contains no *direct, complete, self*-revelation of God. These qualifiers have been examined one by one. The examination does not claim to have proved anything, but perhaps it has shown that the middle qualifier, complete, is inappropriate to the subject and that the either-or of the other two ought instead to be a both-and. Revelation is probably always both indirect and direct; and revelation of self, within the interpersonal analogy, probably always takes place through that which is not directly identifiable with the self. If these reflections are at all persuasive, then we can omit the adjectives and ask simply whether the Bible testifies to revelation—a question that has not been raised here! If it does, then it can be nothing other than the revelation *by* God *of* God. We have suggested that the Bible refers to such revelation in terms of God speaking. But it is not our purpose here to pursue that line of thought, but rather to investigate Pannenberg's own solution, according to which such revelation is found in history, most specifically in Jesus' resurrection.

## III

The intention of Pannenberg's present paper is evidently to set forth just such a revelation: the revelation *by* God *of* God himself through, or in, Jesus. He says "Jesus of Nazareth" inadvisedly, it seems to me, for he shows no disposition to limit the discussion to the historical man of Nazareth but means the whole of what most of us would call "Jesus Christ." But he does begin with Jesus of Nazareth, whom he regards as an apocalyptic prophet. As such Jesus presents nothing that, in itself, is new. The particularity of his apocalyptic message is his exclusive emphasis upon the nearness of the Reign of God, exclusive even of the central concern of Jewish tradition, the pre-eminence of the Law. To accept his diminution and concentration of the Jewish-apocalyptic tradition and his insistence upon its immediately future fulfillment was to accept him. To reject him was to reject it. With it he stood or fell. It fell! His expectations failed to come about either soon or late. Jesus, then already dead, had been an audacious fanatic, or would have been but for one thing—his resurrection from the dead. Jesus had in substance proclaimed the final general resurrection of the dead as imminent. It did not occur. But God vindicated Jesus by raising him from the dead, thus bringing to pass the great eschatological event in token form (my expression) and thereby pronouncing the divine *Yes* upon Jesus and his message.[16] Therefore Pannenberg, with his already great emphasis upon history as *the* medium of revelation, *must* insist upon the historicity of the resurrection of Jesus. For a disciple of Bultmann, that is a challenge which demands discussion. Hence we must ask what a historical event is, what makes a matter historical, and whether there are events of a different order from those that we label historical.

Pannenberg is aware of the difficulty and the complexity of the problem and is appropriately wary. He recognizes time and again, though not radically enough, that our primary datum is the Easter message. In one of his formulations toward the beginning of his paper he refers to "the Easter message which makes us reckon with the historical reality of the event there reported."[17] Here he does not speak simply of Easter itself or claim historical certainty about it. Also, in spite of his later polemic against mere subjective conviction,[18] he cannot avoid (and why should he?) occasionally speaking in subjective terms. Thus he appends as an apposition to "the raising up of Jesus" the following paraphrase: "the certainty that Jesus as the Risen One lives and will die no more."[19] In other words, the resurrection *is* this certainty. Admittedly certainty is ambiguous as to whether it is due to manifest historical fact or refers to unshakable conviction. Nevertheless, the choice of this ambiguous word instead of "proof" or "demonstration" is revealing.

Pannenberg never lets himself get trapped into describing the resurrection (for a very good reason, one should think!)

---

[16] The discrepancy here between the "announcement" and its "fulfillment" does not worry Pannenberg because he has already observed elsewhere, as on p. 120 above, that even perfectly legitimate Biblical predictions are very rarely fulfilled in exact detail—in spite of the solemn and unrestricted words of Deut. 18:22: "When a prophet speaks in the name of the Lord, if the word does not come to pass (*yihyeh*—not 'occur approximately'!) or come true [*ybw'*—'arrive,' not 'more or less arrive'], that is a word which the Lord has not spoken."

[17] Cf. above, Pannenberg, p. 114.

[18] *Ibid.*, p. 131.

[19] *Ibid.*, p. 117.

nor even into characterizing it broadly in regard to the many
riddles the New Testament leaves us. What is the relation between the exaltation to the Father's side and the resurrection?
Is the empty tomb relevant to a "body" that is not stopped by
closed doors and becomes *aphantos,* nonapparent, in the midst
of a group? Does Paul make any basic distinction between
the Easter experiences and the appearance to him? These
central questions he leaves untouched. One can only admire
the reserve in Pannenberg's reflections on the metaphorical
character of the term, resurrection. He means *anastasis* but it
applies to *anistēmi, egeirō,* and *egersis* just as much. The passage is worth quoting.

"Evidently something had happened to the witnesses of the
appearances of the Risen One for which their language had
no other word than that used to characterize the eschatological expectation, i.e., resurrection from the dead. This expression is a metaphor. It suggests the idea of being awakened and
arising from sleep. Hence Jewish traditions often join mention
of the future resurrection of the dead with the metaphorical
description of death as sleep. It is important to notice this
metaphorical meaning of our talk about the resurrection,
though of course not of the *thing* itself. [Here I begin to have
difficulty.] The metaphorical character of our speaking about
resurrection means that we do not know what sort of reality
corresponds to that word. [The previous sentence left the impression that our relation to the thing itself would be shown
to be closer than the distance involved in the metaphor, resurrection, implies. But this next sentence says the opposite: we
are farther from the *reality itself* without the metaphor than
we were with it.] It surpasses our imagination, because we
live on this side of death. Speaking and thinking about a life
on the other side of death is possible only in images of hope
and is legitimate only on the condition that we be aware that
that new 'life' must be completely different from all we now
know as life. So we do not really know even yet what happened to Jesus then nor what kind of reality the Risen One
may have in relation to our present life. Only metaphorically

can we speak of this. The most that we can really *know* is whether or not the Easter witnesses were confronted by a reality which we too can comprehend only in terms of that parabolic word of eschatological expectation: resurrection from the dead."[20]

With most of this, except where I have interpolated, I am in substantial agreement. If the sole point of contention is the happened-ness of Jesus' resurrection—even though we cannot say what happened—I am in agreement with Pannenberg and perhaps in some disagreement with Bultmann.[21] It does seem that the thought-world of the Synoptics requires a different way of speaking about the resurrection than Bultmann's Pauline-Johannine way. Bornkamm has found a way that seems fruitful: "The Easter *message* was in existence earlier

[20] *Ibid.*, p. 115. The word "thing" is not italicized in the original.

[21] That Bultmann would disagree is not so certain as it may seem, e.g., on the basis of such a formulation as the following from "New Testament and Mythology," in *Kerygma and Myth*, trans. by R. H. Fuller (New York: Harper & Row, Torchbook Edition, 1961), I, p. 34: "Side by side with the historical event (*historisches Ereignis*) of the crucifixion it (sc. the New Testament) sets the definitely non-historic event (*kein geschichtliches Ereignis*) of the resurrection." In the light of his habitual distinction between these two adjectives, this was most surprising. However, in German composition it is a virtue (not a vice as in English) to vary one's expression for the same thing in one sentence. Had Bultmann's school-training here conflicted with his own terminology? I wrote him about it. He replied: "Your conjecture is right. The fluctuation between *historisch* and *geschichtlich* on p. 34 is 'a merely stylistic variation.' In order to avoid a misunderstanding I should have written both times *historisch*. You are right: The cross is *historisch* and (for the Christian) *geschichtlich;* the resurrection, though not demonstrable in a *historisch* way, is (for the Christian) *geschichtlich.*" *Geschichtlich* does not mean "without reality"—on the contrary! I take it to mean here that for Bultmann the resurrection is not the happened-*ness* (*Geschehensein*), the past-ness of a past event that can only be described with an algebraic *x*, but an occurrence, a happen-*ing* (*Geschehen*), that takes place when testifying faith proclaims and is met with obedient, submitting faith. This is true for the thought-world of Paul and of John ("I am the resurrection"); and, in Paul, faith-arising-from-proclaimed-faith implies a chain of testifiers that reaches back, not to the time of the Synoptics (that lies ahead!), but to the time of which we try to make the Synoptics exclusively speak but cannot because they do not.

[To some extent Bultmann's position has been further clarified by letters of 1961–62 published by Gilbert E. Bowen, "Toward Understanding Bultmann," *McCormick Quarterly*, XXVII (1964), 26–39, esp. pp. 35–37. Cf. above, Robinson, nn. 74, 92, 94, Eds.]

than the Easter *stories* and experienced in them a greatly varying precipitate. As detached narratives these supply the *occurrence* of the resurrection with sensory expression."[22] Note that Bornkamm speaks of "the *occurrence* (*Geschehen*) of the resurrection!" He states: "We must look for the *Easter message* in the *Easter stories*. By no means does that mean that the proclamation of Jesus' resurrection is simply a product of the community's faith. Of course the form in which it reaches us bears the stamp of that faith. But just as certainly the origin of that faith lies in the appearances of the Risen One and the testimony of his witnesses."[23] In view of what Bornkamm has just said about "sensory expression," presumably he means "appearances" here in a figurative sense.

For the occurrence-character of the resurrection Bornkamm really rests his case on the change it created in the disciples. After Jesus' death, "they regard themselves as defeated, shattered, along with what they hitherto have believed. Those who are confronted with the Risen One in the Easter stories are at their wit's end, frightened and bewildered by his death, mourners. . . . What they experience in fear and dread, what only gradually awakens joy and praise in them, is just this: on Easter day it is they, the disciples, who bear the mark of death, but it is he who was crucified and buried who lives. It is his survivors who are dead, and the deceased who is alive."[24] Something had changed them in a way and to a degree that they were themselves powerless to bring about. Something had happened *to* them, not merely *in* them.

But now the question is: can that something that had happened *to* the disciples properly be called a "historical event"? Perhaps it is only a war of words, once we agree that something *had* happened, and that it was not merely internal, or subjective. Some would maintain (Pannenberg among them?)

---

[22] Gunther Bornkamm, *Jesus von Nazareth* (Stuttgart: W. Kohlhammer Verlag, 1956), p. 167. My own translation. [*Jesus of Nazareth,* trans. by Irene and Fraser McLuskey with James M. Robinson (New York: Harper & Row, 1960), pp. 182–183.]

[23] *Ibid.,* p. 168 of Ger. ed.; p. 183 of Eng. ed.

[24] *Ibid.,* p. 169 of Ger. ed.; pp. 184–85 of Eng. ed.

that any event in space and time is a historical event. But that definition contains a most important *probandum*. The event under discussion must first—within the allowable range of relative historical probability, whatever that range may be —be proved to satisfy that qualification "in space and time." The locus in *time* is here the easier. "After three days" or "on the third day" is pre-Pauline.[25] It is implied in the passion chronologies of both the Synoptics and John, no matter what the month dates were, and it is explicitly present in the Synoptics' *vaticinia ex eventu* (Mark 8, 9, 10, and parallels), in Peter's sermon (Acts 10), and in a fragment of tradition in John (2:19 f.). The "three days" are reckoned from the day of the crucifixion, a Friday, which was either the 14th or the 15th of a Nisan, which could have been almost any Nisan between A.D. 26 and 36. In other words the resurrection is only relatively fixed in time, but with a relativity no greater than that of other events which are not, for that reason alone, denied historical status even by highly positivistic historians.

What about the resurrection in relation to space? First let us be clear that absolutely no witness *of* the resurrection is adduced in the New Testament. There are witnesses *to* its *effects,* but this is a very different matter. Nothing like the waking-of-Lazarus scene is even hinted at in the case of Jesus. The resurrection has already occurred before any witness in any Gospel gets to the tomb. Even in Matthew the still-closed tomb is opened by the angel, not to let Jesus out—he is already not there—but to let the women in. In John, too, even before Mary Magdalene gets there, the Easter event is already complete.

It is often said that not until the Gospel of Peter is there a description of the resurrection of Jesus, but it is not found even there. I do not mean that only the exit from the tomb is described and not the coming-to-life, but rather that what is there mythically described is the *exaltation* to heaven. Two "men" of cosmic proportion, probably Luke's two angels,

---

[25] Embedded in tradition which he quotes at 1 Cor. 15:4, though he happens never to mention the "third day" again.

support a third of even greater stature whose head reached
into heaven, which must be assumed to have opened to receive all three heavenly figures, the two angels and now the
exalted Christ. For shortly afterward heaven opens "again"
and a man comes down from it and enters the tomb. The
man is evidently not the newly exalted heavenly Christ but
one of the angels. Perhaps it is the single one of Mark 16:5,
for it is he who later gives Mary the Easter message—or rather
the Exaltation message (Gospel of Peter, Ch. 13): "See the
place where he lay, that it is not, for he arose and departed
thither whence he was sent forth." Before any resurrection
appearances to any disciple the exaltation is first mythically
described and then nonmythically announced to one disciple,
Mary. Not excluding the Gospel of Peter, then, there is no
account of the actual resurrection. If it happened in space
and time, it happened in the night, remote from any human
eye. Is this simply reverence for "the holy" which man must
not too closely approach? Or is it a tacit avowal that the
occurrence was such that no human witnesses could have seen
anything had they been present?

The Gospel accounts of the appearances are all secondary
and apologetic. They localize the appearances, not the resurrection itself, in Galilee or around Jerusalem, but they do not
establish the resurrection as an event in space. They do insistently raise the question of what was meant when "resurrection" was spoken of. They raise it so insistently that we
cannot be content with the explanation that "resurrection" is
only a human metaphor. One series of appearance-stories
gives the appearances a hard reality which implies that the
unseen resurrection had verily been in space—but at the price
of positing a *resuscitated corpse. This* apologetic series is con-
fined, basically, to Luke-Acts.[26]

---

[26] The exceptions, if they be such, are the seizing of Jesus' feet (Matt.
28:9) and the invitation to Thomas to touch (John 20:27). But the
unemphatic note that the women "seized his feet" (Matt. 28:9) seems
to me to be only one twin in a hendiadys, the other one being "and
prostrated themselves before him." It is the same gesture of imploring
respect that the Shunammite woman made to Elisha (2 Kings 4:27) and

Luke, the historicizer, even though he takes over one story that is inconsistent with it (24:13–32), makes his view perfectly clear: The resurrection of Jesus did occur in space, where matter is, and hence is in the plane of history. For in Luke's apologetic, the risen Jesus has an unmistakably physical body. Lest there be any doubt about it Luke lets him tell us so explicitly (24:39). Here he polemically dispels a rival theory that he is a ghost, offers his bone-supported flesh to their touch, and finally sets up a chemical-physical demonstration of his physical reality by eating before them, eating, not for communion, but solely for the purpose of this demonstration. It is significant that the only other mention of eating on the part of the risen Jesus is also by Luke (Jesus himself does not eat in John's appendix), in his wording of a sermon of Peter: "to us . . . witnesses, who ate and drank with him after he rose from the dead" (Acts 10:41). If this is what the metaphorical $x$ of the resurrection meant, then the stories of the empty tomb become understandable and relevant, for the body that walks about and eats cannot still be in the tomb. But what is the future of that body? It must either die like all flesh or be removed from the earth by a special dispensation. Is it any accident that Luke, and only Luke, knows anything of the Ascension? Only he needed it! Only he had so historicized the resurrection in time and space that he had to deal with this problem.

Undoubtedly, Luke *claims* the resurrection to be history. But many other matters have been claimed by individual historians to be historical which later, according to the relativities of all history writing, turned out to be unhistorical. Is the con-

---

need not imply the presence of palpable feet. In the Johannine case the invitation to Thomas results in utter conviction. To many interpreters the conclusion is inescapable that Thomas had touched and had been thereby convinced, even though the touching is not narrated. However, if actual touching were implied, the words of Jesus which follow ought logically to have been: "Have you believed because you have touched me? Blessed are those who have not touched and yet believe." Furthermore, the word "seen" which twice stands there disparages not merely *tactual* confirmation of the resurrection but even *visual* and, hence, probably *all* kinds of sensory confirmation.

tent of Luke's alleged historical fact such that any neutral historian of today could recognize it as historical matter?

If Luke's historicizing apologetic only leads us astray, can we come any closer to what "happened" from another angle of approach? With all respect for those who deny it, I think 1 Cor. 15 can help us. Admittedly Paul is not speaking in verses 42–50 about Christ's resurrection, but primarily of the general eschatological resurrection. But both here and elsewhere he is greatly concerned with the parallelism between Christ's resurrection and ours. Furthermore, he is setting forth how he conceives resurrection in general, particularly demarcating his conception from certain misconceptions. This unavoidably throws light on how he regarded Christ's resurrection. The chief misunderstanding he is guarding against is that the physical body will be raised from the grave (one strand, at least, of the resurrection tradition which he received from his Jewish past). In the eight staccato clauses of 42ᵇ-44ᵃ, arranged in four pairs, there is no logical subject until the last pair which, finally, contains the missing (or delayed) subjects: *sōma psychikon* and *sōma pneumatikon;* and these subjects work back by a kind of grammatical osmosis into the other three pairs. Their meaning is clearer if we join all the left-hand members and all the right-hand members: "There is sown in decay, disesteem, and weakness a *sōma psychikon.* There is raised up in non-decay, high esteem, and power a *sōma pneumatikon.*" Gnostic invention though *psychikon* probably is, Paul nevertheless thinks it related to the Septuagint of Genesis. A *psychikon* body is one that ought to, and did, have *psychē* but now has lost it—a *corpus exanime* or *exanimatum.* (He could have used *apsychon,* 14:7). When Paul now names the other, the new, reality, he seems to stammer as humans must when they speak of subjects too lofty. He calls it a spiritual body, which may be self-contradictory, but at least clearly indicates that the new reality is not the corpse, and that the corpse remains buried. The new reality is of the nature of *pneuma,* which perhaps never means utter immateriality (except perhaps to the Gnostics), but rather the minimal conceivable degree of materiality. What relevance could an empty grave possibly have to a reality of this kind? Significantly, Paul never mentions the empty tomb even where the Gospels lead us to think he must. It evidently was not in the old tradition (1 Cor. 15:3 ff.) which he is quoting —old already in the 50's A.D. Is it missing because as late as 35 or 40 A.D. not only this block of tradition but the total Christian tradition still lacked it, lacked it because it was not a historical fact? Among the many competing motifs of the Gospel appearance stories, three stories contain a conception that is related to this nonmaterial understanding of resurrection: the pre-Lucan Emmaus story with its vanishing of the recognized Stranger, and the two stories in John 20, "the door being closed."

If there were space, two other themes should be discussed: Paul's "seeing the Lord" (1 Cor. 9:1),[27] and the wide range of testimony that much of the first-century church regarded the *resurrection* and the *exaltation* as synonymous. Can the exaltation even be proposed for recognition as a matter *in history?*

I have suggested that the resurrection of Jesus qualifies as an event in time, but that as an event in space it either does not qualify or does so only as a historically incredible event. For this reason alone it would seem questionable to speak of it as a historical event. In addition to that, a historical event must have some contours by which it can be recognized as a subject of investigation. It is scarcely meaningful to inquire whether an indefinable $x$ took place in history.

[27] Was it a resurrection appearance? How is it related to the tripled story of the Damascus Road?

# 5. The Character of Pannenberg's Theology

## WILLIAM HAMILTON

*Colgate Rochester Divinity School*

This chapter will be primarily a series of comments, questions, and reactions to some of the main themes in Pannenberg's work. It does not pretend to be an analysis of his programmatic essay in this book. If it can serve any purpose at all, it will be to suggest some of the ways in which a German-American dialogue, based on this original and most interesting theological venture, can be set up. This method is made almost inevitable by the very character of Pannenberg's work. His theology is one in the process of being formed. In this fact lies much of its interest for the American scene, where increasingly theology is being treated as a kind of "doing" rather than as the achievement of a finished or systematic product. We are beginning to ask ourselves: "What does doing theology mean?" This is a question that can be put to Pannenberg to get the discussion of his work off the ground.

It can be claimed, I think, that Pannenberg's work has three fundamental themes or motifs. There are others, and he may not even consider these three the central ones. But I found myself moving from perplexity to some sort of clarity as I was able to distinguish three separate strands.

First, Pannenberg works with *a particular conception of history and historical method*. It is at this point that he enters into the current theological debate on the nature of history, and distinguishes himself from most of the antagonists already

176

on the field. Pannenberg rejects the distinction, so beloved by a whole generation of Biblical theologians, between sacred and profane history. A good deal of what he is doing becomes clearer when we take note of this attack on *Heilsgeschichte*. There are not two kinds of history, but one. God works in the ordinary world of profane history. Pannenberg also rejects the Barthian version of the two-types-of-history tradition: the idea of primal history or *Urgeschichte*. And finally, and most emphatically (though, as we shall see, least clearly), he rejects the distinction between mere chronicle or past history (*Historie*) and history as present encounter and meaning (*Geschichte*) that Bultmann and his followers have erected and proclaimed as a self-evident fact. This attack on Bultmann is one of the most useful and needed attacks in our day, but it remains to be seen how effective and decisive has been Pannenberg's attempt to separate himself from the persuasive Bultmannian position.

Second, Pannenberg's theology is *a theology of history*. The goal of his theology is the formulation of a systematic theological interpretation of the whole realm of secular history. This hope may explain the interesting impression one gets from Pannenberg's writing that the tension between Luther and Calvin is not of decisive theological importance to him. The curious absence of some of the Reformation theological substance will be noted later. Here we need only say that Pannenberg seems primarily empowered by the Augustinian vision of theology of history. Luther, because of his eschatology, and Calvin, doubtless because of his doctrine of election, were not really interested in the theological problem of secular history. Pannenberg is, and he rightly finds Augustine to be his most significant model. He is undaunted by the fact that theologies of history have not been fashionable in recent years, as both historians and theologians have enjoyed taking a dim view of the possibility of such endeavors.

Third, Pannenberg's theology is *a theology of the resurrection of Jesus,* and—as I am sure Lutherans have already damned it by that fatal phrase—a *theologia gloriæ*.[1] He takes very seriously the historical character of the resurrection, as we shall observe, and his views of faith, history, and the theology of history all proceed from his interpretation of the resurrection. Because of the resurrection, he would claim, this kind of theology is possible. The goal is a theology of the whole of history; the method stretching from the possibility to the goal is a particular understanding of historical analysis.

These three themes are central to Pannenberg's theological vision. How do they fit together? What does he mean by some of his basic presuppositions? How does this all work out?

## I

I wish to begin by raising an issue that I suspect is quite unimportant to Pannenberg, and that raises questions about what may be to him merely marginal aspects of his theology. It is a question about the nature of man (Americans are supposed to be more interested in man than in God), and it proceeds from a conviction of the theological significance of Bonhoeffer's analysis of the world come of age. Bonhoeffer has cut deeply into contemporary American theological self-consciousness, and perhaps the Germans should be shown how this influence is affecting the way we read our German colleagues today. There is, in Pannenberg's work, a presupposition concerning the natural religiousness of man. At this point he is at one with Bultmann, for whom all existence outside of Christ is, by definition, inauthentic. Pannenberg's is a theology of the religious *a priori,* though in a form more ontological than epistemological (if such charming language may be permitted). In his essay, "The Revelation of God in Jesus of Nazareth," we read: "Only in God's proximity, in community with God, does human existence find its fulfill-

---

[1] [E.g., Günter Klein, "Offenbarung als Geschichte? Marginalien zu einem theologischen Program," *MPTh*, LI (1962), 88, in the final sentence of a critical article. Eds.]

ment."[2] The importance to Pannenberg of this presupposition was shown in the course of an illuminating address he delivered at the Vanderbilt Divinity School in April 1963 on the subject, "Did Jesus Really Rise from the Dead?" In this address he remarked that man's specific human structure, his openness to the world, requires resurrection for his own unique self-understanding.[3] Man must seek his final destiny beyond death, he claimed, and this destiny must be in terms of the unity of body and soul.

This point is an important step in his argument on the resurrection itself, and we will be commenting on that presently. But it is worth noting at this point as a remark about man—all men, apparently, Biblical as well as modern. Man can find fulfillment, true self-understanding, true meaning, only in God. But what kind of statement is this? Is it one concerning the observed religiousness of all men, or is it a structural, perhaps even ontological, fact about man as man, independent of what he knows about himself? What kind of evidence does one cite for the truth of such a statement? If there are men who declare that their fulfillment is not in God, does this invalidate the statement? This presupposition that man can find his fulfillment only in God is, at the very least, not a self-evident truth. It seems to proceed more from some other world rather than from the real world of the twentieth century with its genuine and painful unbelief.

Thus, at the outset, there stands what may well be an unbridgeable gulf between our understandings of what living in the twentieth century really means. I can see no way in which Pannenberg can take seriously the world of modern unbelief, whereas unlike both him and Barth, I suspect that theology needs to take it seriously. I assume that certain rejections of God in our time are real rejections, and that they cannot be taken care of by calling them "negative witnesses to God," or some other such silliness. "No" to God can really mean

---

[2] Cf. above, Pannenberg, p. 118.
[3] This theory is more fully developed in *Was ist der Mensch?* (Göttingen: Vandenhoeck und Ruprecht, 1962), Chs. 1 and 4.

"no," and it need not always refer to the *cor inquietum* that cannot rest till it finds its rest in God.

Secularism for Pannenberg is rather like sin for Barth: it is really impossible. Why? Because, as we shall point out presently, the world of finiteness already contains God, and faith is, primarily, a certain way of finding out what is already there, using the correct technique of historical investigation. For Pannenberg there is no place, no piece of history, and therefore no man, who is without God. It is rather hard to understand, or to take seriously, a theology that can by a definition dispose of the secularism which has been an important segment of Western history for the past four hundred years.

To be sure, if we are compelled to reckon with the reality of the "man come of age" today, we are in for a good deal of theological difficulty. Speaking about God is a much tougher business when we give up assuming that a man somehow must ask the theological question. But the practical difficulties that follow from such an affirmation about the nature of man do not seem to disprove it. If there is really such a thing as being without God, then it simply means that we have a tougher job to do than the kerygmatic or the correlation theologies imagined. But (again assuming that there is such a thing as really being without God) we have no right to tinker with our presuppositions so that speaking about God can be changed from something merely possible to something necessary.

So much for the first, and anthropological, query concerning the natural religiousness of man. If I am right, and if there is emerging a community of men who can do without God—not replacing, but standing alongside the community of men who are longing for him—then the religious theologies of a Bultmann or a Pannenberg are not making adequate connection with the modern world. If I am right (I am not at all sure I am, but I think the issue needs a careful debate), then Pannenberg's theology is a species of theological docetism, a structure of impressive power and originality that does not quite get down into the world we have to live in.

It is, as we have noted, Pannenberg's understanding of the

relation of God to history that makes it possible for him to affirm the impossibility of secularism. We must now turn to this issue and try to see just what he means by faith, history, and the relation of both to God.

## II

Just what does Pannenberg mean by history? At first glance he seems to be simply attacking Bultmann's central distinction between *Geschichte* and *Historie*. This is fine, and it is about time that continental theology began to wonder about the self-evident character of this distinction. But he attacks far more than this Bultmannian distinction. He is calling into question the basic distinction between fact and meaning, event and interpretation, on which most modern historiography has been based. This false distinction he calls neo-Kantian, rightly seeing that in its modern form it emerged from Kant's sharp cleavage between questions of fact and questions of value. So his attack on Bultmann is not primarily that Bultmann obscures the factual element in the historical event, it is that he accepts the false, positivistic fact-meaning distinction in the first place. In this connection we are not surprised that Pannenberg has been influenced by R. G. Collingwood's criticism of nineteenth-century historiography.[4]

Let us examine Pannenberg's approach to a particular historical question by seeing what he makes of the resurrection of Jesus. Pannenberg began his discussion of this subject at Vanderbilt by insisting, against Bultmann, that certainty about the resurrection does not come from the decision of faith. Faith is based on the certainty, which must come from outside of faith. Pannenberg rightly observes that Paul, in 1 Cor. 15:3 ff., cites a list of eye-witnesses as if this kind of evidence were significant. Some of these witnesses were still around and their testimony could be checked. Certainty can come, he con-

---

[4] It is interesting to note that Bultmann also makes extensive appeal to Collingwood in his Gifford lectures on *History and Eschatology* (Edinburgh: University Press, 1957).

cludes, only from "modern" historical research. If proof at first hand is now impossible, at least a kind of secondhand historical proof is available to us.

But the resurrection of Jesus does not emerge in a historical vacuum. Paul has a set of presuppositions that makes it possible for him to interpret both his experience and the evidence in such a way that it leads to the conclusion: Jesus was really raised from the dead. These presuppositions derive from Jewish apocalypticism. Paul's belief is thus partly grounded on that part of the apocalyptic tradition that speaks of an individual resurrection at the last day: Isa. 26, Dan. 12, and the tradition about the resurrection lying behind Jesus' debate with the Sadducees in Mark 12:18–27 and parallels. Thus, Pannenberg notes, we can get at the meaning of 1 Cor. 15:13: "But if there is no resurrection of the dead, then Christ has not been raised." This means that the apocalyptic resurrection tradition in the basis for Paul's faith in Jesus' resurrection. Part of our ability to declare the resurrection a historical event comes from our being able to locate the historical matrix and tradition out of which it emerged. "Historical" means, in part, "having a specific tradition behind it."

But, further, the resurrection of Jesus is historical in a second sense. It not only has a past, but also it is able to meet a genuine need or longing in man. The historical, it might be said, has an ontological color as well. As we mentioned above, it is at this point that Pannenberg introduces his conception of man as basically longing for a destiny beyond this life. Thus the resurrection of Jesus arrives in history and is defined as truly historical in two senses: it is prepared for by Jewish apocalypticism, and it is prepared for by a natural or given longing in the heart of man.

But there is a further problem. The event must find a language appropriate to its reality, and this is what Pannenberg calls the problem of "metaphor." The right metaphor to use in expressing the resurrection's reality is that of waking from sleep. Therefore, the resurrection is "historical" because it contains these three elements: a context we can point to; an ontological analysis of man that guarantees that it can be received; and an adequate metaphorical expression. This procedure is apparently what Pannenberg means by an adequate or a modern historical methodology in the investigation of the resurrection.

After this methodological preface, Pannenberg turns to the resurrection material in the New Testament itself. He is inclined to reject the appearance-traditions of the four Gospels from the start. These, he says, are more legendary than historical, and are obviously designed to heighten the bodily or physical character of the Risen Lord.

First Cor. 15, particularly verses 3–8, is the material Pannenberg subjects to the most careful analysis. This enumeration of eye-witnesses is for Paul an important part of the argument. Their testimony could be checked, and it went back to only a few years after the event itself. Paul, at the close of his list, identifies the appearance he witnessed with these others, and thus we are permitted to infer the character of the earlier appearances from Paul's description of his own experience.

What does the New Testament tell us about Paul's experience on the road to Damascus? He saw Jesus; Jesus was the revelation given by God; he saw a spiritual body; it was an appearance from heaven, not from any natural context; it was probably in the form of a blinding light; and there was an auditory element in it. Thus, this "experience" of Paul's was a decisive event in time. (It is less clearly an event in space, it ought to be noted.) This experience of Paul's, therefore, is what the basic event of the resurrection of Jesus actually was.

But we must now recall Pannenberg's refusal to separate event and meaning. So we have not yet filled out the truly historical character of the resurrection. The brute event takes on its full historical character only when we bring the three methodological components to it. Resurrection becomes the truly historical resurrection of Jesus when to the curious blinding light of Paul's vision we add the apocalyptic background, the analysis of the nature of man who longs for an otherworldly fulfillment, and the metaphor of waking from sleep. All these together permit us to say: Jesus' resurrection was truly historical; he really rose from the dead. Now nothing needs to be added to the historical for it to be "revelatory." Faith does not need to come in from the outside, so to speak, and confer truth on the probable historical affirmations. Historical analysis itself has uncovered its character as a revelation of God. What was the appearance to Paul (and to the others) really like? Perhaps the word "vision" will suffice, Pannenberg states, but we must not think of it as subjective, as illusory, or as explicable in terms of need-and-wish fulfillment.

In his treatment of the resurrection, Pannenberg has a good deal more to say. He looks at the empty-tomb tradition with some care, though he clearly prefers the appearance material in his analysis. He assumes that the empty-tomb tradition arose independently of the appearance tradition, and that the two strands came together some time later. He ascribes to the empty-tomb tradition, however, a historical character, on the grounds that no alternative to the account as actually given in the Gospels seems to be able to explain all the facts.

It is not my purpose to subject Pannenberg's study of the resurrection to a full analysis. We needed to have a look at it because through it we can see just what he means by history, historical, and adequate historical method. Historical method has three main elements: context, ontology, and language. It is brought to a particular event, it tests that event, tests its level of probability, examines the witnesses if any, and in the encounter between method and event, the label "historical" is conferred. Historical means event and meaning, and the two cannot be sundered. Historical method finds the resurrection event to be historical *and* revelatory, together, in the same process and at the same time.

Thus it would seem that there is a place in space and time where God can be said to be self-evident, where his presence can be discerned by a proper investigative technique. If this is pre-eminently the case with the resurrection of Jesus, is there any reason why the same method cannot be used to un-cover the revelatory power of God in every other historical event? For Pannenberg there is no reason why this should not be the case, and this is why the resurrection can become a clue to the theology of history, just as the Exodus served the prophet, just as the fall of Rome served Augustine. In this way Pannenberg is able to move from his statements about the resurrection to his project for a theology of world history. We will comment further on this in a moment.

In spite of some curious similarities between Pannenberg and Bultmann on the meaning of history, Pannenberg claims, with some justification, that he is more willing to allow his-torical investigation to affect faith than is Bultmann. Faith has, he states, no storm-free area which can be immune from historical analysis. This is good, and worth saying, and it is therefore with some feeling of surprise that one finds Pan-nenberg also declaring that historical knowledge can "only slightly impair the certainty of belief."[5] If faith is really in principle vulnerable to historical research, it is hard to see how you can know beforehand just how much damage such research has the power to inflict. If you do know this before-hand, you are not talking about the sort of historical investi-gation that historians undertake (Pannenberg would call this "positivism"); you are talking about a curious mixture of history and metaphysics. Thus it would seem that, in spite of his claim, Pannenberg has constructed just as protected and invulnerable a theological circle as has Bultmann. Man for Bultmann is protected from contingency by the encounter with the preached Christ; man is protected for Pannenberg by his conception of the nearness of God to all men, which virtually means an identification of God with the process of history itself. God, in some sense, *is* history; or at least he is by defi-nition in history, and historical method can find him there.

<hr />

[5] Pannenberg, "Heilsgeschehen und Geschichte," *KuD*, V (1959), 278 [English translation by Shirley C. Guthrie, Jr., "Redemptive Event and History," in *Essays on Old Testament Hermeneutics*, ed. by Claus West-ermann, Eng. edition ed. by James Luther Mays (Richmond, Va.: John Knox Press, 1963)]. Cf. above, Robinson, note 44.

This method can never conclude that God is not there; a method that concluded that would be dismissed as inadequate. The reason that facts cannot count against faith is that there are no such things as facts. A fact (i.e., the appearance to Paul) cannot become intelligible or historical until it is submitted to the proper historical methodology. This method is bound to declare that when an event is seen as truly historical, it is seen as revelatory of God at the same time.

Pannenberg's understanding of history seems to have a number of interesting affinities with the idea of history in the Middle Ages. For the Greeks, history was the pale reflection of the eternal world of ideas. But in the Middle Ages, as Gogarten points out, the eternal world of ideas was replaced by the concept of the divine plan, working itself out in history. Augustine's *City of God* provided the theological basis for this theory of history. Thus, in the Middle Ages, history "was the realization of the eternal, transtemporal divine plan. It was a plan in which all temporal, worldly events not only had their unity but also were grounded in the divine reality."[6]

This is what Tillich calls theonomy, and Pannenberg's view of history is a theonomous one. To be in history is, at the same time, to be in the revelatory power and presence of the divine. Now when one visits the cathedral at Chartres, for example, he can for a moment participate in the reality and power of medieval theonomy. But as soon as he steps out of the cathedral and onto the street, he knows at once that this tremendous vision does not express his own view of himself and the world.

Modern man is able neither to long for an old theonomy nor to build a new one. Non-Christian or Christian, he knows that the power contained in history lies in himself. Technology is a fact to be faced, not to be fled from. Pannenberg does not approve of the disappearance of theonomy, and one can understand a theologian who is like that. But it will no longer do to try to bring a theonomous God-world picture into being

[6] Friedrich Gogarten, *The Reality of Faith*, trans, by Carl Michalson and others (Philadelphia: Westminster Press, 1959), p. 22.

by use of a new set of definitions. We are back again to our argument with Pannenberg in the first section. Is there not something sectarian about this theology: talking much about openness to the world, but out of touch with it from the start? It may well be, as Pannenberg asserts, that the existentialist distinction between *Geschichte* and *Historie* is an ungainly and relatively useless tool for today. But it is hard to see that the methodological refusal to separate fact from meaning is any more useful. Bultmann may be using instruments no longer wholly accurate, but he at least tries to take seriously the world of modern unbelief.

With his high estimate of what historical method can do, we might well suppose that Pannenberg would have some difficulty with the idea of faith. This is just what we do find.

"To be able to have Christian faith one must at least *presuppose* that the message about Jesus Christ is true. This includes primarily the affirmations that Jesus really proclaimed the coming of God's reign and that he really rose from the dead. It may very well be that one cannot always comprehend the truth of this message, but one must be able to *presuppose* that it is correct, and that, at least in principle, its truth is intelligible. In the sense of a logical presupposition (though not always a psychological antecedent), the knowledge of Jesus' history, including his resurrection from the dead, is the basis of faith."[7]

What then can *fides* be? There clearly can be no *fides quaerens intellectum,* and not even an *intellectus quaerens fidem.* True *intellectus* is *fides.* Faith involves presupposing that certain things are true or, more exactly, that certain historical events took place as the New Testament records them. Pannenberg has an admirable antipathy to all forms of *fides implicita*—whether it is faith as unquestioning obedience to the command of Jesus (Bonhoeffer) or as a decision in response to the preached Christ of the church (Bultmann).[8] But it

---

[7] Cf. above, Pannenberg, pp. 128 f. The first "presuppose" is not italicized in the original.

[8] *Ibid.,* p. 102.

seems likely that Pannenberg has been so careful to avoid *fides implicita* that he has tumbled into the brambles of *fides historica*. Faith, he tells us, arises completely from the history in which it is grounded, it requires a presupposition that certain events took place; and the right investigative technique can uncover both the uniqueness and the revelatory character of Jesus.

It is interesting to observe how far we are from the Calvinist doctrine of the inner witness of the Holy Spirit. Calvin states that faith is that event in which God comes to man in the context of Scripture, and that it is God himself who takes the dead word and turns it into a living word for faith. In Pannenberg it almost seems as if the proper methodology has been substituted for the Holy Spirit. History already contains God—"history is reality in its totality"[9] and presumably divine reality is included in that total reality that is history—and man has in his hands the correct tool to dig into that reality and to discover God present there.

A whole family of traditional theological terms has been deprived of its meaning, if the above is anything like a faithful picture of Pannenberg's view of faith and history. Revelation itself has been radically reformulated. If you say that the revelation of God can be discovered in history by the right kind of method, is it not just a verbal luxury to declare that God reveals himself? Revelation has ordinarily meant in Christian theology that there is a place where man cannot find, but can only be found. Where is the blessing to Peter? "For flesh and blood has not revealed this to you, but my Father who is in heaven" (Matt. 16:17). What are we to say of Paul? "No one can say 'Jesus is Lord' except by the Holy Spirit" (1 Cor. 12:3). What can we make of grace, of justification by faith? Justification by faith surely has always meant in part that there is nothing man can bring—not even the proper historical method—that will guarantee faith or participation in the revelatory power of God. To be sure, Bultmann and Gogarten

---

[9] "Heilsgeschehen und Geschichte," p. 222 ["Redemptive Event and History," p. 319].

have read all kinds of silly meanings into the doctrine of justification. They have said, for example, that to search for historical evidence is unfaith, betraying an unwillingness to trust completely in God. But it is not at all clear that Pannenberg's justification by method is an appropriate response to Bultmann's tendentious misuse of Luther.

There is an important element in what Pannenberg means by faith which we have not yet mentioned. Up to now we have been approaching Pannenberg's view of faith in terms of what he considers its presupposition. This means taking the probabilities of history (in particular the history about Jesus) and presupposing that some of them are true, even if we cannot ourselves comprehend the truth. But, Pannenberg states, faith is also hope, trust in the promise of God and his future.[10] How does this fit together with the conception of faith's presupposition? Faith as hope means that the certainty of faith can only be eschatological, only future. Faith's certainty will be established only in the world to come. In this life we have only probability and the Christian life lived as if certain events were truly historical. In this life we have only *fides historica*. But, we also have the confidence that God will, in his good time, transform faith as belief based on probability into full trust.

The profound influence of apocalyptic thought has stood Pannenberg in good stead here, for this is an essential part of any good doctrine of faith. But what does it mean in his case? If faith can be verified only eschatologically, does this mean also that it can be falsified only in the world to come? This would be convenient, and it may partly explain why Pannenberg can be sure that historical research cannot really do too much damage to faith here and now.

One way of clarifying our understanding of Pannenberg's view of faith and history in their contemporary theological setting might be to put a particular theological question to him, and then to try to imagine his answer to it, in comparison with other answers of our day. Let us put to him the

---

[10] Cf. above, Pannenberg, p. 130.

problem that has come to be called the problem of Lessing. Whether or not modern theology has correctly understood Lessing himself, the problem he posed has its own independent existence, and a very decent little theological literature has sprung up around it. The problem is easily stated: How can a series of past historical events, dwelling as do all historical events in the realm of probability and contingency, become transformed into a present reality of faith, for me, now, in the present? There are a number of answers to this question available today.

1. There is the sacramental answer to this problem. The making present of the past is the inner meaning of Lord's Supper, Eucharist, Mass. However one describes what (if anything) happens to the elements, sacramental participation is the way the believer receives the past reality as a present form for faith. This description can be in terms of transubstantiation, of memory, or of a fresh evaluation of the meaning of symbolism.

2. There is what might be called the confessional answer. It can exist alongside the sacramental answer, or it can be independent of it. Faith is not only a present reality and a hope, it is a memory. Thus, to be in faith is to have something now, whatever one calls it: trust, loyalty, believing in God. But faith is also the act of grafting my small autobiography onto a very wide story that stretches into the future and back into the depth of the past, back indeed to the very beginning of time itself. Thus, a whole faith is defined as a telling of my story of faith as part of a wider community of time and space that includes creation, fall, and redemption. Faith is a saying "yes" to the Biblical story as part of my story. That Biblical story becomes more than mere ancient history when I am enabled to see, imaginatively and actually, that it is the story of my life. The world underwent no specifiable metaphysical alteration at the time of the death and resurrection of Jesus. But faith declares that those events are taken as determining what God means, then and now.

3. There are those who would say that anyone worried about the problem of Lessing has a defective doctrine of God. This is the position of Karl Barth, as he works it out in his treatment of the Resurrection in IV/1, para. 59, section 3. In the resurrection, the parousia has begun, the new age is already breaking through, and God is defined as being-for-man. Faith in this God is, by definition, faith in him who has already taken up the past events of redemption and made them present to me. To be perplexed by Lessing's problem is therefore to be in unfaith, since God makes himself known as the one who makes the past redemptive events present to us. Faith is therefore letting his making-present activity happen to me, and so Barth characteristically solves a problem by defining the nature of God in such a way that the problem cannot arise.

4. The past, and investigation of the past, profits nothing; but the living Lord encounters me in my present as his word is proclaimed to me. In *Christus praedicatus,* the past becomes present. This is, of course, Bultmann's position. It presupposes the *Geschichte-Historie* distinction and it is based on his attempt to reduce every form of the God-man relation to the mode of encounter. It is part of his thoroughgoing attempt to secure for Christian faith an invulnerable worldly locus where the contingencies of mere historical fact cannot hurt it. The invulnerable place where the past is made present to me turns out to be the pew (reminding us of the real similarity between this view and what we have called the sacramental view, where the distinctive place is the altar). This is a very Protestant, very ecclesiastical, and very religious solution to the problem, and helps us to understand how Bultmann's theology can be described as the most impressive and complicated system of homiletics ever designed by a Christian.

5. Pannenberg's answer to the problem of Lessing owes something to both Barth and Bultmann, but it is uniquely his own. A summary of his answer might well be the aphorism of Croce: all history is contemporary history. The problem

of Lessing assumes that there is a real gulf between the past and the present, but a careful examination of history reveals no such gulf. Thus, Pannenberg does not need a doctrine of God to deny the gulf, and he does not need a project of demythologizing to bridge the gulf. He needs only to define history as an interconnected system of events in which any one thing can be shown to be connected with anything else. If I extend the context in which I stand—the present time— the New Testament itself becomes part of my present and the difference of time between then and now becomes irrelevant. The resurrection is the clue here, for in it a future event has already begun to happen.

In his treatment of the resurrection we have already observed that there is no attempt to distinguish the historical and the theological issues. "Did the New Testament writers believe that Jesus really rose from the dead?" and "Can we so believe?" are one and the same question. But it is important to recall what Pannenberg does not intend by collapsing this distinction. This is not historicism, such as one can find yoked to both conservative and radical theology today. It is not historicism because, as we have already observed, Pannenberg does not really believe there is such a thing as a mere historical fact. Such a category betrays one into neo-Kantian positivism. The collapsing of the theological and historical questions could be a species of theologism—a position in which theological statements are made without any recourse to historical facts at all. But such a label would be closer to Bultmann than to Pannenberg, who rightly claims that he can allow more weight to historical investigation than Bultmann. Nevertheless, it would seem that Pannenberg, with his special understanding of historical method, is doing much the same thing as Bultmann is doing with his distinction between *Geschichte* and *Historie*. He, too, is seeking in the sphere of the subject an escape from the radical contingency of our situation. He is looking for a way to translate statements concerning past events into statements about the present life of faith.

Pannenberg's subjectivism is not that of experience but of historical methodology. But his way seems fully as escapist as does Bultmann's.

## III

Though we have tried to show that Pannenberg's theology, unlike Bultmann's, does not try to reckon with the reality of modern unbelief, and though we have deemed this a serious flaw, it does not follow that his theological work is merely an academic exercise. Pannenberg is not primarily interested in proposing an alternative to the systems of Barth and Bultmann. He is, as we have seen, setting about a very specific theological task—the creation of a theology of history. This is an admirable goal, particularly when so many are telling us it is impossible. What many men say is impossible must be worth doing.

How will he move from his understanding of faith, history, and resurrection to a theology of history? Is the threefold historical method, developed in relation to the resurrection, to be the clue? Is the resurrection of Jesus, both a unique and a revelatory event as he says, to be paradigmatic for the way all events are to be related to God? Can an event be both unique and paradigmatic?

This apparently is Pannenberg's hope: to discover a way of describing God's presence in all of history along the lines that were used to describe his presence in the resurrection. Thus, a theology of history will involve three things. First, every event to be so described must have a particular context or past, and it must be a context that is theological. As Jewish apocalyptic was to the resurrection, so there must be some context for every other event. May it not be that Pannenberg will use the resurrection itself as the context-event for all subsequent events? Second, every finite event must be shown to have a particular susceptibility to the idea of God. This is the metaphysical part of Pannenberg's method, and we recall how he had to assume, in his argument for the resurrection, that all men long for a fulfillment beyond this life. If the participants in the, let us say, contemporary events that are to be related to a theology of history do not happen to agree with this analysis of their longing for God, what happens? Do they have to be persuaded of a particular metaphysic before the theology of history can get moving?

Just how is God to be uncovered in finite events? That he is in fact the Lord of history and that he cannot be restricted to some special and sacred type of history is one of Pannenberg's soundest contentions. From Jesus, he tells us, "all history receives its due light."[11] True, but this does not constitute a theology of history. As it stands, it is just a theological truism of no particular use. As we look at Pannenberg's method and Pannenberg's goal, the first seems almost perfectly unsuited to the second. It is rather like bringing a ping-pong paddle to the dinner table. There is nothing wrong with a ping-pong paddle, if you want to play ping-pong. But it is not made for eating chicken noodle soup.

However, Pannenberg has taken tough and unconventional problems in hand, problems that we have not solved either. Here is a question that might usefully be raised: What is the relation between what Pannenberg calls theology of history and what we in America are inclined to call theology of culture? One of the most interesting things in American theology today is the wide variety of conversations going on between theology and other disciplines and vocations. There is no particular methodology determining these discussions with science, psychoanalysis, literary criticism, history, sociology. They are just taking place, and, as a matter of fact, we are rapidly junking a good deal of the inherited theological method that we brought to these discussions in the first place: "there is no gulf between science and religion," "faith is like a scientific presupposition," "every man has an ultimate concern," "the gaps in our knowledge of the external world show that the universe is open to God," etc., etc.

[11] *Ibid.*, p. 125.

We do not always know exactly what we are doing or what we are learning; no one metaphysic controls us, and no common presuppositions about the nature of man can be assumed. As a matter of fact, we are involved in this kind of thing because these are just the things we want to find out. These conversations are probably the most important theological activity in America right now, far more important than the often dreary discussions theologians feel obliged (from time to time) to carry on among themselves. I have the impression that Pannenberg is working in his way toward the same kind of goal. Yet I cannot conceal the feeling that it is too likely he is entering into such a dialogue to persuade rather than to learn. There are too few places in the structure of his thought where the voices of strangers can be expected to have much effect.

In any case, the most fruitful element in the fascinating and complex thought of Pannenberg seems to lie not in his views on faith, history, or resurrection, but in his utter willingness to take the whole of history as his workbench.

I am optimistic, therefore, as to the extent to which American theologians can share Pannenberg's goal and can learn from it. I am much less optimistic about the possibility of real dialogue on the theological level itself. For many of us, the theological task contains far more surprise, mystery, and agony than he seems willing to allow. We cannot understand what it means to say that the revelation of God can be discovered by an adequate historical method. We miss the note of grace and the substance of justification by faith. Perhaps what we miss more than anything else is any confession of the mystery of the incarnation. To be sure, a lot of mumbo jumbo has been uttered in the name of the mystery of the incarnation. But for us, on this side of that theological abyss known as the Atlantic Ocean, there is the conviction that the struggle for faith is "quirky," unexpected, and passionate; and when it comes, it comes as something given. There are some lines in Eliot's "The Dry Salvages" (IV) that say this. Could we un-

derstand each other if we met to wrestle with these lines for
about a year?

                                    But to apprehend
The point of intersection of the timeless
With time, is an occupation for the saint—
No occupation either, but something given
And taken, in a lifetime's death in love,
Ardour and selflessness and self-surrender.
For most of us, there is only the unattended
Moment, the moment in and out of time,
The distraction fit, lost in a shaft of sunlight,
The wild thyme unseen, or the winter lightning
Or the waterfall, or music heard so deeply
That it is not heard at all, but you are the music
While the music lasts. There are only hints and guesses,
Hints followed by guesses; and the rest
Is prayer, observance, discipline, thought and action.
The hint half guessed, the gift half understood, is Incarnation.[12]

Erich Kähler recently remarked that only blasphemers or
near-unbelievers can have genuine healing power for faith
today. It is this anguish that one misses in the work of Pannenberg. It seems interesting, without being important. Such
a statement may say more about the one who makes it than
it says about the one of whom it is made. But I feel Kähler
is right, and this may explain the fact that the only truly
helpful theological fragments that we have received from
Europe in the last four or five decades are those that came
from a Swiss parsonage and a Berlin prison.

---

[12] From *Four Quartets,* in *Collected Poems 1909–1962* by T. S. Eliot.
Copyright 1936 by Harcourt, Brace & World, Inc.; copyright © 1963,
1964 by T. S. Eliot. Reprinted by permission of Harcourt, Brace &
World, Inc. and of Faber & Faber Ltd.

# PART III. Reappraisal and Response

## 6. Past, Present, and Future

JOHN B. COBB, JR.

*School of Theology at Claremont*

The theology of Wolfhart Pannenberg has opened a quite new front in the theological scene on both sides of the Atlantic. A good many issues that theologians had widely assumed to be more or less settled have suddenly been brought vigorously to the fore. While much contemporary work continues to build upon the foundations established by the dialectical theology of the twenties, Pannenberg takes a critical look at those foundations and proposes a quite different direction for theological development. As a result, one senses a somewhat pained surprise in the reactions to his thought. After an initial effort to write off this theological movement as falling under some no longer acceptable rubric, other theologians have recognized that they must deal seriously with the issues that have been raised. This fresh posing of basic questions may well introduce a new vitality into the discussion both within the theological community and between theologians and representatives of other disciplines. Perhaps a critical restatement of the issues that emerged in the American criticisms of Pannenberg will help promote such discussion.

## I

The essay by Martin Buss on "The Meaning of History" is an argument for an understanding of the relation of Christian faith and history in sharp opposition to that of Pannenberg. Pannenberg sees the course of events as a meaningful progression in which man's true nature and destiny become apparent to him. God is the ultimate actor in these events which thus manifest his will and purpose for man. Especially in the history of Israel can we discern the progressive emergence of the understanding that God is the God of all history and that, therefore, all history must eventuate in universal fellowship with him.

As over against this affirmation of history as the work of God destined for consummation in him, Buss argues that in the Old Testament, history is more often viewed negatively as the work of human disobedience.[1] God contends against history rather than revealing himself through it as its bearer. The fundamental significance of apocalyptic in this connection is not, as Pannenberg supposes, the discovery of meaning and revelation in universal history, but the intensification of the negative attitude toward history and the denial of its value.[2] In the New Testament the all-important story of Jesus again displays the futility of history, as it leads, and can only lead, to the cross.[3]

Buss knows that the Bible also witnesses to moments of fulfillment, chief of which is the resurrection of Jesus. But Buss regards the resurrection, like the apocalyptic hope and the idealized eras of Israel's past, as mythical in character.[4] At these points the divine is seen as active, but for just these reasons they are not historical.

At a certain level of this discussion the problem may be as

[1] Cf. above, Buss, pp. 144–146.
[2] *Ibid.*, pp. 146 f.
[3] *Ibid.*, p. 150.
[4] *Ibid.*, p. 150.

much terminological as real. Pannenberg, of course, knows of the repeated disobedience of Israel and of the sins of all nations and peoples, and he includes all this in what he calls history. That God is the bearer of history never means for him that human freedom and responsibility are set aside and that God in some simple and direct way effects an ideal course of events. But it does mean that man's sin is not the final word, that God works through it and around it so that history moves toward its fulfillment in God in spite of what man does as much as because of it. For Pannenberg "history" includes both those events which the Old Testament attributes primarily to man and those events attributed explicitly to God. Thus what Buss calls mythical is for Pannenberg included within history on the sole condition that the event in question actually took place. It is this total course of events and not any segment abstracted from the whole that reveals God and his destiny for man.

At this level, terminological agreement would help. Since "history" is not a Biblical term, it would be possible to identify "history" either with what is understood in the Bible as the totality of man's acts or with what is understood as the totality of all that took place. Clearly "history" must receive differing evaluation in the two cases, but since what is thus differently evaluated is different, no substantial disagreement is entailed.

However, deeper issues do manifest themselves in substantive differences. Buss believes that the modern categories of history and myth point to two quite distinct structures of meaning and reality that can and must be distinguished also in the Bible. History speaks of before and after in terms of chronological sequence, whereas myth speaks of the Beginning and the End as a quite different order of reality to which historical time is irrelevant.[5] If this is so, then it is a matter of utmost moment for the understanding of Scripture or other ancient records, to determine when one is reading history—an account of human action—and when one is reading myth—

[5] *Ibid.,* pp. 139 f.

an account of the sacred and transcendent reality. If, as Buss believes, apocalyptic must be read as myth, then the expected End cannot be thought of as historically future. Then, also, the resurrection of Jesus must speak to us of the everlasting contradiction of the sacred and historical dimensions rather than as an assurance that resurrection awaits us all at a chronologically future moment.

Pannenberg, of course, cannot accept this distinction of history and myth as a basis for understanding the Biblical faith. For him history is the encompassing horizon, and history means the whole of what has occurred. This cannot be subdivided into a course of historical events and something distinct therefrom which is a dimension of sacred reality.

In part this issue is one which study of the Biblical texts can settle, but only in part. Scholars can debate the extent to which apocalyptic pointed to an End that stands in temporal-sequential relation to historical time and the extent to which it pointed away from history altogether. But agreement as to the conscious intention of the apocalyptic writers would settle only secondary aspects of the issue. If we should agree that the apocalypticists themselves thought in terms of something that is chronologically future, it might still be objected that this represented only a superficial and irrelevant confusion in their minds, owing to the excessive historicization of Hebrew thought. Their deeper intention, it might be held, is to negate all history in favor of the transcendent reality to which chronology is irrelevant. This understanding assumes that the religious experience of Israel is sufficiently like that of other peoples that it can be illumined by a study of religious experiences generally. It is of a piece with Buss's statement that the religious history of India and the East parallels in great detail that of Israel and the West.[6]

Pannenberg, in contrast, while recognizing that Israel's religion emerged out of a common matrix and through interaction with other religions, also takes a special interest in that

[6] *Ibid.,* pp. 141, 151, 153.

which is peculiar to it as a new emergent.[7] Whereas Buss sees apocalyptic as another expression of a common religious phenomenon,[8] Pannenberg sees it as a special development out of Hebrew prophetism.[9] Buss focuses attention upon the apocalyptic negation of the historical world, a negation that can certainly be readily paralleled in other religions. Pannenberg calls attention to the more unusual features of apocalypticism, its concern for universal historical developments and its promise of resurrection for all.

The issue between Buss and Pannenberg, and one which is of course far more widespread in its significance than the naming of any two representatives could indicate, is one of the nature of man and his essential need. The understandings of man that underlie the two positions are, on the one hand, products of historical study and, on the other hand, presuppositions of such study. One view, encouraged in recent decades by the existentialist analysis, is that the meaning of existence must be found anew in each moment, and that the structure of each moment is essentially the same as that of every other moment. Each moment embodies the possibility of authenticity or eternity, and thus of a nonhistorical fulfillment.[10] Whereas if man seeks fulfillment in a historical future, he must forego the possibility of being touched by infinity and participate in the futility that is history. A second view is that man is a future-oriented being who cannot but be concerned for the attainment in the future of a fulfillment that is not available in the present. From this perspective it is the attempt to escape the problem of the historically future in the name of eternity that is illusory and futile. Christian faith has been, and today is, understood in the context of both of these views of man.

The extensive ramifications of this issue are seen in the very wide context into which Buss sets his argument against Pan-

[7] Cf. above, Pannenberg, p. 106.
[8] Cf. above, Buss, pp. 147 f.
[9] Cf. above, Pannenberg, pp. 121–122.
[10] Cf. above, Buss, pp. 153 f.

nenberg. He attempts to show not only the futility of all attempts to find salvation in progression toward a goal in the course of history but also that there is finally no common reality of time. Macrocosmic categories of time do not apply to the subatomic world in which even the phenomenon of "negative time" may be found.[11] In the macrocosmic physical world, time is a dimension of events, and its distinction from the other dimensions is relatively unimportant.[12] All this suggests, in Buss's view, that any notion of a final cosmic consummation runs counter to our best knowledge of the physical universe.

Buss recognizes that at the biological level time does involve a goal-seeking future-directed process.[13] Here he seems to give some support to Pannenberg. However, according to Buss, the situation changes again with the appearance of culture. The biological future orientation finds here its continuation in historical development, but man's self-transcendence, through which he is related to the sacred reality, points away from this biological-historical time toward a new dimension of being.[14] Pannenberg, Buss believes, has insufficiently differentiated historical time and sacred or mythical time.[15] A clear distinction here would draw attention away from a historically future End toward the self-transcending dimensions of man at any moment.

Although Pannenberg has not, so far as I know, discussed the question of physical time, he is in principle open also to this extension of the discussion. Hence one might enter into consideration as to whether, ontologically at least, there is not a common conception of time applicable to all levels of reality. I personally believe this to be the case, and I assume that Pannenberg shares my view against that of Buss. If we are right, the plausibility of affirming a quite different kind of time as mythical or sacred time may be somewhat reduced,

11 *Ibid.*, p. 137.
12 *Ibid.*, p. 137.
13 *Ibid.*, p. 138.
14 *Ibid.*, p. 139.
15 *Ibid.*, pp. 139 f.

although the reality of very diverse modes of apprehending and interpreting the temporal flow cannot be denied. Since Buss's argument could be pursued almost as well at the level of the meaning of temporal experience to man as by his defense of the existence of different types of time, a more appropriate focus of discussion is the nature and meaning of transcendence in relation to time. Does man's power of self-transcendence, as Buss holds, direct his quest for salvation away from the future of biological and historical time? Or does this transcendence greatly intensify man's ultimate concern with the historical future?

In these ways Buss's paper throws into relief the great importance of Pannenberg's anthropological conviction that man must seek his fulfillment in the historical future. So long as we are discussing the *importance* of the factuality of the resurrection, this anthropological question is the one that comes primarily into view. When, however, we turn to the question of the evidence supporting the claim of factuality, other issues arise. Here we can turn to Grobel's discussion, as it constitutes a quite different criticism of Pannenberg.

## II

Grobel agrees with Pannenberg that in the resurrection appearances something happened to the witnesses which was more than a change in their subjective state.[16] But he denies that what happened to the disciples, in distinction from its subjective effects upon them, can be called historical. He recognizes that the occurrences of this reality were temporal,[17] but he denies that they were spatial.[18] For him, a spatial occurrence would be one that involves matter that can be sensuously experienced. A resurrection with spatial dimensions would presumably involve a resuscitated or transformed corpse, and Grobel is convinced that the New Testament

[16] Cf. above, Grobel, pp. 169 f.
[17] *Ibid.*, p. 171.
[18] *Ibid.*, p. 175.

stories pointing in that direction are late and misleading interpretations of the original Easter event. Moreover, even the apocryphal accounts never pretend to describe the resurrection itself, that is, the physical event of the revivification of the body of Jesus.[19] Assuming that what appeared to the disciples did not have sensuous, spatial, material character, Grobel does not believe that it can be regarded as historical.

Since it is a main thesis of Pannenberg's theology that the resurrection is historical in character, we have here an apparent direct confrontation between the two men. However, some analysis is needed to determine just what the real issues between them are.

First, Pannenberg believes that the primary Biblical witness is that the tomb was empty, that the resurrection did involve a transformation of Jesus' physical body into what can only be called a spiritual body. That we have no account of the process of this transformation and that the stories of the empty tomb are late, Pannenberg agrees. But he argues that Paul's understanding of resurrection is such that the physical body of the resurrected one could not remain in existence, and that it is most reasonable to suppose that he reflects, in this respect, the general view of the first generation of Christians, including the Jerusalem community. The debate here is largely an exegetical one, based on 1 Cor. 15:42–50, since both accept this as a key passage.[20]

Second, Grobel agrees that a resurrection involving an empty tomb would be spatial as well as temporal, and hence would qualify as a historical event, but he regards any claim that such an event occurred as incredible.[21] He does not explain just why this is historically incredible, but we may assume that he means that it falls outside the range of possibility allowed by the modern historian. The historian must operate by the principle of analogy, and lacking all analogies in our

[19] *Ibid.*, p. 171.
[20] *Ibid.*, pp. 174 f. Pannenberg engaged Grobel in exegetical debate on this passage at the Vanderbilt meeting.
[21] *Ibid.*, p. 175.

experience for bodily resurrections of this sort, we cannot as historians make any affirmation about them. Presumably Grobel also rejects the possibility of some other standpoint from which what is incredible to him as historian appears possible.

Pannenberg, in contrast, insists that historical methodology must not be such as to exclude unique occurrences, even such radically unique occurrences as Jesus' resurrection, from its purview. He rejects any absolutization of a contemporary world view that would in advance settle negatively the question of the occurrence of a past event. Like Grobel, he identifies what he can believe about the past with what he can believe as historian. Unlike Grobel, as man and as historian, he can believe that the tomb was empty.

Third, however, we must avoid exaggerating the importance of the doctrine of the empty tomb in considering the relations of these two positions. In Pannenberg's paper on "The Revelation of God in Jesus of Nazareth" nothing is said that clearly requires an empty tomb. Pannenberg does not rest his case for the historical character of the resurrection on this doctrine. What seems essential with respect to the resurrection is that something happened to the disciples that caused their subjective change and was not dependent upon it. To this Grobel also agrees. For Pannenberg I assume that this objective reality must involve the personal presence of the risen Jesus, but the involvement of the crucified body in this presence might not be essential. For example, we might speculate that the risen Jesus so impressed himself directly on the minds of the disciples that sensuous experiences were produced as a by-product.[22] Whether Grobel would agree to such a possibility is not clear, but it seems doubtful that he would make a major issue of this point. Hence, the primary issue here seems to be terminological.[23] For Grobel, historical means

---

[22] In *Grundzüge der Christologie* Pannenberg characterizes the resurrection appearances as a special type of vision, insisting only on their involvement of extra-subjective reality; pp. 88–93.

[23] Grobel recognizes this as a possibility; above, p. 170.

spatial (in the sense of sensory and material). For Pannenberg, historical means past event of any kind at all. For Grobel, a self-presentation of the resurrected Jesus as immaterial spirit would not qualify as historical event; for Pannenberg, it would. A substantial issue remains as to the limits of the proper work of the historian, but it may be that the issue as to what in fact occurred is far less crucial than it appears.

At the very end of his paper Grobel raises another issue which can count as the fourth in this series. If a historian is to undertake to determine whether or not something took place, he must have some specifiable idea of what he is looking for. He cannot be looking indiscriminately for just "something." In this case the question is that of the presence of a resurrected one as a reality objective to those who witness to his appearances. But what would count as such a presence? If it were affirmed that the resurrected one must be a revived corpse, that would give the historian a clear indication as to what he should seek, but this is not essential for Pannenberg. Indeed Pannenberg tells us that we can only describe what the historian seeks in metaphorical language. But can any evidence count for or against an affirmation that has no literally specifiable meaning? It seems that we would be reduced to saying that something happened to the disciples and, negatively, that this was not a merely subjective experience. But how can the historian either support or reject one metaphor or another which describes the posited $x$?

I have suggested above that the required literal affirmation is that the spirit of the human Jesus was personally present to the disciples. We could further specify this as meaning the presence of Jesus' conscious selfhood at the particular times and places of the appearances. If this did in fact occur, then it was one of those occurrences that make up the sum total of occurrence and, hence, was part of history in this broadest sense. The problem for the historian who accepts the total sphere of past occurrence as his field, and who does not exclude in advance the possibility of radically unique occurrences, is to determine whether the evidence in favor of the claim that this occurred is sufficient to cause it to be regarded as a probability. Other historians, who rule out in advance the possibility of such occurrences, or who so define history as to exclude them, will not participate in this inquiry.

Grobel's paper raises another quite different kind of issue. Pannenberg denies that the Bible speaks of a direct self-revelation of God in his essence. Grobel counters that the Bible speaks frequently of God's speaking to men and of man hearing.[24] In such speaking God communicates his will, which is his self in a particular focus.[25] If the word, reveal, suggests too much a visual experience, then other terminology may be needed, but the directness of personal communication should not be denied.

Once again, the issue between Grobel and Pannenberg appears to be partly substantial and partly terminological. Grobel means by a direct revelation one in which there is no medium, one in which God acts directly upon the recipient;[26] and when he insists that what is revealed is God himself, he means that God's purpose or will for man is made known to him.[27]

Pannenberg, in contrast, states that the question of the presence or absence of a mediator is not at issue in the question of directness or indirectness.[28] Directness and indirectness have to do with the content that is imparted. A direct revelation would be one in which the content imparted directly coincides with the intention of the revealer and does not require any secondary interpretation. A direct self-revelation of God would be one which revealed directly the nature or character of God. Pannenberg's point is that when the Bible tells us of God's disclosures, the content of these disclosures is characteristically something about human events and actions, not

[24] *Ibid.*, p. 159.
[25] *Ibid.*, pp. 164 f.
[26] *Ibid.*, pp. 160 f.
[27] *Ibid.*, pp. 164 f.
[28] Pannenberg, *Offenbarung als Geschichte* (*KuD, Beiheft* 1; Göttingen: Vandenhoeck und Ruprecht, 1961), p. 16.

directly information about himself. When elsewhere the Bible speaks directly of what God is like, it does so on the basis of interpretation of those events.

The problem is somewhat subtler when we consider God's communication of his will. Grobel and Pannenberg agree that God's will is essentially God himself,[29] and that in some sense God reveals his will. For Grobel this means that God does directly communicate himself, but Pannenberg insists that directly and specifically what is revealed is a law or command dealing with human events. God does not communicate information about his will, and only that would constitute direct self-revelation.

For these reasons, Grobel's arguments do not contradict Pannenberg's position substantively, even where verbally they seem to do so. Indeed, Grobel recognizes this in advance. Given Pannenberg's exact way of defining what direct self-revelation of God's essence would be, the concept is largely absent from the Bible. Grobel grants Pannenberg the right to define his terms and draw his conclusions accordingly, but he points out the danger that such a methodology may lead to neglect of important material and oversimplification of the alternatives.[30] This can be illustrated in several ways.

First, what is communicated by God that has to do with his will could have three forms. It could be a simple statement as to how men should act. This would be clearly indirect as revelation of God. It could be an explicit affirmation about his will. This would be clearly direct in Pannenberg's terms. It could be a statement that a particular course of action is God's will. This would be less easily classified. It seems directly to communicate something about God's will as such although its content is not simply a statement about that will. Pannenberg demonstrates that the Biblical understanding of revelation does not take the second of these three forms. From this he seems to draw the conclusion that it must take the form of the first, or that the third is not significantly different

[29] *Ibid.*, p. 15; above, Grobel, pp. 164 f.
[30] Cf. above, Grobel, p. 157.

from the first in crucial respects, but Grobel's work suggests that the third possibility may be a quite distinctive and defensible one and may lead to markedly different conclusions.

Second, by distinguishing the question of the directness or indirectness of revelation from that of the presence or absence of a mediator, Pannenberg directs attention away from the question of God's immediate dealings with individuals. It is, of course, quite permissible to select one's problems, but one must not then draw negative conclusions based on one's nonattention to other problems. By focusing attention on the content communicated in revelation and minimizing its reference to God, Pannenberg shows that this revelation always has to do directly with history. From this he concludes that a merely verbal revelation must depend upon the course of events to which it points for its vindication and that it is these events themselves that are fundamentally revelatory. Of course, he emphasizes also that these events are in turn influenced by the interpretations of earlier events and the concomitant expectations, and that they can only be seen as revelatory of God in the context of interpretation that has thus arisen.[31] But he wishes to deny that the prophetic word can have any *self*-validating power to reveal God even indirectly.

It is my impression that having denied the importance of the question of *how* a revelation is communicated (mediately or immediately), Pannenberg then tacitly assumes that all verbal statements arise as interpretations or reactions to public historical events and without any immediate divine action upon or communication to the speaker. Grobel, on the other hand, points to the necessity of some divine self-presentation to a man if he is to see the public events as revelatory of God.[32] Here the immediacy of God to the believer in distinction from man's unaided powers of insight, reflection, and interpretation is a matter of utmost importance.

Pannenberg resists this approach chiefly because of the way it has been employed in modern theology. It has led to a dis-

[31] Cf. above, Pannenberg, pp. 119 f.
[32] Cf. above, Grobel, p. 162.

tinction between profane history, the story of what really took place in the publicly observable sphere, and the account of faith which sees events in the light of God's activity, but never in such a way that God's activity is an explanatory factor in profane history. Pannenberg sees this, rightly, I believe, as an unhappy abandonment of the sphere of public knowledge to interpretations that are alien to Christian faith and an attempt to find a safe place for Christian belief in the sphere of the unverifiable.

I suggest that a third possibility be considered. Perhaps we could understand God's immediate self-presentation as opening the eyes of men to the revelatory character of the public events in such a way that the course of events is in its turn affected by this act of God. God's self-revelation to the prophet (direct or indirect in Pannenberg's terms) then must be recognized as a part of history and as a distinctive locus of God's working in history. This complicates the total picture considerably as over against either Grobel's or Pannenberg's views, but it might allow us to see the truth in each.

## III

Fundamental among the questions posed by Hamilton's paper is that of the nature of modernity. Pannenberg presents his thought as completely open to all that the modern world has to teach him and as a means of persuading open-minded modern men of the superior truth of Christianity. Yet to Hamilton the whole enterprise seems strangely out of keeping with the modern temper. To him it seems that the course of secularization has proceeded to such a point that there is little place any longer for theological system building. The theologian must enter the world and express his solidarity with it rather than work out the implications of his traditional faith and offer the results for acceptance. He can engage in unstructured conversation with secular man, can learn from him, and in unexpected ways make his own witness. But he cannot approach the conversation as though he had some settled and

established truth to present. From such a perspective Hamilton can only view the ambitious program of Pannenberg as
"interesting, without being important."[33]

Pannenberg might reply to such criticism that if indeed
modern man is so far estranged from historic Christian faith,
this may well be the fault of the theologian. Modern man is
willing to look at the evidence and discuss its most plausible
interpretation. Theologians have done their cause great damage by appealing to private and subjective grounds for faith,
for onto this ground modern man cannot follow. If participation in Christ depends upon faith, and if faith is inaccessible
apart from a special act of God, then the man who can recognize no such act of God within his own life must learn also
to do without Christ. To challenge modern man to rethink
his interpretation of history in terms of his own accepted
methods is not to fail to take modernity seriously.

The difficulty with any such argument, of course, is that
"modern man" has taken many forms. Even if we limit "modern man" to man estranged from his historic religious faith,
the variety remains. There are indeed moderns who will take
no interest in any systematic restructuring of history. They
are too deeply convinced of the absence of any pattern or
meaning in history to be concerned with a new attempt to
display history as revelatory of God. Equally, the very word,
God, has lost all intelligibility for many, such that arguments
about the directness or indirectness of his revelation can only
appear as literally nonsensical. But there are other moderns
who have utmost faith in reason and complete openness to the
discussion of any idea so long as no arbitrary or private cri-
teria are introduced. To such moderns Pannenberg may well
speak as few recent Protestant theologians have.

This very general question as to the character of modernity
and what this implies for the responsibility of the theologian
can be made more pointed by treating particular points of
criticism. Hamilton believes that Pannenberg's theology presupposes that man is naturally religious, that he can only find

[33] Cf. above, Hamilton, p. 196.

the fulfillment which as man he must seek in relation to God.[34] Hamilton knows that many moderns cannot recognize themselves in any such description and assure us that what they seek has nothing to do with God. If men can thus, in full awareness of what they are doing, reject God as the fulfillment of their lives, does this not mean that Christianity must surrender its presupposition of man's natural religiousness? And if so, are not fundamental assumptions of Pannenberg's thought shaken?

I assume here that there are no disagreements as to the facts. Pannenberg well knows that many intelligent persons consciously seek fulfillment elsewhere than in God. Indeed his own youth was spent among such people quite outside of the sphere of Christian influence. The question is whether the fulfillment that is so sought can be true fulfillment or can indeed be found at all where it is sought. That men now seek fulfillment elsewhere than in resurrection to new life with God may show only how the church has failed to witness clearly to its faith and to display its reasonableness. It may not mean that there are real alternatives to resurrection.

We are confronted here with the fundamental question of human nature as such. Pannenberg does not rest his case on some peculiar religious faculty in man. He argues from man's nature as a future-directed individual and from the kind of future that alone can make men's life meaningful. But this does assume a constancy and universality of man's nature, at least in this respect. If there are men who are not oriented to a temporal future but simply take each moment as it is, finding therein all the meaning that they require, then Pannenberg's analysis seems irrelevant to them. The question would have to be pressed as to whether it is really possible to find adequate meaning for life in each new momentary present, or whether human nature is such that this is an illusory ideal. The latter view, which is Pannenberg's, depends on the assumption that there is in this sense a common and universal human nature. But perhaps man is so deeply deter-

---

[34] *Ibid.*, pp. 178 f.

mined by his involvement in particular cultures, formed by particular histories, that no such universals can be affirmed. In this case there may be emerging, as Hamilton seems to think, a modern man whose needs are genuinely different from those with which traditional Christian faith has had to do. Hence, although Pannenberg assumes no religious *a priori,* he does presuppose a characteristic of common human nature that may turn out to be formed in a particular history and subject to loss in our post-Christian era.

Partly because of his far lesser confidence in the power of reason to deal coherently and adequately with ultimate and comprehensive questions, Hamilton is suspicious of the very close connection established by Pannenberg between faith and reason. Pannenberg insists that faith must presuppose certain things about history, the truth of which can only be established by rational investigation of the evidence. Thus, faith presupposes that Jesus taught the coming of the reign of God and that he was raised from the dead. These assertions must be justified as probable by historical investigation. Since they are established historically not as mere facts but as facts laden with meaning, the belief that they are true is also the belief that in the last day all men will be raised. Thus the whole structure of Christian belief, as Pannenberg understands it, seems to be given even apart from faith, and faith is little more than living as if these probabilities are true.[35] Hamilton sees this understanding of faith as the existential acceptance of probability as far removed from the historic Protestant emphasis upon the witness of the Spirit.[36] Whereas the Reformers believed that acquiescence to all manner of right doctrine profits nothing if a special miracle is not worked by God in the depths of the heart, Pannenberg seems to see nothing more as needed than an intelligent response to the acceptance of historical probabilities.

In his vehement rejection of the appeal to private and inaccessible sources as justification for Christian belief, Pan-

[35] Cf. above, p. 189.
[36] Cf. above, p. 188.

nenberg has certainly left himself open to Hamilton's criticism. He does really mean to say that belief in Jesus' resurrection and its meaning as first-fruit of universal resurrection is established historically and that faith follows from it.[37] But the faith that follows from it is not so much some greater confidence that these propositions are true as it is confidence in the God who raised Jesus Christ and who will raise all men. We cannot know in advance the course of our own life, individually or as a community, but we can trust the one who raised Jesus from the dead and believe that he also gives our lives some place in the comprehensive scheme of things. If history gave us no basis for trusting him, such trust would be absurd credulity, and such credulity is not what Christianity demands. The more confident we can become through our rational reflection about the past that God really is trustworthy, the freer we can become in the present to put our lives in his hands.

If faith really *presupposes* certain beliefs that must be rationally justified through historical investigation, then an additional problem arises to which Hamilton directs our attention.[38] Does it not follow that Christian faith is wholly at the mercy of historians? If historians decide that the factual presuppositions of Christian faith are not true, or are not highly probable, then must we not in all honesty lock the doors of our churches and surrender the name Christian?

If the facts presupposed by faith were relatively unquestioned ones, this challenge might seem largely academic. But Pannenberg includes among the historical facts presupposed by faith that Jesus rose from the dead.[39] Since the great majority of historians now refuse, at least as historians, to make this assertion, the plight of faith seems very serious indeed. Is it not, then, even now the case that we should abandon our faith?

Pannenberg, of course, does not view the situation in this

---

[37] Cf. above, Pannenberg, p. 129.
[38] Cf. above, Hamilton, p. 185.
[39] Cf. above, Pannenberg, p. 129.

way, and we have already seen some of the reasons for his drawing quite different conclusions. Insofar as the reason for the historian's failure to support the Christian belief in the resurrection arises from prior belief in its impossibility or from exclusion of this kind of event from the province of history, his rejection of the historical character of the resurrection is irrelevant. The question is only whether an honest and open inquiry into the evidence points to the reality of the resurrection. The relevant evidence is the New Testament witness read in the light of what we know of the traditions in terms of which men then lived. When one does not approach this evidence with prior incredulity, Pannenberg insists, it points overwhelmingly toward the actuality of Jesus' resurrection. The progress of historical investigation is not likely to change this situation drastically. The way in which we are led to think of resurrection may continue to be modified by further historical study, but the fact is well-established. On such grounds as these Pannenberg is able to say that historical knowledge can "only slightly impair the certainty of belief."[40]

Nevertheless, Pannenberg's understanding of the relation of faith to beliefs about past occurrences seems to leave faith considerably more vulnerable to the course of historical research than he himself affirms. For example, one cannot rule out the possibility of the discovery of additional ancient documents that would throw a quite different light upon the events of Jesus' life and resurrection. Perhaps they might make the hypothesis of conscious deception more plausible than it now appears; or perhaps they might point in a way that our present records do not to the employment of techniques of autosuggestion in the earliest community as a way of inducing resurrection appearances. As of now, I assume, we are right in rejecting such theories as highly improbable in light of existing evidence. But it is hard to see how one can affirm in advance that the certainty of faith could be impaired only slightly by further developments in historical research.

More important is the point treated earlier in this chapter

---

[40] Cf. above, Hamilton, p. 185.

in connection with Grobel's criticisms. If all that is required as the presupposition of faith is that *something* occurred at Easter, then this is not a particularly vulnerable affirmation. On the other hand, very little follows from the mere fact that *something* happened. Unless this something is further specified in its character, one can draw no conclusions with respect to our own destiny with God. To whatever degree this something is specified, the affirmation that it occurred becomes less indubitable. Although it may help at one level to show that "resurrection" is a metaphor, the problem cannot either be solved or avoided in that way.

## IV

One of the striking features of the present theological scene is the dawning realization that the leaders of the theological revival of the previous generation were not—or at least are not now—so skeptical or indifferent as they long seemed with respect to hope for a temporally future personal fulfillment. Karl Barth, Reinhold Niebuhr, and Paul Tillich have all published statements in recent years for which their earlier writings had not fully prepared us. Even Rudolf Bultmann apparently believes that the Christian rightly looks forward to a personal future beyond death.[41] Nevertheless, in the case of all these senior theologians the future hope appears rather as a postscript to their theology than as its integrating principle.

The belated acknowledgment of concern with this subject, however, raises a serious question as to the appropriateness of its secondary character in their thought. If one does believe that death is not simply the end for man, then should not this belief be more integrally related with one's understanding of the gospel than has been characteristic in recent decades? Should not the gospel be recast as a promise of a future with God?

During the same period that we have been learning of the openness of the senior theologians to this aspect of traditional

[41] Cf. above, Grobel, p. 169, note 21.

Christian faith, new voices have been raised for whom the future is the clear center of attention. The Catholic Teilhard de Chardin has commanded a wide hearing among Protestants for his understanding of the whole course of nature and history as moving toward an eschatological consummation in God. Ernst Fuchs has focused the kerygma as a promise of life beyond death. And Wolfhart Pannenberg has brilliantly rethought the whole meaning of Biblical history in the light of the conviction that only a promise of future fulfillment could be authentically good news for man.

From this point of view many of the basic issues between Pannenberg and his critics are illumined. These critics for the most part understand faith as the fulfillment of man in the here and now. Such a faith is self-authenticating. Fundamentally it has no propositional content and needs no rational support. The decisive relationship of God to man is seen in the awakening of faith. The resurrection of Jesus is understood as the occasion in which Christian faith arose. From this perspective detailed questioning as to just what the events were to which the resurrection points is unimportant and even undesirable. God's work is not primarily related to the temporal-sequential character of the flow of events. If any event is seen as an act of God, this is by virtue of the faith of the perceiver, not by virtue of any public, visible aspect of the event. Concern for a future fulfillment is failure to accept what is offered in the present. Even if one believes that God has some further gift in store in the future, that belief is only a postscript to theology.

If, on the other hand, one sees man as a fundamentally future-oriented being who requires for his fulfillment a condition that is unattainable in this life, then everything must appear quite differently. Faith must be trust in God that he will grant to man in the future that apart from which man's life is incomplete and without adequate meaning. Since such a faith cannot be self-authenticating, it must either be arbitrary or else find its basis in evidence. The Christian claim of the resurrection of Jesus points us to that one place where

man may gain adequate confidence that God is indeed lord
over history, that he loves all men, and that he will one day
raise us to new life with him. To discover just what took
place in the Easter event and just what it meant and means
in the light of the total context of tradition in which it occurred is a matter of ultimate concern. Furthermore, since
trust in God depends upon belief in his trustworthiness, the
evidence of his trustworthiness cannot itself be a product of
the trust. Man properly demands objective evidence of God's
power and love.

Along with all the other deep differences that are involved
in these two ways of understanding man's fulfillment—as
primarily present and as decisively future—there is a radical
difference with respect to the role of the historian. From the
first of these two perspectives, the historian expects his work
to be irrelevant to faith. He seeks no evidence of God's character in history. He is quite content to explain all that he finds
in history in terms that make no reference to God. To speak
of God would be to intrude a faith perspective and lose the
objectivity of historical study. For Pannenberg, in contrast,
we must depend upon the study of history to learn the answers to those questions that are of ultimate concern to us. To
exclude God from history is to preclude in advance the possibility of learning from history that which makes it the su-
premely important object of study. To approach the study of
the past open to the possibility that it will teach us about God
is to be genuinely objective. And Pannenberg is convinced
that when we study the past with that objectivity it *will* teach
us about God and give us grounds to trust him.

I personally find Pannenberg's dramatic challenge of what
had become an emerging consensus both exciting and disturb-
ing. I am excited by it because I see Christian man as far
more oriented toward the future than recent theology has
usually acknowledged. I see this, as Pannenberg does, as en-
tailing concern for many questions about the past, the present,
and the future that have been suppressed by those who have
understood faith as fulfillment in the present. I am disturbed

by Pannenberg's position because it subordinates the present too much to the future and the past. Pannenberg, of course, finds meaning in present Christian existence. But this meaning depends decisively on a confidence in the future based on beliefs about the past. This relationship of past, present, and future is important, but it must be supplemented by others which move directly from the past to the present, and also from the present to the past and future.

I share with Pannenberg the view that the resurrection appearances of Jesus were probably nonhallucinatory visions on the part of the disciples. I agree also that they carried with them the conviction that the hope for general resurrection was vindicated and that hence the early Christians found the meaning of their present in their faith in the future based on beliefs about the past. I also believe, however, that the kind of existence they shared in the eschatological communities came rapidly to have for them a self-authenticating meaning and validity partly independent of their beliefs about the future and past and partly supportive of these beliefs. Other beliefs about Jesus than those dependent on his resurrection also played a role as a direct influence of past upon present not mediated by convictions about the future.

This complex blending of factors in ever-changing ratios and interconnections has characterized the Christian community to the present day. On the one hand, there have been those for whom loss of the assurance of future consummation would be tantamount to total loss of Christian faith. On the other hand, there have been those for whom deep devotion to the God revealed in Jesus is completely separated from any hope of future fulfillment. Between lie the far larger number for whom belief in God's future vindication and completion of his work is a major and cherished factor in their faith but not its one indispensable cornerstone.

My concern is that Pannenberg's position is too near the first of these alternatives. In reaction against the prevalence of the other emphasis, in which the self-validating character of present faith has been polemically employed against concern for both past and future, this counteremphasis has some justification. But it places a very heavy burden upon the establishment by correct historiography of the factuality of the resurrection of Jesus.

In another respect, however, Pannenberg is very keenly interested in the present. He knows that the historical demonstration of the resurrection of Jesus and of the fact that it originally carried with it its meaning as verification of the expectation of universal resurrection does not in itself determine the truth of this doctrine for us. It is equally important to justify in our day an expectation analogous to that provided by apocalypticism in Jesus' day. Only as we today recognize that our best knowledge of ourselves and of history points to a future consummation as its only ground of meaning can the fact of Jesus' resurrection carry eschatological meaning for us as it did in its own context.

Pannenberg sees in German idealism a powerful apprehension of the truth he wants to bring home in our day. This philosophy was itself a penetrating expression of Christian thought. In the light of more recent developments in Christian theology and in anthropology generally, this nineteenth-century movement requires correction and reformulation. But it is through the immense undertaking of reestablishing for us the persuasive power of major aspects of this philosophical tradition that Pannenberg proposes to set the context for our appropriation of the truth of Christianity. To one committed like Pannenberg to the importance of speculative thought and to the quest for comprehensiveness of vision, but schooled far more in the empiricism and naturalism of the English-speaking world, this vast undertaking appears awe-inspiring, but also somewhat foreign. We may be grateful that its architect is also sensitively and perceptively open to the other philosophical currents of our time.

# 7. *Response to the Discussion*

## WOLFHART PANNENBERG

In any discussion which does not deal directly with substantive problems, but with the conceptuality used in their description, the danger is especially great that the conceptuality will unintentionally take on other nuances of meaning in the perspective of the critics than in that held by the author who is being criticized. In confronting the arguments of my critics with my own views, Cobb has called attention to this kind of shifting of perspective in the discussions in this volume. I agree with his presentation for the most part, and I think that through it the actual differences have emerged more clearly out of those which are only apparent. In light of the results of this confrontation, I intend now to take up the central themes of the discussion once again, in dialogue with the criticism that has been brought forward. If I understand the issue correctly, we are especially concerned with the understanding of revelation and history, and with the relation of faith and knowledge.

These themes are of a more abstract nature than the subject of my introductory essay.[1] There I attempted to clarify the question common to all contemporary theology, namely, what Jesus of Nazareth really means to us today. This essay focused particularly on the problems concerning the relation of the beginnings of Christianity to contemporary truth. The question of the relevance of Jesus for our time can be clarified

[1] The article, "The Revelation of God in Jesus of Nazareth," was concluded in 1963 and hence does not take up literature that appeared after that time.

221

only if one first makes explicit what the appeal of Jesus means. One must begin with the historical Jesus—otherwise we bring in all sorts of experiences and ideas that have little to do with the actual, historical Jesus of Nazareth. But in raising the question about Jesus, one cannot for a moment bypass the God whose coming lordship Jesus proclaimed. Hence the question about Jesus is transformed into another question: To what extent can the God of Jesus still be regarded by us today as the all-determining reality? This question is unanswerable if one tries to relate the message of Jesus and that of the earliest Christian community to the present by leaping abruptly over two thousand years. In a completely altered context, in a situation that has been radically transformed, a message cast in precisely the same words no longer means the same thing. For this reason I pursued the question of how the message and history of Jesus were proclaimed for the first time in a non-Jewish sphere of tradition, namely, in the context of Hellenism. It was in this connection that the problems arose which are bound up with the position of the Christian message in the world of the other religions. Since the time of the formation of the Hellenistic community, the issue of truth which begins here has been answerable for non-Jews only in the realm of philosophical questioning. Does not this step into the Hellenistic world hold something that is paradigmatic for Christianity even today?

In the second section of my essay I attempted to indicate the features of the appearing and history of Jesus which made it possible for him to be accepted in the Hellenistic world as the revealer of the true God. My concern here was much less with the manifold factors then actually effecting the turning to Christianity, than with what makes understandable the acceptance of the Christian message by Hellenistic man as meaningful, given what we know today about his characteristic consciousness of the truth. Already implied in the question in terms of its Greek-Hellenistic counterpart was our modern, philosophically-reflected consciousness of truth. Therefore in

the third section I went on to a more general discussion of
the concept of revelation, oriented toward contemporary problems. This concept of revelation was in part related back to
Biblical-exegetical findings, not in order to introduce it as a
concept to be established exegetically, but rather merely to
ascertain its current systematic (or philosophical) applicability
to the history of Jesus, with regard to the concrete religious-
historical context of this history that found expression in the
Biblical texts. Only then was it possible in the course of the
article to develop the fourth section on faith and the knowledge of revelation.

This particular train of thought of the initial essay, oriented
to the historical difference between primitive Christianity and
the present, and to the bridging of the gap between them,
was scarcely touched upon in the subsequent critical contributions. Yet, in my essay it is not simply a question of historical
reminiscences, unimportant for the interpretation of the subject itself. Rather my contention is precisely this, that the
truth of the Christian message is not separable from the historicality of the relation of our present to primitive Christianity. The truth itself is embodied in this historical relationship.
The critical contributions to this volume have for the most
part discussed the structure of the concepts of revelation, history, and faith without reference to this relationship. Certainly
a critique of concepts has its proper place. The concepts one
employs must be able to stand examination to determine
whether they are appropriate to the subject to which they
refer. The discussion becomes problematic only when another
substantive understanding comes into play in the process.
Without overlooking this difficulty, I shall seek in what follows
to clarify the substantive reference of the concepts of revelation, history, and faith, in dialogue with the criticism that has
been advanced. Since the introduction by Robinson reports
comprehensively on the German discussion of my theses, and
since some of the viewpoints that appear in this volume touch
on certain views that play a role in the German discussion, I

will also include German publications in my considerations here, especially those that are recent and to which I have not yet responded elsewhere.

## I

Under the theme of revelation, two questions are currently being raised together: who God is and whether he is. In making such a statement, I am taking for granted that both questions are not already regarded as having been already settled. Otherwise the theme of revelation would lose its significance. To one who is convinced that all talk about God has today become utterly meaningless, any consideration of whether God has revealed himself as God must be judged irrelevant from the outset. And conversely, for one who already thinks he knows from another context—perhaps from a philosophical theology—that God is and what it means that *God* is (hence who he is), all talk about a revelation of the divinity of this God can only be of subordinate significance. In the supernaturalism of the Middle Ages and of orthodox Protestantism it was only ostensibly otherwise. More decisive for the salvation of man than the mere *existence* of God were his *will* and its revelation to man. But the enveloping of the supernatural doctrine of God by a philosophical, natural theology, together with the crisis which has arisen from this combination in modern times, has its ultimate cause in the fact that God's will cannot be conceived as something externally added to his existence. The problem of revelation has gained its fundamental significance for the knowledge of God only in a historical situation in which on the one hand it is no longer certain in some other way who God is and that he is, nor on the other hand has it been definitively decided that all talk about God is illusory, so that the mere question about a possible self-confirmation of divine reality would have become irrelevant. It is characteristic of our situation that this problem is still open on both sides. Because he has outgrown the cocoon of an authoritarian tradition and thus has become a question for himself, a question that points him beyond himself and beyond everything finite, man himself exists as *questioning* toward God. But one cannot simply deduce from the openness of the question that God exists. Indeed, even the claim that by his questioning concerning himself and the meaning of his existence and of everything that has being, man is questioning concerning *God*, can, strictly speaking, only be justified if the reality on which man turns out to be dependent in the openness of his questioning meets him personally and hence as "God."[2]

[2] Cf. my essay, "Die Frage nach Gott," *EvTh*, XXV (1965), 238–62, esp. 254 ff. That man is a "question" that finds its answer in the encountering reality of God does not signify a "theology of the religious *a priori*," as Hamilton claims (p. 178). The truth of religious experience—especially as experience of God—is not to be derived from man's structure as question, but from his *being met by* the reality that is experienced as the answer to the open question of his existence, and thus claims his ultimate confidence as the ground of his existence. That a *recognition* of the reality presupposed in man's self-transcending personal dependency comes to pass only through the *experience* of this reality itself as concrete meeting, I emphasized in *Was ist der Mensch? Die Anthropologie der Gegenwart im Lichte der Theologie* (Göttingen: Vandenhoeck und Ruprecht, 1962), p. 12. I also called attention in that essay to the character of personhood connected with such meeting that first makes it possible to call the reality thus experienced "God" (*ibid.*, p. 26; now more clearly in *EvTh*, XXV [1965], 259 ff.). H. Gollwitzer, too, is mistaken in thinking that I assert the personal character of the reality presupposed in the open dependency of human existence, different from all that is finite and manipulable, and thus the ground of our existence, through a "decree as to the alleged rational necessity of the personality of God" (cf. H. Gollwitzer, *Die Existenz Gottes im Bekenntnis des Glaubens* [Munich: Christian Kaiser Verlag, 1963, 3rd ed., 1964], p. 155, English translation of 3rd ed. by James W. Leitch, *The Existence of God as Confessed by Faith* [Philadelphia: Westminster Press, 1965], p. 193). To the contrary, I base it on man's being met by this reality. Of course, it is here that the question of human existence first finds its proper answer, since it is through the personality of the divine power encountering him that man is himself awakened to personhood. I have certainly not held it to be "a self-evident truth," as Hamilton insinuates (p. 179), that man is always an open question transcending everything finite. Rather I have established my claim in *Was ist der Mensch?* through considerations of the structure of the so-called "world-openness" of man, in which, along with anthropologists like M. Scheler, A. Gehlen, A. Portmann, M. Landmann, and others, I see the specific structure of human behavior summarized. Buss rightly notes that my view of this matter differs from that of Scheler. This is because I have generally followed A. Gehlen in describing the anthropological phenomenon. Against Scheler, Gehlen endeavors to exclude the mysterious assumption of a "spirit" wholly different from nature. For the

The question has thus been raised, whether a god exists as the reality that bears our existence, and if so, which god. One may now ask whether this question can be answered by a reference to revelation, so that some one religious tradition would be put forward as authoritative truth. Until the Enlightenment, Christian theology was doubtless a theology of revelation in this sense, appealing to revelation as a supernatural authority. The authoritative revelation was found in the "Word of God," i.e., in the inspired word of the Bible. As the product of the divine Spirit, this word was regarded in a strongly literal sense as the "Word of God." In the twentieth century the neo-orthodox theology of the Word no longer sought the "Word of God" primarily in the Bible. It was found rather in the event of Christian proclamation, in the kerygma (Bultmann), or else in Jesus' history, also interpreted as the "Word" of God, which as revelation is the origin both of the word of the Bible and the word of proclamation (Barth). In both cases the authoritarian character of the appeal to revelation remained untouched. But for men who live in the sphere in which the Enlightenment has become effective, authoritarian claims are no longer acceptable, in intellectual as little as in political life. All authoritarian claims are on principle subject to the suspicion that they clothe human thoughts and institutions with the splendor of divine majesty. Thus they are defenseless against the reproach of interchanging the divine and the human, and to the accusation of absolutizing what in truth is finite in content, with the result of subjugating all other men to those who represent this authority. On this point I am much more in accord than Hamilton seems to think with his positive valuation of the secular self-

---

justification of my interpretation in the sense of a "God-openness" of the phenomenon otherwise described as "world-openness"—in contrast to Gehlen, Landmann, or even Sartre—cf. *EvTh,* XXV (1965), 252 f., and already in *Was ist der Mensch?* (1962), pp. 10 f. One might have expected Hamilton to come into dialogue with my anthropological argumentation instead of simply imputing to me that I hold the God-relatedness of man to be "a self-evident truth." I know as well as Hamilton or anyone else that talk about God no longer is—or is not yet once again—taken by modern man to be self-evident truth.

understanding of the contemporary man who lives on the basis of the Enlightenment. I do not believe, to be sure, that the new coming of age of man (in Bonhoeffer's sense) grounded in the Enlightenment makes religion in every sense and all talk about God impossible or even merely superfluous. But it does make many forms of religion and faith in God incredible, certainly including all those which rest exclusively upon authoritarian claims to revelation and which exempt themselves from questions of critical rationality.

It was for this reason that I finally turned away from the "theology of the Word of God" in its different present-day forms; I was able to see in it only the modern expression of such an authoritarian theology of revelation. Therefore I cannot agree with the opinion of Grobel that "word" or "speech" corresponds in the Biblical writings with what can be meaningfully discussed today under the heading of a self-revelation of God.[3] It is certainly undeniable that authoritarian forms of tradition play a significant role in the Old and New Testaments. This could not possibly be otherwise in documents from a period in which the entire social and intellectual life was stamped by authoritarianism. It also belongs to the authoritarian features that the foundations of law and ethics were stylized and passed on traditionally as words of God, that the prophets received and presented their words directly as words of God, and that the early Christian apostles, such as Paul, proclaimed their message as the "Word of God," certainly in a more differentiated sense, but nonetheless with the claim to represent the authority of God himself to their hearers and readers.[4] Motifs of this kind determined the structure of Chris-

[3] Cf. above, pp. 158 f.

[4] The question of the theological meaning of the "word," or better, of "language," is certainly not settled with the critique of the authoritarian structure of the traditional—and in dialectical theology, current—appeal to be the divine word. But the positive meaning of language and word, to be adhered to by theology, will only be ascertainable through a decided rejection of the authoritarian features of the traditional understanding of the word. The efforts of G. Ebeling and E. Fuchs to develop a theology of the word event have doubtless accomplished an important step in the direction of an interpretation of "word" and "language" more strongly oriented toward the phenomenon itself, and thus brought about a miti-

tian tradition not only in the early and medieval church, but also in the Reformation churches up to the Enlightenment. One can see authoritarian features not only in the medieval understanding of episcopal and papal authority, but also in the positivism of the Reformation's *sola scriptura* and in the understanding of the proclamation of the Word in the churches of the Reformation. Since the Enlightenment, on the other hand, the question of the freedom of the spirit over against all merely "positive," i.e., established, authority has been posed—not only from the outside, but also as a demand of Christian faith itself. Man's recent coming of age must itself be recognized as a fruit of the Christian spirit. Hence one must ask whether the basic ingredients in the Biblical experience of God are not independent of the authoritarian features, which of course did not first of all appear in the later church tradition and proclamation, but already adhere to the Biblical texts themselves. Before any "demythologizing" is undertaken, it would seem reasonable for Christian theology to strip away the authoritarian forms of the premodern Christian tradition. Only after such *depositivization* would it be possible to determine the extent to which a "demythologization" would still be necessary, or whether the latter would not already be accomplished in the over-all task of the former. Perhaps in this way demythologization would reveal itself to be a program that has remained, on the one hand, too fainthearted because it did not include the authoritarian character of Christian tradition in its critique, and on the other hand, too undifferentiated with regard to the extremely heterogeneous contents of the Christian tradition. The immense task of translating and interpreting the actually-intended contents of the Christian tradition into the language and thought-forms of a period issuing from the Enlightenment was attacked at the start with

---

gation of the authoritarian understanding of the word once more stubbornly maintained by dialectical theology. It would be too much to say that it has already been overcome, however. Yet, perhaps even the talk of the "word of God," on the other hand, could be interpreted within an understanding of language freed from authoritarian features, in the direction of its phenomenal moment of truth.

a decided vehemence, the result of an all-too-simple separation between an allegedly mythical worldview and an allegedly detachable self-understanding, retainable without alteration. The insight into the artificiality of this separation does not nullify the task of translating the Christian message, however. This task must be continued on the basis of a depositivization of the Christian tradition.

The question concerning the revelation of God, as it has been reformulated on the basis of the Enlightenment,[5] is not seeking for some authoritarian court of appeal which suppresses critical questioning and individual judgment, but for a manifestation of divine reality which meets the test of man's matured understanding as such. For that reason I feel that the stress on the distinction between "hearing" and "seeing," as well as the preference for "hearing" above "seeing," is doubtful, even when it appeals to a Biblical understanding of the Word.[6] Insofar as in hearing, one is "entirely dependent on something happening outside his control,"[7] I can only understand such hearing to be a cipher for that abandonment of

[5] Whether following Locke or—exclusively as *self*-revelation—under the influence of German Idealism.

[6] Thus Grobel, pp. 158 ff. Cf. the similar argumentation of G. Klein reported by Robinson, p. 74. In his *Zukunft und Verheissung. Das Problem der Zukunft in der gegenwärtigen theologischen und philosophischen Diskussion* (Zürich/Stuttgart: Zwingli Verlag, 1965), pp. 221 ff., G. Sauter rightly criticizes this (also otherwise popular) antithesis of hearing and seeing, word and picture, as "an understanding of cognition that splits up reality." There remains to faith "only the 'no' to phenomena" (*ibid.*). To be sure, seeing is "in danger, because it is always an anticipatory act" (p. 222) and thus is subject to the temptation that it "already wants to grasp God in the world" (p. 224). The Christian promise does not check this danger by discrediting sight altogether, but by preparing "men for a seeing of the world which is looking out for that which it has not yet become . . ." (*ibid.*). The continuation of the sentence, "and should become, by virtue of the word that calls non-being into being," I of course cannot agree with, for reasons mentioned above, just as I am also frightened away by the features of an authoritarian and half-mythological concept of word in Sauter's understanding of promise. But the cited rejection of a dualism of hearing and seeing, of faith and reason, is especially noteworthy particularly in the case of a theologian of the word, and one would wish that Sauter himself had followed this direction throughout.

[7] Grobel (pp. 158 f.) appropriates positively for himself this characteristic of "hearing" intended by Jonas as discrediting.

one's own judgment which is required in submission to authoritarian claims. I confess that for similar reasons I mistrust the characterization of faith as "obedience" and by the same token also the celebrated prohibition against questioning behind the kerygma for its legitimation.

On the basis of the Enlightenment, the question of a revelation of God can only be asked in the sense of the self-manifestation of divine reality to human understanding. It is out of such a self-manifestation of divine reality that the Biblical writings of both the Old and New Testaments, as they understand themselves, actually seem to emerge. Such self-manifestation, furthermore, may have been much more fundamental for the Israelite and early Christian bearers of tradition than all the authoritarian features of their thought and of their ways of handing down tradition. Indeed, the self-manifestation of divine reality in a preauthoritarian sense was a central *theme* of Israelite and early Christian thought. Several different kinds of self-manifestation can be distinguished: Divine reality manifests itself in its most obvious form in the theophany of the deity, but also in the institutions and orders of life that legitimate themselves through such appearances or which appeal to prophetic inspiration.[8] Divine reality further

[8] Prophetic inspiration as a manner of human experience, which as such is still to be questioned as to its adequacy, does not become meaningless through a critique of its authoritarian claim. Rather, as a specific form of religious experience, it then first becomes accessible to impartial understanding at all. Such reduction of supernatural sayings of the tradition to their phenomenally exhibitable content forms the element of truth in K. Schwarzwäller's characterization of my theology as "phenomenological" (*Theologie oder Phänomenologie. Erwägungen zur Methodik theologischen Verstehens* [*Beiträge zur evangelischen Theologie,* 42; Munich: Christian Kaiser Verlag, 1966], pp. 90–118). But such a way of thinking which has compelled acceptance in modern thought above and beyond individual philosophical programs, does not specifically have anything to do with the phenomenological philosophy of Husserl or its development by Heidegger. Above all, I am not bound to the specifically phenomenological "bracketing" of the question of being-in-itself (Ansichsein) in the analysis of phenomena. Consequently, it does not hold true, as Schwarzwäller thinks, that I methodically neglect something standing "behind" the phenomena, or even—what a Husserlian would also dispute—that I would have to deny "apodictically something 'that stands behind the object' " (p. 92, cf. p. 106). However, whatever it is

manifests itself in the communication of the "name" of the deity. Finally, divine reality manifests itself in all events in which the believer experiences the action of the deity to whom he knows himself to be bound as helpful or destructive, and in which it is given to him—and to others as well—to "know" the greatness and uniqueness of the divine power.

I have intentionally chosen general categories from religious phenomenology for a provisional characterization of the Biblical experience of God.[9] The idea of a theophany of the deity, for example, as the starting point for a cult etiology, was shared by ancient Israel with her religious environment. The science of religion is accustomed to designate as "revelation" such a self-manifestation of divine reality in the ancient experience, as well as all forms of inspired communication. But such an imprecise use of language is not adequate for the problem of revelation in the philosophy of religion and in theology. For philosophy of religion and systematic theology, the question is that of a self-manifestation of divine reality, one which was not only experienced as such by men of earlier cultures at some time or another, but one which is capable of being convincing for our present-day understanding of existence as the deity's self-confirmation of his reality. Against all the deities *claimed* by the religions, the doubt is directed whether they can also be regarded by us as God, as the power

that stands behind the phenomena is certainly not simply to be identified with the supernatural claims of the theological tradition!

[9] Only a supernatural theology can single the God of Israel out of the history of religions from the outset as different from all other deities. For this reason the appearances of Yahweh that the Old Testament reports from early Israelite history must be understood as appearances of a numen, as the history of religion knows them elsewhere, in spite of the protest that Schwarzwäller raises to the contrary (pp. 98 f.). This does not exclude the possibility that this numen has proved itself in the further history of Israel and, through Jesus, also for non-Jews, to be the one true God, so that now in retrospect it can actually be said: even then, in Israel's origins, the one true God was at work—though not yet revealed as such. Schwarzwäller himself substantiates just this (pp. 141 ff.) in reference to the later identification of the "hitherto worshipped deities" of the individual tribes with Yahweh as the covenantal God of Israel after the merging of the tribes. This example is rightly to be assessed as of fundamental significance.

over everything.[10] But how, under such circumstances, can a deity claimed by others prove himself as God in the full sense, as the power over everything? For the individual it is a question of the personal experiences that make him disposed to trust "everything" to a particular deity claimed by others. For reflection at the level of generality it is a question of whether it is possible to *think* a deity claimed to be the power over everything. Both forms of the question can be oriented toward particular Biblical texts, indeed, even toward the same texts, since theological thought has to do precisely with reflection upon what is encountered in religious experience. It is explicitly stated in some Israelite texts that Yahweh will prove his divinity, for Israel and for all other people, through events which will show that the God of Israel is powerful over all things. In distinction from other forms of divine self-manifestation, this "word of demonstration" corresponds to the systematic-theological or, as the case may be, the religious-philosophical problem of revelation: whether an alleged deity is really God, i.e., powerful over all things, a matter that can only be demonstrated in the event in which, according to the assertion, he is supposed to be powerful. It can finally be demonstrated only in the totality of all events, insofar as what we mean by the word "God" is the power that is powerful over everything that has being. This is the reason why I have related none of the other traditionally-asserted forms of divine self-manifestation to the modern problem of revelation, but rather precisely this idea of the self-confirmation of God through his action. Other forms of self-manifestation are not able to convince us today of the divinity of what appeared at a time in the past; they can only be convincing for those who were the immediate recipients of such experiences. The

[10] In this the aspect of power should by no means be stressed at the expense of the love, justice, and wisdom of God and the salvation grounded therein. In Christian theology it can always be a matter only of the power (and therewith the divinity) of *the* God whose essence is revealed through Jesus as love. However, if this love were powerless, then it would not be God; and if it were only one power among others, then it would not be the one God from whom and to whom are all things and who alone can in all seriousness be called God.

thoughts of the Biblical writers moved in this direction, too, when they regarded all self-manifestations of God in epiphanies and even the communication of his name as something merely provisional, compared with the way in which the one who had so appeared and become namable was to make his divinity known in the future.[11] In that respect the question put by philosophy of religion and theology does not simply bypass the self-understanding of the Biblical text when, with its modern presuppositions, it searches in the history to which these texts refer for the answer to our modern question of revelation.

This is related to the issue of whether in the Biblical texts the idea of a self-revelation of God is to be found in the sense of a direct or only of an indirect self-manifestation. Like some of my German critics,[12] Grobel has endeavored to demon-

---

[11] Cf. in this connection my introductory essay, pp. 118 ff., also Robinson, pp. 42 ff., and on Exod. 3, esp. pp. 49 f. and 53 f. R. Rendtorff (*Offenbarung als Geschichte, KuD, Beiheft* 1 [Göttingen: Vandenhoeck und Ruprecht, 2nd ed., 1963], p. 25) notes that the conception of a *self-showing* of God was felt in later times to be inappropriate. This corresponds with the (direct) "appearance" of God that is spoken of in this text. In the Priestly Document this is replaced by Yahweh's making himself known from Moses on "as himself," as Rendtorff says (*ibid.*). But this does not occur through the isolated act of communicating his name, but rather through the future guidance of the God who from now on is known by name—through guidance that is announced with the formulalike motivation, "that you shall know that I am the Lord" (Exod. 6:7). The mere announcement of the name "Yahweh" does not yet reveal what this name comprises. P says this in Exod. 3 in referring to future events from which Israel will recognize what the name of Yahweh means concretely for this people. J. Moltmann, *Theologie der Hoffnung. Untersuchungen zur Begründung und zu den Konsequenzen einer christlichen Eschatologie (Beiträge zur evangelischen Theologie,* 38; Munich: Christian Kaiser Verlag, 1964), pp. 102 f. and 104, in agreement with Rendtorff's exegesis at this point, believes that the communication of the name may not be personalistically isolated, but must be taken together with the promise of future self-confirmations of Yahweh through his dealing. "The recognition 'I am the Lord,' and the recognition of his glory, which happens, are one and the same" (p. 104). To be sure, Moltmann has not been able to express this asserted unity through a unified concept of revelation, but has stopped with a "both-and" (p. 103). With regard to his critique of Rendtorff's (and my) conception of revelation history, cf. below.

[12] For example, recently F. Hesse, "Wolfhart Pannenberg und das Alte Testament," *Neue Zeitschrift für systematische Theologie,* VII (1965), 174–199, esp. 186 f. Hesse admits that the "self-confirmation" of Yahweh

(which he would like to distinguish terminologically from "self-disclo-sure," p. 195) as a rule "comes to pass in an event" (p. 198)—hence in any case indirectly, in my terminology. However, he also calls "revelation" the "self-disclosure" through which Yahweh unveils his "essence and his intentions with his appointed people" (p. 195). Now I do not dispute that Israel was always coming from events in which she had experienced self-manifestations of Yahweh—be it the "appearances" of the gods of the fathers, which were later understood as forms of appearance of Yah-weh, or be it the announcement of the name or of the will of Yahweh. At any rate I would not be able to see this right off as an unveiling of the "essence" of Yahweh. For unveiling of essence is something ultimate, and if one claims such for an event of divine self-manifestation witnessed to in the Old Testament, it becomes impossible to understand the God of Jesus as identical with the God of Israel, at least in a Christian the-ology that first ascribes finality to Jesus' message of God and not already to the Old Testament. Furthermore, at least for us as non-Israelites, the divinity of Yahweh is not convincing on the basis of those self-manifesta-tions attested to in the Old Testament. Many religions tell of appearances of deities and of the communication of the divine name—how will one decide from this that precisely the God of Israel is the true God? For this reason I limit the concept of *revelation* to the *self-confirmation* of Yahweh through his deeds, which were to prove his divinity to Israel and—according to Israelite expectation—also to the nations.

That Hesse finds direct self-revelation of Yahweh in the Old Testa-ment is connected with his broader definition of the concept of revelation. This is also evident in that he does not see the *uniqueness* of revelation given in its strict sense as self-revelation and can speak of a plurality of revelations (p. 185), instead of speaking of provisional anticipations of the one revelation that is still to come. With such divergent understand-ings of revelation, it is no wonder that Hesse and I arrive at different results. But at least he should not make that a charge against me! How broadly he confirms my interpretation substantially, can be seen in that as far as self-confirmation is concerned, he explicitly admits the thesis he so vehemently contests, i.e., that God will first be revealed at the end of history (p. 196, cf. 192 f.): The "revealing of God's doxa" remains "in many cases (sic!) still expected"; the Old Testament moves "toward the revealing of his doxa" (p. 196). But what I call revelation becomes thematic in the Old Testament just here, with self-confirmation. A deeper conflict in the matter results from Hesse's view that even the self-confir-mation of Yahweh is always in need "of the interpreting word" (p. 198). The category of interpretation already presupposes that abstract separa-tion between event and linguistically articulated understanding, which Hesse surely intends to exclude when he emphasizes (rightly) that the apprehension of an event as a deed of Yahweh's power always presupposes "what we might in the broadest sense describe as 'word' ": presupposed, namely, is that "event is not only event, also not an act of power of any deities whatsoever, but rather that Yahweh, their God, is at work for his people in such events" (p. 172). The category of "interpretation" is not helpful for the intention expressed here (with which I agree). This cate-gory implies as its corollary exactly that understanding of reality that Hesse would like to forestall, namely, that apart from appended interpre-tations, event would be "only event." Like others of my critics, Hesse does not seem to see that my (and also Rendtorff's) skepticism toward strate that the Biblical writings are aware of a direct as well as an indirect self-revelation of God. Now there is no question that particularly the Old Testament reports various direct self-manifestations of God. What is questionable is whether such self-manifestations as the theophany of Yahweh or the announcement of his name already have the strict character of self-*revelation,* in the sense of the manifestation of the divinity of God as the power over everything in a way that is at least virtually universally valid. The announcement of Yahweh's self-confirmation through his acts points to this latter understanding, however. In his discussion of the concept of self-unveiling, Grobel has nicely formulated—apparently without intending to—the manner in which self-revelation and indirectness belong together.[13] He wants to show that a person seldom simply reveals "himself"; instead, he ordinarily reveals his "kindness or cruelty, goodwill or spite, genuineness or sham, depth or shallowness."[14] All of these expressions refer to what the person does: ". . . his doing reveals the doer"—although the deed and the doer are not simply identical. In this sense God reveals his will, his life, his son,[15] and *in* all these he reveals himself. This is an excellent description of the indirectness of the self-revelation of God through his deeds, the exclusive validity of which Grobel had previously disputed.[16] Grobel even says expressly: "Revelation of self, within the inter-personal analogy, probably always (sic!) takes place through that which is not directly (sic!) identifiable with the self."[17] Precisely this is what my thesis of the indirectness of the self-revelation of God asserts. The reason for this Grobel himself indicates in the peculiar nature of the self—related to others and just therein wholly one with itself:

---

the call for the interpreting word does not arise from a preference for a positivistic concept of facts. Quite to the contrary, it arises from the insight that the concept of "interpretation" usually represents only the correlative complement of a positivistic conception of the "real."

[13] Cf. above, pp. 163 ff.
[14] *Ibid.,* p. 163.
[15] *Ibid.,* pp. 164 f.
[16] *Ibid.,* pp. 160 f.
[17] *Ibid.,* p. 166.

"Must we not say, that a person *can* only reveal himself by revealing something other than himself, something *about* himself, *pertaining* to himself, issuing *from* himself, but not identical with himself?"[18] In fact, this is the case, and for this reason the *self*-revelation of a *person* (but what besides a person could reveal itself?) can only be an indirect revelation.[19] Where a theophany or a self-presentation of the deity is represented as its self-revelation, the deity *in its appearance* is not yet understood to be a self that is different from its appearance! Only impersonal things may be directly identical with the sheer obviousness of their appearance—and perhaps not even they, insofar as they have an "essence" that remains distinguishable from their mere presence-at-hand. A person, a self, cannot be directly, but always only indirectly, identical with the physical appearance, the existential milieu, and the modes of behavior, in which he expresses himself.

When Grobel insists on speaking of a *direct* revelation, in spite of his insight that the revelation of a self is only possible through something that is "not directly identifiable with the self,"[20] then he is no longer talking about revelation in the same sense (as self-disclosure), but about the necessity of a divine illumination—as I would say—that bestows upon men the "willingness"[21] to recognize acts of God in particular historical events.[22] This kind of inspiration should by no means be disputed. But for this one does not have to think immediately of something supernatural, of a miracle in the psychic life. The phenomenon of inspiration is rather to be understood

18 *Ibid.*, p. 164.
19 Accordingly, all manifestation of the *will* of God—understood as the expression of his essence, of his self—always already contains a factor of indirectness. To reply to Cobb's considerations (pp. 208 ff.): Neither a statement about what God wills, nor the judgment, that a certain course of events is God's will—howsoever such talk might be substantiated—can designate a *direct* self-manifestation of God. For will always refers to a goal different from the one who wills and to that extent has the structure of indirect announcement described above, which characterizes all personal behavior.
20 Cf. above, pp. 160 ff.
21 *Ibid.*, p. 161.
22 *Ibid.*, p. 161.

in the broader context of imagination and its efficacy in all human thought and perception. Inspirations which we are accustomed to designating as impulses of imagination often open up to us for the first time an understanding of reality. But even if reasons could be cited why the spiritual life of the individual is admitted at just this point to that "dimension" to which the question of God refers,[23] such inspirations would not for that reason be a revelation (much less revelations) of God in the sense of self-revelation. This would not even be the case if they allowed a historical event to be seen as an act of God: the question remains whether one's inspirations are not deceptive. This can only be decided, in a concrete case, on the basis of the object to which they refer. But a single event cannot by itself reveal the power over all that is real—even if it is seen as an "act of God." On the contrary, it is rather only justifiable to speak of a single event as an act of God if the power over everything is already known in another way to be identical with God. The question can be discussed, whether an inspiration that allows someone to understand a particular happening as God's dealing is more than a religious self-deception, only if the divinity of God is already proven and evident as reality from another context. As true as it is that all cognition lives from intuition and from inspirations in the broadest sense, nevertheless, inspirations cannot *establish* why and by what right an event should be understood as an act of God, much less as a revelation of God. That would lead once again to an authoritarian claim of revelation. Inspiration is only genuinely illuminating if the true meaning of an object is to be grasped in its light from the thing itself, in contrast to so-called interpretations that are only externally tacked on to the thing that has been interpreted. In formal theological language, related to the central "object" of Christian theology, this means: the Spirit comes through the Son, and to the extent that the Word refers to this object by speaking of Jesus and his destiny, also through the Word.[24]

23 Cf. also *Was ist der Mensch?* (1962), pp. 21 f.
24 In emphasizing the relation of the word to its object, I am in agree-

In this way it must be shown whether various spirits and in-spirations are touched by the *Holy* Spirit, the spirit which causes the self-evidence of the history of Jesus to radiate. This is why I cannot agree with Grobel's formulation that the ex-perience of the facts "did not come *from* the fact, but was brought *to* it."[25] This formulation leaves untouched the cru-cial point that the true cognition of an object is not added externally to the object, but expresses its very essence,[26] and does so in such a way that it becomes demonstrable in the object itself: how else should it be its very essence?

Like Grobel, who misses in my thinking the idea of a direct revelation of God to the individual, somewhat in the sense of the *testimonium Spiritus Sancti internum,* Cobb is of the opin-ion that I direct "attention away from the question of God's immediate dealings with individuals."[27] Far be it from me to contest the immediacy of contingent divine activity in indi-viduals. Where this activity becomes the content of conscious-ness, certainly an immediate individual experience of God occurs. I would certainly want to add at once that such direct experience—like all consciousness—is itself mediated through the previous history of individuals within their environment, as well as through their relation to the future toward which their anxieties and hopes are directed. But above all, even when such a direct self-manifestation appears in the form of prophetic inspiration, I cannot attribute to it an autonomous status as revelation. For at least for contemporary critical re-flection, it must remain a question, even for one who himself has this kind of direct experiences, whether that which he has experienced is really *God*—or whether the word "God" might

ment with A. Wilder's presentation in *The New Hermeneutic* (*New Frontiers in Theology;* New York: Harper & Row, 1964), II, 198 ff., esp. 208 ff., "The Word as Address and Meaning."

[25] Cf. above, p. 161.

[26] It is a very difficult task to understand how it is possible for human words—even though they are spontaneous and freely formed—to express the essence of the objects with which we have to do. I will discuss this fully in my *Theologie der Vernunft* (*Theology of Reason*).

[27] Cf. above, p. 209.

not here be merely a conventional cipher, or one reproduced by personal necessity, for something, the actual reality of which should be described quite differently, perhaps in the sense of Feuerbach or Freud. Immediate religious experience cannot *by itself alone* establish the certainty of the truth of its content. At this point religious experience is in a totally different situation from sense experience, for instance. If one is at all justified in speaking of God as the power over everything, it is only in view of the *whole* of reality, and not of certain special experiences. On this basis, then, those direct experiences could certainly be confirmed, in some circumstances, as true. And at any rate they do belong to that entirety of reality that is at stake the moment we speak of "God." This is also true of the words of the prophets and of their special experiences connected with the reception of the Word. They participate in the history that is revealing the divinity of God. But they have the character of revelation not in and of themselves, but at most as the anticipation of the whole of reality, in the prophetic announcement of final judgment or salvation. Thus I agree with Cobb that the prophetic word and prophetic inspiration are certainly elements, indeed, very significant elements, in the whole of history, in the totality of which the divinity of God will reveal itself as the power over everything. To the extent that the prophetic word anticipates this whole by announcing final things, to that extent it is actually a proleptic revelation. But it is a revelation of God not as an isolated supernatural inspiration, but only by virtue of its relation to the entirety of all that occurs, since the divinity of God is determined by his power over *all* events.

My distinction between partial and complete revelation, to which Grobel has objected, is connected with this indispensable reference to the *totality* of all occurrence: If the God of Israel can be revealed as the power over *everything* and thus revealed in his *divinity* only in the totality of all events, but if on the other hand the course of history is not yet complete and all events are not yet gathered up in their totality, then the divinity of the God of Israel is, strictly speaking, not yet revealed but still hidden—assuming that sometime, at the end of all things, it will be clear to everyone. Single events can nevertheless anticipate the entirety of all events, in different modes of advance representation or of announcement, which is also a representation in advance. To this extent anticipatory revelations (or better: anticipations of the one revelation) of the power over everything are thinkable. Since these anticipations point forward only more or less clearly to the totality of all events and moreover are different from one another, although they also form elements of the whole of all occurrences in which God will be revealed as the power over everything, I have spoken of such a provisional, anticipatory revelation also as a "partial" revelation. Such partial revelation allows the divinity of God to appear only under a finite *aspect* in some one given case. Since revelation in the full sense has to do with the entirety of all occurrence, the concept of "part" lends itself for the characterization of these provisional anticipations of this revelation, especially in view of their plurality and their own one-sidedness that looks to other partial aspects for completion. Although the notion of "parts" may wrongly suggest a mechanical assemblage of the whole from such parts, and is inadequate to the dynamic character of the history of revelation, this expression should nevertheless not be rejected merely because of its quantitative character, as Grobel thinks. Only in the abstract can quantity and quality be so fully separated as the terminology of some theologians following Kierkegaard suggests.

The final, although still anticipatory, revelation of God in Jesus Christ is to be distinguished from the provisional and partial anticipations of revelation. The difference consists not only in the way in which a special event (comprising the ministry of Jesus and what happened to him) anticipates the end of all events and their completion, as I described this difference at one time. Above and beyond this, I now see the distinctiveness of the history of Jesus, which establishes its finality as the revelation of God, in the fact that it is itself the event uniting and reconciling all other events to the whole.[28]

## II

The theme of "history" is relevant for the question of the reality of God, to which the modern problem of revelation is related, insofar as history characterizes reality as a whole. If it does, then God is only really God, that is, the power over all things, if he shows himself to be the lord of history. Since a God who was not the lord of all things would not really be God, theology must strive to think of the God of Israel and of Jesus as the one who is lord of all things, and therefore in relation to the entirety of all reality—provided that it is theology's task to take the responsibility for speaking about God in critical thought. The divinity of God can only be conceived in relation to the whole of reality. Theology can only claim to have thought the thought "God" when everything that exists is conceived as from God or tending toward God, when, that is, the God of Israel and of Jesus of Nazareth is thought of as the creator of the world, and this quite concretely in view of everything that makes up the world in our contemporary knowledge of it. Even then theology will never have thought this thought through to the end.[29] Now if all

[28] This is described in greater detail in the concluding section of my *Grundzüge der Christologie* (Gerd Mohn: Gütersloher Verlaghaus, 2nd ed., 1966), pp. 379–430, in connection with the theme "Herrschaft Christi."

[29] Buss contests this (above, p. 137) when he stresses the inapplicability of our macroscopic conceptions of time and space to microphysical processes and, appealing to B. Russell, declares the question of a finite beginning of the known universe to be dependent on arbitrarily exchangeable systems of measurement. Nevertheless, I cannot think that the explanation of the red shift in the spectrum by reference to a finite beginning of the expansion of the known astronomical universe is solely arbitrary, and above all, Buss's argument that the law of entropy is not rigidly applicable because of its *statistical character* ("being statistical," p. 138) is quite unconvincing. With C. F. von Weizsäcker, *Die Geschichte der Natur* (Zürich: S. Hirzel Verlag, 2nd ed., 1954) [*The History of Nature* (Chicago: The University of Chicago Press, 1949), trans. by Fred D. Wieck from the 1st German edition], I accept not only the explanation of the red shift (Hubbel effect) by reference to a finite beginning of our uni-

reality, and not only the level of human life, is marked by historicality, then the divinity of God can only be thought of in relation to the whole of reality understood as history, and in this sense in relation to universal history. This is so in spite of the fact that the whole of history is not present as complete, but is incomplete, directed toward an open future. And only if the whole of all reality is history can one speak meaningfully of a revelation of the divinity of God as a particular event in relation to this whole. For if reality as a whole were cosmos, timeless order, then the divinity of God (if it is not a fiction) would have to be already manifest in it. That was, of course, the basic conviction of ancient Greek piety.

Any discussion of the whole of reality sounds dubious to many, and presumptuous in view of the finiteness of human knowledge. There is no doubt that no one can know or survey the whole of all reality. That is impossible not only because of the finiteness of human knowledge, but also because of the historicality of reality. As long as the future brings something new, reality is not yet complete even in its existence. Nevertheless it is indispensable to *think* of the whole of reality, and everyone does so, even if for the most part in an unreflective way. The anticipation of the whole cannot be evaded, for the reason that the individual entity is not really any more easily available than the whole. Each individual entity has its meaning only in relation to the whole to which it belongs. Therefore we can attain only provisional knowledge, which is subject to constant revision, both of the individual entity and of the whole.

Because every individual entity has meaning only in relation to a greater whole, universal history in the sense of the total meaning of all history is an inescapable theme of histor-

---

verse, but also the general validity of the law of entropy. The irreversibility of time, and to that extent also the "historicality" of time, is thereby given for all physical processes. Perhaps the irreversibility of time becomes intelligible on the basis of the contingency characterizing all physical occurrence, since every contingent event clearly defines a before and after, insofar as it—as contingent—entails something new with respect to everything previous.

ical work. Buss doubts that historians have linked this meaning of universality to the concept of universal history.[30] To this one can reply that, e.g., Dilthey, in his effort to sum up the principles of historicism, recognized the relation of part to whole as constitutive for the category of meaning which is fundamental for historical thought, and therefore he conceived "universal history" or world history as the highest task of historical writing.[31] Ernst Troeltsch thought the same.[32] Wolfgang Mommsen has recently defined "universal history in the narrower sense" as "the attempt to secure an overall view of the whole process of history from the beginning of human

[30] Cf. above, p. 136.

[31] Cf. W. Dilthey, *Gesammelte Schriften,* VII (Leipzig and Berlin: B. G. Tuebner, 1927), 233: "The category of meaning denotes the relation, grounded in the nature of life itself, of parts of life to the whole." Similarly, *ibid.,* pp. 238 f. H. G. Gadamer sees in this the application of a principle that has passed from the hermeneutical tradition into historicism, which, for example, is also detectable in Schleiermacher's hermeneutic (*Wahrheit und Methode. Grundzüge einer philosophischen Hermeneutik* (Tübingen: J.C.B. Mohr, 1960), pp. 178 f., p. 186). In this way of thinking, according to Gadamer, there can be for Dilthey "at bottom no other history than universal history . . . since a single thing is defined in its individual significance only in relation to the whole" p. 187). Cf. in this connection Dilthey, *Ges. Schriften,* VII, 257 f. and 233; and also J. G. Droysen, *Historik. Vorlesungen über Enzyklopädie und Methodologie der Geschichte* (Darmstadt: Wissenschaftliche Buchgesellschaft, ed. by R. Hubner, 1937, 3rd ed. 1958), pp. 306 f., further his *Grundriss der Historik, [Outline of the Principles of History* (Boston: Ginn and Company, 1893)], Sec. 74, p. 354.

[32] Troeltsch's fundamental concept of development (Entwicklung), particularly in his earlier works, is always related to the idea of a general unity of all history (cf. E. Lessing, *Die Geschichtsphilosophie Ernst Troeltschs* [*Theologische Forschung,* 30; Hamburg-Bergstedt: Herbert Reich, Evangelischer Verlag, 1965], pp. 27 ff. and 139). In his *Die Absolutheit des Christentums und die Religionsgeschichte* (Tübingen: J.C.B. Mohr [Paul Siebeck], 1902), Troeltsch writes that modern history strives to unite all phenomena "in a total picture of the continuous becoming of humanity, in which all individual phenomena condition each other reciprocally" (2nd ed., 1912, pp. 3 f.). This happens precisely through "developmental history" (*ibid.*). Such a "total picture" (p. 4) of the "entire history of humanity" (p. 6) Troeltsch designates as the "presupposition of all judgments about norms and ideals of humanity" (p. 3). Quite in accord with Dilthey is the similar statement on p. 57 that from individual formations "the view is opened to a broader context and therewith finally to the whole, so that only their synopsis in the whole makes a valuation and a judgment possible."

culture."[33] He speaks further of "the practical impossibility of actually grasping the totality of the historical world, and of the theoretical difficulty of finding a universal standing point, which would honestly permit one to recast the profusion of facts into a history of the whole of mankind."[34] Hence every "attempt at a concrete realization of a universal history must . . . today, more than ever, remain fragmentary." But as a "guiding principle," the "principle of universal history is today more timely than ever before."[35] And even the Göttingen historian Reinhard Wittram, who in discussion with me affirmed that it was impossible that "the 'whole of history' should be reconstructed by research,"[36] nevertheless holds that the unity of history (as world history, or human history) is the "presupposition" without which we "can scarcely any longer think historically."[37] He even admits, "perhaps we have made it too easy for ourselves, in that we have lost the relationship to world history from consciousness and have left secularized designs in possession of the field."[38]

Today there is widespread consent to the view that the specific consciousness of universal history has its origin in the Jewish and Christian theology of history. Thus Mommsen affirms that the intention of universal history in a Thucydides or a Herodotus lay in the "presentation of concrete events as exemplary," and not in the comprehension and interpretation

---

[33] Mommsen, "Universalgeschichte" in: *Fischer-Lexikon* No. 24: Geschichte (Frankfurt: Fischer Bücherei, ed. by W. Besson, 1961), 322–332, esp. 328.

[34] *Ibid.*, p. 331.

[35] *Ibid.*

[36] Wittram, "Die Verantwortung des evangelischen Historikers in der Gegenwart," in *Im Lichte der Reformation (Jahrbuch des Evangelischen Bundes,* Bd. 5) (Göttingen: 1962), pp. 26–43, quotation from p. 40. In the meantime, in a lecture on "Möglichkeiten und Grenzen der Geschichtswissenschaft in der Gegenwart" (*ZThK*, LXII [1965], 43–57), Wittram supported the view that precisely the Christian conviction that "God makes history" makes any "total interpretation superfluous" (p. 455). But then the question remains how one arrives at the conviction that God makes history, and whether such a "total interpretation" is not already implied in this.

[37] *Ibid.*, p. 39.

[38] *Ibid.*, p. 40.

the denial of any distinction in principle between sacred and profane history has for my understanding of history.[47] He agrees with my related proposition that Christian faith cannot retreat to some sheltered area where it would be immune from historical criticism.[48] In fact I quite concur with Hamilton's

"Every time a new event supervenes, the whole perspective is altered in its light, including the relation to the still outstanding final event" (p. 104). In this sense, in the interrelationship between event and interpretation Cullmann ascribes "a certain primacy" to the event (p. 117, cf. p. 79). These observations of Cullmann come into close contact with my conception of the transformations that take place in the history of the transmission of traditions, which continually arise from new experiences. Here, too, belongs the "inclusion," emphatically worked out by Cullmann, of the bearer of tradition into the series of events which he interprets and passes on in his interpretation (pp. 97 ff.). But in my opinion there is an unresolvable tension between this description of the process of interpretation from the point of view of a certain "primacy of the event," and the already-mentioned thesis that the special character of *heilsgeschichtlich* events is constituted by the fact that certain events are experienced and interpreted as divine revelation (p. 133). Does this not mean that *this* interpretation of the events does not come from the events or from further, new events, but is added to them as a supplement? If the event is "already revelation *as such*" only "for the believer" (p. 133 n. 1), does not the interpretation brought by the believer, of certain events as revelation of God, effect their isolation into *Heilsgeschichte* by separating them off from all other events? Therein would consist the difference between Cullmann's and my conception of the theology of history, that with Cullmann—in contrast to his general definition of the relation between event and interpretation, in which I can concur—a supplementary added interpretation is constitutive for the quality of an event as a salvation event and thus for the isolation from profane history of a qualitatively unique *Heilsgeschichte*. In my view of things every interpretation of an event must be justified from the context in which it was experienced and from the context of new experiences which call forth new interpretations. Of course the implications of such experience have to be considered, namely, that as linguistically articulated it has anticipated a whole of reality (cf. above in text, pp. 242 ff.). Only in this way is a speaking of finite events as divine acts possible, and indeed not in a supernatural one, but in a phenomenological one, namely, as an understanding description of the manner in which religious language in general (and not the specifically Christian or Israelite language) can come to make that kind of assertion. The special character of the Israelite and Christian appeal to God's action in historical events and to its "truth" over against analogous assertions of other religions raises further problems, which can be clarified in the context of the comparative history of religion, just as the case with respect to the special character and the truth of the Israelite and Christian faith in God in general.

[Cf.] above, p. 177.
[O]n the question of the "certainty" of faith in regard to definite see below, pp. 272 ff.

of the whole of "the historical process in its spatial and temporal totality." It was Christianity that first offered "the interpretation of world-history as a dynamic process that was unique and unrepeatable."[39] This observation should be supplemented by reference to the Israelite roots of this understanding of the world as a unique and unrepeatable process. Israelite thought is thereby characteristically distinguished from other sorts of understanding of history, not only those of the Greeks, but also from the spirit of the historiography of the Ancient Near East. In this situation it is strange that Buss ascribes a negative attitude toward history to Israel and even more decisively to the Christians.[40] This judgment is made only partly comprehensible by the fact that Buss understands "history" as completely secular, more in dependence on the humanistic historiography of ancient Greece than on the Biblical understanding of history.[41] He classifies the latter, with its interest in "beginning" and "end," as mythical.[42] By doing this he brings a dualism into the historical thought of the Old Testament that is completely foreign to it, in spite of its knowledge of the wanton antagonism of man against God. When Buss holds that the Old Testament links what he calls myth to historical event only "because God is pictured as battling against man,"[43] he overlooks the foundation of Israelite historical writing in the ideas of election and covenant, as well as in concrete promises of Yahweh. A dualistic relationship to the world can be ascribed even to apocalyptic thought with its "progressively downward" view of history,[44] only if apocalyptic is interpreted from Persian dualism and not from

[39] "Universalgeschichte," *Fischer-Lexicon* No. 24, p. 324. Cf. in this connection especially K. Löwith, *Meaning in History* (Chicago: University of Chicago, 1949), above all his remarks on pp. 18 f. and 6 ff. with regard to Greek historiography (published later in German as *Weltgeschichte und Heilsgeschehen* [Stuttgart: W. Kohlhammer Verlag, 1953], cf. pp. 25 f. and 14 ff.).
[40] Cf. above, Buss, *passim,* especially pp. 145 f., 150.
[41] *Ibid.*, p. 136.
[42] *Ibid.*, pp. 139 f., 144.
[43] *Ibid.*, p. 144.
[44] *Ibid.*, p. 146.

Old Testament historical thought. The dualistic opposition which Buss affirms between God and world, between God and human history, is suspiciously similar to Manichaeism and Marcionite gnosis, in its contradiction to the Christian faith in the creation and reconciliation of the world, *this* world in the course of its historical time.[45]

---

[45] Although Buss sees God struggling against man and history already in the Old Testament, in order to create a "new mythical period" (p. 145)—"The chaotic dragon that has been slain is human history itself"—it remained for Christianity, under the sign of the cross, to alienate man completely from himself and from the world of objects, and thus to break even more thoroughly with history (p. 150). How unhistorical this way of thinking is becomes clear when Buss can compare Christianity with Buddhism in its negative attitude toward history and then appraise the similarity to be greater with the latter than with the Old Testament (p. 151, cf. p. 142). But the Old Testament thereby becomes the analogue of Hinduism, thus strangely contradicting Buss's tendency to point already in the Old Testament to a negative valuation of man and history. Buss would like to make the influence of wisdom responsible for the attention to matter-of-fact occurrences in Israelite historiography (pp. 148 f.). Indeed, the influence of wisdom thought on the Yahwist, for instance, and on the narration of the succession to David's throne, has long been accepted. But only he who with Buss could judge the prediction of future events by the prophets as unessential for the understanding of prophecy (pp. 147 f.), would be able to deny that the understanding of actual events as acts of God has its basis at least as much in prophecy as in wisdom. Understandably, Buss has particular difficulties in this connection with the cognition formula (p. 149), which even he must assign to prophetic and priestly but in any case not to wisdom traditions. His assertion of its origin *first in the time of the Exile* (p. 149) lacks persuasive power, not only in view of 1 Kings 20, but above all in view of the Yahwistic examples in Ex. 7:17, 8:18, 10:2; cf. also 8:6 and 9:14. The further claim that a self-presentation formula of priestly origin has here been combined with the term "knowledge" not only passes over Rendtorff's thesis (against Zimmerli) of the primitiveness of the longer as opposed to the shorter formula without discussion. It must also leave open the question *why* the prophets who used the cognition formula combined the term "knowledge" with the allegedly primary self-presentation, "I am the Lord," and expected this recognition from an occurrence that they had predicted. Buss seems to suggest that it is here a secondary wisdom interpretation that first records a cognition of God out of events of history (pp. 149 f.). But in view of such a combination of self-presentation, knowledge of Yahweh, and future occurrence, executed in the prophetic circles of the Exile, this would really be incredible. What meaning other than a cognition of God from events of history is such a combination likely to have had originally? Hence attributing the positive theological appropriation of historical events exclusively to wisdom traditions of Israel, in contrast to prophecy, remains a false track. It is even more astonishing when Buss wants to exclude all wisdom elements from the teaching of Jesus (pp. 150 f.)—as if the great influence of wisdom motifs on the para-

---

The dualism between Biblical myth (including historic myth) and history which Buss advocates seems to me to an extreme form of the antithesis which is much more quently encountered between *Heilsgeschichte* and profane tory.[46] Hamilton has rightly emphasized the importance w

---

bles and on the language of the oldest strata of the synoptic traditio not long since found general recognition in critical research.

[46] The difference between *Heilsgeschichte* and profane history i most emphatically stressed by Oscar Cullmann (*Heil als Ges Heilsgeschichtliche Existenz im Neuen Testament* [Tübingen: Mohr (Paul Siebeck), 1965], pp. 58 ff., 133 ff.). Yet Cullmann excludes a complete dualism by the fact that the goal of the *Heilsgeschichte,* the "salvation of all mankind," establishes outset an "inner bond between *Heilsgeschichte* and history" While *Heilsgeschichte* forms only "a very narrow line" of ever for this purpose by God, it tends toward a "flowing of all h this line," into an "absorption of profane history into *Heilsges* 146)." One must concede to this conception that the events reported by the Biblical writings as decisive acts of God pr took place strikingly off the main highroad of world history and succession of the great powers, although according to and Christian conviction their import reached to all mankir less, the exclusion in principle of this series of events fro history, which Cullmann has effected, is questionable, for appearance that these events were different from others no historical peculiarity, but also qualitatively different in physical sense. A qualitative difference of *heilsgeschichtli* other events cannot be adequately established by the s Biblical presentation of history of such events which w the main line of historical occurrence (pp. 58 f., 134 ff.) is clearer that these events—and according to Cullmann experienced as divine revelation" and that the account as their interpretation are traced back to divine revelati thus established qualitative peculiarity of *heilsgeschich* expression especially forcefully in Cullmann's thesis t currence" also belongs to *Heilsgeschichte;* it is "analog withdrawn from any historical testing" (p. 123). It is cile this affirmation with the explanation found a few the myths (exclusively?) contribute to "the *interpr geschichtlich relationship* of the separate events of If the myths only supply categories of interpretation establish the persuasive power of the nonhistorical e may mean) which go beyond the historical whose i to mediate? Cullmann's concept of interpretation ties, especially confusing for me because in Culln not "paid enough attention to the distinction bet pretation effected by the Spirit" (p. 40, cf. p. 1 Cullmann has emphasized that the interpretatio seen "in connection with new events" (p. 40), v interpretations and at the same time are taken up

concern that the Christian faith must be engaged with the reality in which the "secular" man lives—otherwise the Christian message will be irrelevant to our time. On the other hand Hamilton criticizes me for understanding this secular reality "theonomously," and not leaving it as secular.[49] This statement is right in a certain sense, but not in the sense that I want to transform the modern experience of reality, and in particular the modern understanding of history, back into the medieval mode of thinking, as Hamilton assumes.[50] In the most varied areas of life, medieval thought took its departure from authority, while modern man intends to judge for himself. By distancing myself from any authoritarian mode of thought, especially in theology, I move rather on the plane of modern thought. It is in its criticism of the "positivism" of the authority principle that I see what is valid in so-called "secularism."[51]

But, as the example of a John Locke already shows, orientation toward the reality which is available to everyone and obligation to make one's own judgment in intellectual honesty do not necessarily mean renouncing every positive relation-

[49] Hamilton, above, pp. 186 f.

[50] *Ibid.*, pp. 186 f.

[51] Friedrich Gogarten has distinguished the "secularism" which turns itself against the Christian gospel from the "secularizing" of the world which was made possible by this gospel and partly brought about by it (Gogarten, *Verhängnis und Hoffnung der Neuzeit: Die Säkularisierung als theologisches Problem* [Stuttgart: Friedrich Vorwerk Verlag, 1953, 2nd ed. 1958], esp. pp. 134 ff.). In the critique of authority by the Enlightenment there lies a motif and an element of truth even of the so-called secularism in its sharp attack upon the Christian tradition. The emancipation from the authoritarian structure of premodern forms of Christian tradition does not at all need to have as its consequence a break with the real content of Christian tradition. In this sense secularity can mean precisely the understanding appropriation of the Christian tradition by a society which has come of age, in contrast to a formally respected sacral authority, which stood over against the society of "laymen" and was administered by priests and theologians. Hamilton's sentence, "secularism for Pannenberg is rather like sin for Barth" (p. 180), in any case does not get the point of my conception. Hamilton could have attained a more balanced opinion by reading the article by T. Rendtorff, "Säkularisierung als theologisches Problem," *NZsystTh,* IV (1962), 318–339. See now also H. Lubbe, *"Säkularisierung. Geschichte eines ideenpolitischen Begriffs* (Freiberg/Munich: Alber, 1965), esp. pp. 112 ff.

ship with Christian tradition and with a "theonomous" understanding of reality. For the contemporary period, the example of Paul Tillich should be proof enough that the endeavor to achieve a "theonomous" understanding of reality does not have to be reactionary. Further, a theonomous understanding of reality does not have to mean that "the world of finiteness already contains God."[52] Theology of history does not in any case, in my view, mean any such "identification of God with the process of history itself."[53] The very historicality of all that is real means rather that the power working in events in every moment separates what is actual (as the finite) from itself, casts it off from itself, in that it passes on to the bringing forth of new, hitherto not present, events.[54] Thus: the transcendence of God is not to be understood as a lifeless beyondness, but as a living, ever new carrying out of his freedom, and thus as the making possible of future, life, new event in the world. In his critique, Hamilton agrees at this point with Buss, who likewise thinks that I localize the infinite "in time and space" and have no "vision of the transcendent,"[55] so that I supposedly do not see the religious meaning of human surrender in God. Correspondingly Ham-

[52] Cf. above, p. 180.
[53] *Ibid.*, p. 185.
[54] Further in my article, "Der Gott der Hoffnung," in *Ernst Bloch zu ehren* (*Festschrift* for Ernst Bloch; Frankfurt: Suhrkamp Verlag, 1965), pp. 209–225, esp. p. 219. The ideas of this article come in contact with the thesis of Thomas J. J. Altizer, *The Gospel of Christian Atheism* (Philadelphia: Westminster Press, 1966), pp. 18, 82 f., 105 ff., that today Christian theology has to speak of God in relation to the future, and not in relation to the primordial past of myth, or to the timeless present of metaphysics. To be sure, it seems to me that in the manner in which Altizer himself proceeds to speak about God, the break with the traditional problems of the philosophical doctrine of God is less complete than his passionate denial of the God of theism would lead one to suspect. That is shown by Altizer's positive evaluation of Hegel and of Hegel's concept of the truly infinite. On the other hand, in Altizer's discussion of the death of God in conjunction with the theme of incarnation and of a kenotic Christology, I can find only an intellectually indefensible mythological imagery: a "God" who (in contrast to Hegel's) has definitively died and thus been done away with, was never God in earnest, and to speak of his "incarnation" amounts to a mere literary-aesthetic reminiscence.
[55] Cf. above, pp. 153 f.

ilton misses in my thought the sense of the "mysterium" of the incarnation,[56] and thinks that by faith I mean the discovery of what is already actual.[57] That is obviously a misunderstanding of the unity of revelation and history which I assert, and even a misunderstanding of my concept of history. The transcendence (or incommensurability) of the infinite over against the finite forms the theme of my writings on the idea of the analogy between God and the world. The thesis of analogy appeared suspicious to me precisely as an infringement of God's transcendence. This point of view has not been lost from sight in my theology of history: far rather it was developed as an alternative to the classical determination of the relationship between God and the world as it is worked out in the doctrine of analogy. The relation between the finite and the infinite is always, even in the case of Jesus, mediated negatively.[58] In this way I take up the element of truth in such a dualistic conception as that represented in extreme form by Buss. The very negativity fulfills itself nevertheless in history itself, and indeed as history, viz., in the collapse and in the transformation of all institutions and forms of political life as well as of individuals. History is not the field of a finitude which is enclosed within itself, an "immanence" to which one could and indeed would have to oppose a "transcendence."[59]

[56] Cf. above, p. 195.
[57] *Ibid.*, p. 180.
[58] Cf. *Grundzüge der Christologie*, 2nd ed. (1966), pp. 346 ff., for a description of the unity of Jesus with God as an *indirect* or *dialectical* identity.
[59] Thus K. Schwarzwäller, *Theologie oder Phänomenologie* (1966), p. 102 n. 315, calls my method of grounding theological affirmations in the historical phenomena and the meaning which is given to them "completely immanental and correspondingly relativistic" (p. 114), corresponding to the phenomenological "dogma of exclusive immanence" (cf. pp. 18 and 25 f., 40, etc.). But "exclusive immanence" is a contradiction in terms, which is shown by the fact that immanence generally is conceivable only as a correlate of transcendence, and vice versa. Only inconsistent thinking can isolate one of these definitions from the other, as if it were meaningful in itself. The same is to be said against Altizer, who, in somewhat the sense of the conception which is attributed to me by Schwarzwäller, expressly rejects the transcendent God (to which concept Schwarzwäller appeals against me), and affirms the immanence of God (*The Gospel of Christian Atheism*, p. 151, cf. pp. 73, 42, 86, etc.). But

History is far rather the ongoing collapse of the existing reality
which is enclosed in its own "immanence" (because centered
on itself). The power of the infinite is active and present in
this collapse of the finite. Thus the infinite expresses itself in
the first place negatively. But because the finite lives not by
clinging to itself, but only in transformation of itself—in contradiction of itself, and of its tendency to cling to itself—
insofar the power of the infinite expresses itself also positively,
as reconciliation and preservation of the finite in the midst of
its collapse. If one regards history only as the sum of the self-
contained finite, and understands it in this way as the total
panorama of human deeds and sufferings, then it really becomes incomprehensible how it can be said of history that
God is revealed in it. Can the finite disclose the infinite? Is
it not the case that asserting such a capacity of revelation
obscures the sovereignty of God? Such questions arise.[60] But
what sort of conception of history is this? Surely the men of
whose acting and suffering history is full are finite beings.
Likewise all human creations are finite. But history is not
finite in this sense. Rather, it accomplishes the crisis of the
finite throughout time. Hence man shows himself to be finite
in his history. History is not merely the history of his *deeds*,
for in that case the doer would not himself have a history.
Rather, his own history happens to the doer—of course not
only as an external happening but in large measure in such
a way that his own action reflects back on him. Both aspects
show his finitude, and form him in his individuality as this

___

such a position cannot be held consistently. It falls to the ground from
its inner contradictions for the person who tries to hold it, for the reasons
suggested above. Transcendence can only be explained in relation to immanence and vice versa.

[60] The thesis of *Offenbarung als Geschichte* is misunderstood in this
way by J. Moltmann, in that he reads into it an untheological concept
of history, one which is not constituted by God's action and therefore
can be opposed to the latter. Moltmann says, in reference to R. Rendtorff, "Here history not only has an assisting function for the personal
encounter with God, but history 'itself' reveals" (*Theologie der Hoffnung*
[1964], p. 104, similarly pp. 100 and 254). As if the finite, that which is
brought forth by God's action, could at the same time be something in
itself, independent of him over against God's action!

particular finite being. Such finitude, however, has nothing to do with an immanence which is at rest within itself, which can thus only be thought of as for itself alone. It is rather the opposite of this. The man who acts and suffers historically is not understandable in isolation in his finitude and also is not left to himself, because the finite does not exist in and of itself. It is constitutive of the concept of finitude that in spite of all its efforts at self-assertion, finitude nevertheless does not exist or subsist of and through itself. Therefore there takes place in the action and suffering of man not only his relation to other finitude, but simultaneously his relation to the infinite reality of God—as threat and as protection, as transformation, as rise and fall, as judgment and as a reconciliation in the midst of the pain of failure. To this extent the very concept of history, precisely as human and profane history, is constituted by the presence of the infinite in the midst of the finite, and in this sense by "God's action." History is not initially conceivable as complete in itself, as the sum of human finitude, as if God's action in history then were added somehow "vertically from above." So conceived, any talk of God's action in history would be superfluous; there would be no further occasion for it, if everything that happened were comprehensible without it. In truth the history of a finite being means in every way its crisis, and self-assertion, failure, and transforming preservation are aspects of such crisis and overcoming of the finite. Only because the infinite reality, which as personal can be called God, is present and active in the history of the finite, can one speak of a revelation of God in history. For it is thereby concretely shown that the finite is not left to itself. Hence it is misleading to say that history reveals God. For history is not a subject which subsists independently over against God. In its very idea, history is constituted by the active presence of the infinite God, and therefore one can only say that God reveals himself in history. At any rate he reveals *his divinity* through history, by showing himself to be the power over everything finite which enters into history—both by the splendor that shines upon the finite and yet is not comprehensible from its mere finiteness, and by the perishing of the finite, which is not a mere decline. In addition, revelation means that God joins himself to the finite. This was first conceivable, as the meaning of the concept of the truly infinite, through the Christian idea of the incarnation, which originated in the experience of the anticipation of the eschaton in the history of Jesus. It is only from this point of origin that it becomes clear *how*, in his revelation of himself through history, God joins himself to the finite, namely, through the future of his rule proclaimed by Jesus. Thus converge the most general meaning of the self-revelation of God (grounded in the general concept of history), and the special meaning, made possible only from the history of Jesus. One should reflect on the fact that the general meaning can be asserted only from the special factor of the anticipation of the eschaton in Jesus' history, because only through that event did history become present reality as a whole and thus as revelation of the divinity of God. Further, the idea is erroneous that God is known by means of an "inference" from history.[61] At least it is erroneous insofar as it suggests that history

[61] This idea is ascribed to me by J. Moltmann (*ibid.*, pp. 68 f.); similarly by Robinson, pp. 89 ff., and indeed in the sense of an eschatologizing transformation of the cosmological proof of the existence of God. While Moltmann elsewhere presupposes in my thought a self-sufficiency of the relevatory history over against God, here on the contrary he protests against the "unresolved union of God with history" (*Theologie der Hoffnung*, p. 68, n. 98), which first makes the "inference-procedure" possible. In these contradictory statements Moltmann presupposes an understanding of history that does not correspond to mine in either case. In fact, I cannot think of the whole of history without God, but its totality is not available, but rather a matter of the eschatological future. Only individual historical events and finite relations between occurrences are available in the present. I do at most recognize an "unresolved union" of the individual historical events with God in the sense that such events do not exist by themselves in their finitude, nor can they be wholly grounded in or comprehensible by their relationships to other finite entities. In this negativity of their finitude they point to "God" as their origin and their truth. But on account of the contingency of the individual events, which is constitutive of the concept of history, and in which the freedom of their divine origin comes to expression, it is nevertheless not possible to infer the original cause (or creator) by analogy from the events as effects. I presented this critique of the "procedure of inference" of Greek natural theology and of the doctrine of analogy between God and the world as early as 1959 (*Zeitschrift für Kirchengeschichte*, LXX

could be conceived as the sum of its finite parts, and from these one could infer back to God as the originator of this totality. This crude model overlooks what historical occurrence really means, namely, that in every individual event of history the crisis of the finite element which is effected by it is accomplished, as shown above. Thus in every individual event, but in each in its own particular way, the infinite power which as personal may be called God, is already at work. This power is not first discovered upon reflection by means of an inference, which could equally well be ignored. As infinite power it makes itself immediately perceptible to men, because neither threat nor preservation points merely to some other finite being, which would not be capable of such effects by its own power. They are the occurrence of the power of being, to which man is related at least in the manner of lack of being (Sartre) and in the open question of what he is dependent on in order to be.

The idea that the power over all things, the infinite God,

---

[1959], 28 f., 37 f.). Therefore I cannot repress a certain mild surprise when I see my own assertions interpreted, without close inspection, in this sense which I have rejected. Moltmann himself in a later context touches on the salient point of the problem, namely that, corresponding to the freedom of God, the "still open and therefore (!) historical reality" of the world and of man "is not yet 'whole,' but its wholeness is rather at stake" (*Theologie der Hoffnung*, p. 255). That is also my view. When Moltmann affirms: "Therefore it would be better to relinquish the intentions of the cosmological proof," (*ibid.*), this advice applies less to me—since I have separated myself from this intention— than rather to the interpretation which Moltmann attributes to me. Further, this dispute should not cause us to forget that all thought, insofar as it combines propositions, moves in inferences. It would lead to a laughable self-deception if one tried to exclude reasoning from knowledge of God altogether. And as far as the inference is concerned, the "recognition of the identity of God from promise to fulfillment," which Moltmann (*ibid.*, p. 104) "opposes to the inference from the effect to the cause," this itself has the same logical structure as an inference. A mere opposition between recognition and inference can hardly be affirmed without inconsistency, even if it is not a question of the same thing in both cases. It cannot be a matter of contention whether or not reasoning may or may not *have a share* in knowledge of God, but only whether in a historically open reality, knowledge of God can be brought to a conclusion by reasoning. Only in the sense of such a claim to totality or adequacy can the inferential method in ancient Greek philosophy be meaningfully contested.

is present in an event which will soon be overtaken by other events and revised by them so far as the relevance of its content is concerned, always reaches beyond the isolated event. That is not a unique situation, in view of the relation between fact and meaning. Every experience, as it finds its precipitation in language, in word, has already reached beyond the particular occasion with which it began. In this way historical experience and language belong together. The word, which reaches beyond the particular event in selection and in anticipation, also says that—and how—God, the power over all things, is present in the individual event. The word can be corrected by further events, which in a similar way give occasion for experiences that reach beyond themselves, precisely because in this way the word comprehends the "general" in the individual.[62]

The relationship just noted between historical experience and language makes it comprehensible that history takes place as *history of the transmission of traditions.* In the individual event something of *general* import is experienced, something relevant for other individuals. Therefore it is passed on in tradition and received by others. But because these others experience the general differently in new events, tradition is continually modified, even when, as is usually the case in archaic cultures, these alternations are repressed from consciousness. It is a consequence of the language-character of historical experience that human history always accomplishes itself as history of the transmission of traditions, in dialogue with the heritage of a past which is either adopted as one's own or else rejected, and in anticipation of a future which is more than the future of the particular individual concerned.[63]

[62] The universal is not to be understood here as a timeless universal, but as the summation of the events which follow one another contingently in time. The universal thus understood is itself related to time and in a specific way related to the future.

[63] It is perhaps not superfluous to note at this point that the concept of the history of the transmission of traditions formulated above is perhaps not fully congruent with what is understood as research in the history of the transmission of traditions in exegetical and form-critical work. The systematic concept, "history of the transmission of traditions," arose from

The thesis that history seen as the transmission of traditions is the deeper meaning of history in general naturally does not justify any traditionalism, as if the "language of tradition" always still unequivocally determined our present.[64] In opposition to all Christian tradition which presented itself as authoritative the Enlightenment accomplished a truly revolutionary "break with tradition," which is one of the presup-

---

an extension by philosophy of history (or theology of history) of a methodological concept which the work of such men as Martin Noth has defined. But the extension implies a transformation. When K. Koch says, "Research in the history of the transmission of traditions begins from the final stage of a literary unit and elucidates first the prior written stages, and then the oral ones" (*Was ist Formgeschichte? Neue Wege der Bibelexegese* [Neunkirchen-Vluyn: Neukirchener Verlag, 1964], p. 54), it is clear that the systematic concept of the history of the transmission of traditions has been distinguished from this by a process of abstraction. The systematic concept does not begin with the final stage of a text in order to inquire back about the derivation of the material that has been fashioned into it. Rather it begins at the points of origin reached through such historical research and inquires into an *open future* of transformations, mixtures, or ramifications of traditions, and what is more, it inquires in such a way that the "materials" cannot be separated from the concrete behavior of the individuals. History of the transmission of traditions in the current historical-exegetical sense of the term includes only a partial aspect of this process, insofar as it inquires only about the history of the literary and oral material. But if the whole implied behavior of the participating individuals is included in the investigation, the transition to the broader, systematic meaning of the concept of the history of the transmission of traditions results. Many of the criticisms which K. Schwarzwäller makes against my method (*Theologie oder Phänomenologie* [1966], pp. 97 ff.) seem to be connected with the fact that he does not direct enough attention to the transformation of the concept of the history of the transmission of traditions that takes place through its extension by philosophy of history. It should be possible, over against an analysis of the history of the transmission of traditions in the usual technical sense, to ask what does stand behind the phenomena which are being studied. But with the extension of the concept of the history of the transmission of traditions by the philosophy of history, questions of this sort are already included or are to be included, as well as the question of "identity in phenomenal discontinuity and lack of identity in formal continuity" (*ibid.*, p. 98). The behavior of the bearers of tradition, and the events and realities which determined their behavior—from which in this procedure one cannot abstract in favor of the contents which have been passed down—can be put into relation to the contents which have been passed down in numerous ways.

[64] Moltmann, *Theologie der Hoffnung*, 1964, pp. 72 and 83, has misunderstood the concept of the history of the transmission of traditions in this way (reported by Robinson above, p. 93).

positions of modern historical criticism.[65] Since then, tradition, in the sense of holding fast to what has been handed down, has no longer been "self-evident." Yet this break with tradition is itself an occurrence in the history of transmitting tradition. The history of the transmission of traditions has precisely to do with the transformations in traditions, not only with the process of their formation, but also with the processes of their criticism, modification, and dissolution. Tradition-bound thought usually will not admit the existence of such transformations. It holds that what has been handed down is unalterably valid, or conversely thinks that what is currently valid has been passed on traditionally for ages. Therefore the *history* of the transmission of traditions accomplishes the criticism of the traditional self-understanding, both as a real process and as a theme of research and historical reconstruction. It does this by bringing to consciousness the transformation which has taken place in transmitting tradition. It is only in such a process of transformation that continuity is to be found.[66]

It is not the case, as has been asserted, that the understanding of history as the history of the transmission of traditions forms a second phase of the development of the program of *Revelation as History*.[67] However, a material shift had already

[65] *Theologie der Hoffnung*, p. 72.

[66] Therefore on closer inspection Moltmann could have discovered, in my concept of the *history* of the transmission of traditions, his postulated new concept of "tradition," which "takes up into itself historical criticism and its consciousness of the crisis in history without negating them or rendering them harmless" (*ibid.*, 1964, p. 72). G. Klein has also misunderstood this critical meaning of the history of tradition, both as a real process and as the reconstructing representation of this process; cf. the report by Robinson above, pp. 82 f.

[67] So Moltmann, *Theologie der Hoffnung*, p. 71; cf. Robinson, p. 92. Compare however *Offenbarung als Geschichte*, (1st ed., 1961), p. 112: "History is never made out of so called *bruta facta*. As human history, its occurrence is always interwoven with understanding, in hope and memory, and the transformations (!) of understanding are themselves events of history. The two cannot be separated even in the initial occurrences of a history. Thus history is always also the history of the transmission of traditions, and even the natural events which affect the history of a people do not have their meaning outside of their positive or negative relationship to the traditions and expectations in which the men of that history live."

taken place at that time, away from my original effort to establish a theological understanding of history as constituted by the tension of promise and fulfillment.[68] Jürgen Moltmann has recently expressed his regret that I later gave up this conception of promise and fulfillment which he has followed up.[69] But why did I give it up? Because as a rule the promises do not enter so literally into a fulfillment as one would assume that they would if they were the word of God effecting history, in accord with the Old Testament self-understanding. Rather, history has "overtaken" promises understood in this sense.[70] Originally unforeseen events cast a new light on the promises which have been passed on by tradition, so that their "fulfillment" could be affirmed in a way that deviates from their original literal meaning. The older way of presenting the "schema" underlying the history of the Old Testament offered a correspondence between effective divine Word and historical event. It is no longer possible to hold this view, since it is irreconcilable with the real historical situation, from which a consciousness trained in historical criticism cannot withdraw.[71] Now we

[68] *KuD*, V (1959), 220 ff. Robinson correctly observed that—to be sure, not only in my presentation, but also in the Old Testament historical writing, the characteristic features of which I was still then reporting without penetrating criticism—this "structure . . . functions . . . as another instance of a timeless principle being used to replace the actual history" ("The Historicality of Biblical Language," *The Old Testament and Christian Faith: A Theological Discussion,* ed. by Bernard W. Anderson [New York: Harper & Row, 1963], p. 128). On the basis of similar considerations I had already in 1961 (in *Offenbarung als Geschichte*) given up this "schema" and, in conjunction with R. Rendtorff, replaced it with the concept of the history of the transmission of traditions (see previous note).

[69] *Theologie der Hoffnung* (1964), p. 69. It is not the case, as Moltmann thinks, that the place of the schema of "promise and fulfillment" has been taken by outdoing the Greek cosmos theology with a universal-historical eschatology, but rather by the concept of the history of the transmission of traditions. In addition, Moltmann erroneously cites Robinson's critique as parallel to his own (*ibid.,* p. 76, n. 101). While Robinson criticized the understanding of history developed under the rubric of the "schema" of promise and fulfillment, Moltmann, on the contrary, objects that I have later departed from this "fundamental perception of the Old Testament" (p. 69).

[70] See my introductory article in this volume, p. 120 and note 14, and cf. esp. Moltmann, *Theologie der Hoffnung,* pp. 99 ff.

[71] In this sense I concur in the remarks of Robinson in his article, "The Historicality of Biblical Language" (see above, note 68).

can only grasp the continuity of "fulfillment" with the preceding promise or threat in terms of the history of the transmission of traditions. It is only in this way that one incorporates into the idea of a relationship between proclaiming word and proclaimed event the critical element of each new historical experience over against the word passed on by tradition.

I have in the meantime gone more deeply into the question of the relationship between word and event in the process of transmitting tradition, to examine this relationship with regard to the connection, on the one hand, of the individual events, and on the other, of the words which bring them to expression, to the whole of reality, which by virtue of its historicality is not yet complete. This further problem area has already been touched on above. On the one hand every individual event has its meaning and thereby its essence (i.e., what it is) only in relation to the whole. But the whole of reality is not yet completed, by virtue of its historicality. Nevertheless words ascribe to events, things, and even persons whom we encounter their essence, their meaning. In consequence of the above, that implies an *anticipation* of the whole of reality. Though it is a question whether the attributed meaning proves correct—which is often debatable and always a question which remains open—all occurrence has to be understood, right into its ontological structure, as anticipation of future finality (both for the good and for the evil), insofar as the event already has any such meaning attributed to it by the word. The word brings to expression this essence, which is not immediately to be found in the event. The category of anticipation or prolepsis, which was originally introduced to describe the distinctive structure of the history of Jesus, especially of his resurrection, thus shows itself to be a fundamental structural element both of cognition and of language, and of the being of beings in their temporality.[72] Thus the

[72] It is incomprehensible to me how Gerhard Sauter can assert that in my thought the concept of prolepsis serves as a "mobile teleological concept of totality" (*Zukunft und Verheissung* [1965], p. 266). After all, I already in 1959 emphasized that the interconnection of occurrence constantly forms itself backward, through the retrospective attachment of

the particular contingent new events to what was earlier, "but not, on the contrary, as forward-reaching direction and action" (*KuD,* V [1959], p. 285). In this way is accomplished the "responsibility of man for the heritage which comes to him with regard to the future, with regard to the 'coming God' . . . who by his coming both creates the contingent and points to what has been" (*ibid.,* n. 68). The discussion of Sauter about prophetic thought corresponds in substance to this (*ibid.,* pp. 197 ff.), in which connection, however, one should note that this term "thought," judged exegetically, may be tied to a "protological" conception much more strongly than Sauter's interpretation will admit. However that may be, Sauter really did not have to miss the opposition between my conception of historical continuity as continually created backward by the retrospective attachment of the new to the earlier, and a teleologically-stamped idea of development. To be sure, the typesetter had to a certain degree deformed my express rejection of the catchword "teleology" in connection with my critique of the concept of development (*KuD,* V [1959], p. 283), by the ingenious exchange of "theology" for "teleology," as I have only recently noted. Even so, it should be clear from the tenor of my argument there that I largely agree with Sauter's critique, which has points of contact with that of N. Hartmann, of a teleological interpretation of occurrence (*Zukunft und Verheissung,* pp. 178 ff.), which tries to grasp "the individual activities in their goal-directedness" from the "primordially established purpose of the whole world" (*ibid.,* p. 179). That remains untouched by the question which has been occupying me recently, whether the function of *telos* in Aristotle's doctrine of motion does not itself contain aspects which stand in direct contradiction to the received mode of teleological thought which appeals to Aristotle. I ask myself with some perplexity how it is that Sauter's agreement with me in the critique of this teleology has remained hidden from him, and instead he has erected an opposition in principle on this point. In view of my emphasis on the contingent new as the starting point for the current experience of the historical relationship to the past, his assertion is off the point, that the approach in terms of the history of the transmission of traditions "*ipso facto* makes what has been the creative ground for that which is coming" (so Sauter, *ibid.,* p. 210); for the procedure of the history of the transmission of traditions inquires how the heritage of tradition is seen and grasped anew from ever new experiences (in the sense of the procedure described abstractly by me in 1959). Thus the conception attributed to me by Sauter presupposes a "teleology of history" (p. 244), from which I have expressly distanced myself. My theological concept of prolepsis, which both Moltmann and Sauter have taken over in the meantime, naturally has nothing to do with such a teleology. The concept of prolepsis, especially as anticipatory *occurring* of the end (cf., e.g., *Offenbarung als Geschichte,* [1st ed. 1961], p. 98), forms exactly the counterconcept to a "protologically" founded teleology (cf. also the connection between prolepsis and "retroaction" [*Rückwirkung*] in my *Grundzüge der Christologie* [1964], esp. pp. 332 f., also p. 407). The thesis that the whole is constitutive for the meaning of every individual event within its scope, in my works regularly has the meaning that this whole is grounded in the future of its end and thus, in Sauter's formulation of his own view, is "that which again and again is anticipatorily given from the future back" (*Zukunft und Verheissung,* p. 217). What else than this is the sentence to mean, that the whole of history is

task is also posed of distinguishing the prolepsis of eschatological future in the ministry of Jesus and above all in his resurrection, in its distinctiveness over against other sorts of ontic and noetic anticipation of eschatological fulfillment. No doubt those forms of anticipation of final reality are predominant which are immediately distinguishable, in their finiteness, from the final reality; their relationship to final reality is similar to

---

accessible only from its end? (*Offenbarung als Geschichte* [1961], p. 104). That this—as Sauter expresses it—"contemporaneity" of totality and end has to be "a teleological, and not an eschatological axiom" (*Zukunft und Verheissung*, p. 256), is incomprehensible to me. The idea affirms that the whole of history is grounded in the eschaton, and therefore in the final future. Does not Sauter say the same in the formulation (p. 217) cited above? The real differences between us may lie elsewhere, not in the thesis of a noetically and ontologically constitutive meaning of the eschaton as the final future for all preceding occurrence, but rather in the question whether the eschatological future so understood has to be conceived in pure opposition to the logic of the phenomena. The assertions of Sauter on this theme are particularly contradictory. Sharply antithetical formulations (*ibid.*, pp. 155 f., 203, 221, 223) are set over against other statements according to which promise and presently-existing world are not to be opposed to each other "rigidly and statically" (p. 228), and which cast as a reproach against the metaphysical view of the phenomena, that it does not do justice "to the creation itself (!) in its longing" (pp. 157 f.). A similar finding appears characteristically in Moltmann's *Theologie der Hoffnung:* compare dualistic-sounding antitheses (e.g., pp. 34, 70, 127, 256, 262) with a statement such as: that Christian theology can demonstrate "its truth in terms of the reality of man and the reality of the world which surrounds man," by "taking up the questionableness of reality as a whole and including it in the eschatological questionableness of human existence and the world, which is laid open by the event of promise" (pp. 83 f., cf. 76, 79, 250 f.). It may be that the motivation for the antithetical assertions in Moltmann as in Sauter is to be sought in the tendency to oppose the "promise" to the whole "natural" situation of man. But this supernaturalism cannot be carried through without depriving the promise itself of its meaning as promise. For a future that is *only* opposed to the presently existing world cannot be a "promise" for it, but can only mean threat and destruction. Sauter has himself observed that the idea of promise implies a positive relationship to the presently existing reality to which the promise applies (*Zukunft und Verheissung*, p. 227). If this insight is taken seriously, then the dualism cannot be maintained between eschatological future (and promise) on the one hand, and the presently existing world of "phenomena" on the other. The new, eschatologically-oriented theology must liberate itself from such remnants of a reactionary supernaturalism, which are reactionary because they arise as a reaction against the problematic of the Enlightenment. Then it will perhaps be able to encounter with less prejudice talk of future, prolepsis, and totality, when presented purely phenomenally.

that of the copies of Platonic ideas to the ideas themselves. In contrast to such broken anticipations of the eschatological future, there seem to be unbroken, so to speak pure, anticipations of eschatological reality in such realities as peace, spirit, love, and life, and also in the mystery of moral evil. This is the case even though our *participation* in these realities remains a broken one in the present life. In contrast to such partial participation, the special character of the proleptic event of the resurrection of Jesus should then be sought in its full participation in the reality of eschatological life. The provisional aspect, by which even this event is still only prolepsis,[73] consists simply in this—but what does "simply" mean here!—that here the eschatological reality of life appeared only in an individual, and not yet in all mankind and the world as a whole.[74] The difficulty of recognizing such an event

[73] G. Klein has constructed an opposition between provisionalness and prolepsis which is foreign to my concept of prolepsis (*Theologie des Wortes Gottes und die Hypothese der Universalgeschichte* (*Beiträge zur evangelischen Theologie*, 37 [Munich: Christian Kaiser Verlag, 1964], pp. 39 f.; cf. Robinson, above, p. 85). The element of provisionalness is included in the concept of prolepsis, insofar as every anticipation remains distinct from what is anticipated. Otherwise it would no longer be anticipation, but the thing itself. Thus an anticipation of the eschaton is only an anticipation as long as it is not completely and in every respect identical with the reality of the eschaton itself. Nevertheless, an anticipation of the final can mean the presence of the reality of the eschaton, unsurpassable in its content. In this respect the proleptic presence of the eschatological reality of life in the resurrection of Jesus is distinguished from all other proleptic phenomena. In the postscript to *Offenbarung und Geschichte*, to which Klein refers, I did not assert that the proleptic character of "the whole reality of being" is "structured similarly" to the Christ event, as Klein avers (Klein, p. 39; against this see *Offenbarung als Geschichte* [2nd ed., 1963], pp. 143 f.). That the proleptic character of all that has being in general becomes comprehensible from the Christ event does not displace the specific particularity of the latter over against all other occurrence. Rather it makes it possible to understand this particularity in relationship with all other reality, while the limitation of the concept of prolepsis to the Christ event would have to isolate the latter from all other reality and thereby render it incomprehensible.

[74] In this provisionalness of anticipation, even in the case of the resurrection of Jesus, it is included that "the risen Christ himself" also "still has a future, a universal future for the nations" (Moltmann, *Theologie der Hoffnung* [1964], p. 73). The resurrection of Jesus is what it is only as a "pre-appearing" of the universal resurrection of the righteous for salvation, and thus as guarantee of future salvation for those who are now joined with Jesus. The union of his church with his own eschato-

as historical, and of speaking with some degree of adequacy about the special reality which appeared already in it, is connected with the unbrokenness of the presence of the final in the resurrection of Jesus, which must be in this respect without parallel. Commonsense reason, like historical judgment in its own special way, moves on the level of what is accessible by analogy with what is already known elsewhere. We can only speak of what is totally different and extraordinary by drawing something apparently similar, even though perhaps only remotely similar, out of the sphere that is known to us, so that we can at least characterize metaphorically what is otherwise unknown and remains mysterious. As far as historical judgments are concerned, there is always a tendency, not only to scrutinize especially skeptically anything that is unprecedented and eludes all analogy, but to declare that it is impossible in principle. But this latter is a transgression of the limits of historical criticism in the use of the principle of analogy.[75] If historical study keeps itself free from the dogmatic

logical life is still future also for the Resurrected One. It is therefore not correct when Moltmann concludes from my idea of the anticipatory occurrence of the end of all history in the resurrection of Jesus, that then "the resurrected Jesus himself wound have no further future" (*ibid.,* p. 73). I have already emphasized in *Offenbarung als Geschichte* (1963, pp. 98, 106, and esp. 109 ff.; see also *Grundzüge der Christologie,* 1964, pp. 65 ff.) that the tension between the anticipation of the end in the raising of Jesus, on the one hand, and the general end-event, on the other, itself opened the path of church history, which is particularly directed by the universal missionary task of the church, and is therefore qualified in the sense of Moltmann's "history of promise and mission." There may be a difference with Moltmann's conception in my conviction that the ultimate reality of eschatological life has appeared in Jesus himself in the *past* event of the resurrection, to which we can look back as in past time and thus as a historical event. For early Christianity the resurrection of Jesus was not only the "putting into force" of the promise (so Moltmann, pp. 132 f., 137, 139), but the shift of aeons, in which the Old Testament promises have found their fulfillment, and not only a "supposed fulfillment" (so Moltmann, pp. 143, 208). The happenedness of the ultimate, the perfect tense of the resurrection of Jesus—in the double sense of the word perfect—became the basis of the Christian doctrine of the incarnation, which distinguishes Christianity from the mere knowledge of hope of the Jewish faith.

[75] It is important to note that only the absence of analogies is regarded as an insufficient argument for contesting the historicity of an event (cf. Robinson, above, pp. 30 f.). My criticism is not directed against the critical use of the principle of analogy, which is basic to the critical historical

postulate that all events are of the same kind, and at the same time remains critical toward its own procedure, there does not have to be any impossibility *in principle* in asserting the historicity of the resurrection of Jesus. No doubt the remaining methodological problems are difficult, as are the questions which arise with the critical scrutiny of the status of the tradition in detail.[76]

---

method. This use is merely restricted. The instrument of analogy gains precision, if judgments about the historicity or nonhistoricity of events asserted in the tradition are based only on *positive* analogies between the tradition which is being studied and situations known elsewhere, but not on the *lack* of such analogies. In the meantime Daniel P. Fuller has developed my brief observations on the principle of analogy by very careful methodological considerations in his article, "The Resurrection of Jesus and the Historical [Method]," *The Journal of Bible and Religion,* XXXIV (1966), pp. 18–24.

[76] Since my argument on the question of the historicity of the resurrection of Jesus is now available in detail elsewhere, I do not have to go into the historical details in answer to Grobel's exposition. In reference to the happenedness of the raising of Jesus as a distinct event separate from Jesus' death on the cross, Grobel expressly agrees with me (p. 169). A particular agreement exists with reference to the appearances of the Resurrected One to the apostles recorded in 1 Cor. 15: something happened *"to* them, . . . not merely in them" (Grobel, p. 170). On the other hand Grobel holds that the tradition of the empty tomb is unhistorical. He bases his skepticism above all on Paul. An empty tomb would have scarcely any relevance for a resurrection-reality in the sense of the Pauline *soma pneumatikon.* Accordingly it is characteristic that Paul never refers to the empty tomb of Jesus. Now I am so far in agreement with Grobel, that the parallelism which Paul always emphasizes between Jesus and the believer requires us to infer, from his general statements about the reality of the resurrection as *soma pneumatikon,* a corresponding understanding of the resurrection of Jesus in Paul (*Grundzüge der Christologie,* 1964, pp. 72 f.). To be sure, the conception of a *soma pneumatikon* seems to me to have a more definite sense than Grobel, with Bultmann, assumes (*ibid.,* p. 172). I contest, however, that the assumption of an empty tomb could be irrelevant for this conception, which is thoroughly at home in Jewish tradition (*ibid.,* pp. 74 ff.). As far as I can see, in early Jewish tradition there is no discussion of resurrection of the dead which does not presuppose that the tombs (so far as they exist) become empty. Also in the Syriac Apocalypse of Baruch, which stands so close to Paul, it says that at the resurrection the earth will give back the dead which it has kept up till then (Syr. Bar. 50:2, 44:4, and IV Ezra 7:32). If in consequence of the above one must consider, that for Paul the grave of Jesus becoming empty was a matter-of-course implication of his discussion of the resurrection of Jesus, then the circumstance that he does not expressly mention the empty tomb of Jesus loses the meaning which is now often attributed to it. In the central question, whether the event of the resurrection of Jesus, which Grobel in partial agreement with me presupposes, is to be pronounced historical or not, I am like Grobel of the opinion that his-

torical events must be locatable in time and space (Grobel, p. 170). There is no argument between us so far as the temporal location of the event of the resurrection is concerned, in view of the relative exactness of the traditional formula "after three days" (*ibid.*). Grobel's skepticism about the relationship of this event to space is incomprehensible to me. Presupposing the tradition of the empty tomb, the relationship to space is already given. But even if one wanted to follow Grobel in this question, it could be said at least that the event of the resurrection took place in Palestine. I cannot see what is opposed to this, the moment one asserts the event as such and as locatable in time. I do understand that Grobel regards the resurrection-reality as not material and thus nonspatial (cf. Cobb's remarks to this point, pp. 204 f.), and I could agree with him in this. But the *event* of the resurrection of Jesus, in contrast to the reality which results from this event, has to do with the transition from our earthly reality to that resurrection-reality which is no longer locatable in space. Thus at least its initial point must be sought in the historical Jesus which was located in space, and thus far at least it is itself related to space. If it really took place, it took place in Palestine and not for instance in America. Beyond this it should be asked whether an event that took place only in time and not in any way in space, would be conceivable at all by us, and not rather an intellectual abstraction. Do not space and time belong indissolubly together in reality? The difficult problem which I see in relation to the relationship of the event of the resurrection of Jesus to time and space lies in the fact that this event, unlike other events, has a continuation in time and space. But this problem affects the temporality of the event equally with its spatiality, and does not hinder us from understanding the event itself as locatable in space and time. To the term "abstraction" a further note should be added to the work of W. Marxsen, *Die Auferstehung Jesu als historisches und als theologisches Problem* (Gerd Mohn: Gütersloher Verlaghaus, 1964), which Robinson cites (nn. 100 and 108). Its thesis, that "resurrection" is an interpretive category for the appearances of the living Jesus which were encountered by Paul (and others), seems at first sight to express a truism, since no early Christian witness observed the event of the resurrection itself or claimed to. The only question is whether this "interpretive category" is exchangeable at will for other ones. Were profound considerations about the relativity of the then-current ways of thinking really necessary to explain the early Christian talk about the resurrection on the basis of the appearances of Jesus? How should this "interpretive category" be avoided, once one reflects that he who appeared as living had previously died? Since Marxsen avers that this tracing back of the appearances to Jesus' being dead was a reflection which in understanding these appearances themselves could have been evaded (p. 24), his argument takes on something of the abstractly artificial. On the other hand, the function of the apostolate which Marxsen also emphasizes is in no way independent of that so-called superfluous "reflection." This latter did not somehow come in at a second stage—there are no grounds for supposing this—but was immediately occasioned by the context of the experience in which the appearances of Jesus were given to those who received them—who of course knew of his death. With Marxsen's method, could not the assertion that the appearances were appearances of *Jesus* also be easily proved to be a secondary "interpretive category"?

## III

The correct definition of the relation between knowledge and faith is bound up *inter alias* with the understanding of the specific anticipation of the eschaton in the person and history of Jesus as the presence of the final in and through him.[77] Knowledge of the history of Jesus as an anticipation of the future general definition of humanity, which appeared in him and especially in his resurrection from the dead and has become accessible through him, is a knowledge of the meaning of this history as promise, and thus leads to trust in "the God, who raised Jesus from the dead." This view is more precisely set forth in my introductory article,[78] and does not have to be repeated here. The clearer the knowledge of this unique character of the history of Jesus is, the more clearly it points beyond its own form as theoretical knowledge into faith.

[77] The distinctive characteristic of the message of Jesus is that the future of the rule of God is not separated from the present as still outstanding, but that precisely as the future it becomes the power that determines the present and thus comes to appearance in the present (cf. *Grundzüge der Christologie,* pp. 234 ff.). Here J. Wirsching has mistaken the point of my understanding of the eschatology of Jesus and of the concept of prolepsis, when he wonders whether the present does not take on "a gnostic or docetic appearance" in my thought ("Ein neues theologischen System?", *Deutsches Pfarrerblatt,* LXIV [1964], p. 609, cited above by Robinson, p. 70). The critique of Cobb (above, pp. 219 f.) has a different accent, namely, that I subordinate the present too fully to the future and to the past. In this it is correct that I see the present as laid open by the future and connected with the heritage of the past, which for its part refers again toward the future. These connections seem to me to be constitutive of the present itself. A present isolated from the past and future would be empty, at least for a finite being. The present always receives its tension-filled content from the interaction with the heritage of the past in the light of a perspective toward the future. And the future comes to be relevant through the fact that it "comes into" the present (and through the "how" it comes), when what the future brings happens in the present. The confession of the incarnation of God in Jesus Christ affirms, in this sense, that in him the future of God has become present among us, and not only a transitory present (in an event which in the meantime has become past once more for us), but an enduring present— through the spirit of Jesus—because it is a present that has an unbounded future. On the ontological aspects of this theme, cf. my article, "Appearance as Arrival of That Which is Future," *JBR,* XXXV (1967).

[78] Cf. above, p. 130.

For thus it will be more clearly recognized that the only ultimately appropriate behavior toward this history is not mere
cognizance, but trust in the God proclaimed by Jesus. But
precisely this knowledge is indispensable, where the freedom
for faith is to be won in the face of doubt of the truth of the
Christian gospel. It sets the sight free on the ground of faith
in Jesus himself *"extra me"* and thus protects the "decision"
of faith from the suspicion that it rests on pious self-deception.

It is incomprehensible to me, in the face of this repeated
explanation of the transition from knowledge of the history
of Jesus to faith, how Hamilton can assert that for me knowledge and faith so coincide that faith in my sense means only
*fides historica.*[79] Obviously Hamilton has not found worthy of
consideration my explanation of how the knowledge of the
history of Jesus, in view of its eschatological-proleptic meaning, leads beyond mere historical cognizance to faith in the
sense of trust.[80] It also seems to have escaped his attention that
the openness of the knowledge of the history of Jesus as eschatological establishes an ultimate identity between the situation of the theologian and that of the unreflective believer.
This is the exact opposite of that "justification by method"
which he wants to make out as my opinion.[81] Hamilton's parallel assertion, that "the proper methodology has been substi-

---

[79] Cf. above, p. 188.

[80] In reformation terminology—to which Hamilton refers me—that
means: historical knowledge must not only be taken cognizance of as
such (*notitio historiae*), but must be understood in terms of its specific
effects (*effectus*): *Estque referenda historia ad promissionem seu effectum*
(Melanchthon, *Loci praecipui theologici,* 1559 [*Corpus Reformatorum* 21,
743], Ch. 20, sec. 23). It corresponds to this that in his *Apology,* Melanchthon characterizes the forgiveness of sins as the *causa finalis historiae,*
the goal of the history of Jesus himself (*Apology,* IV, 51). Cobb has
given a first-rate formulation of the difference between my conception
and Hamilton's interpretation of it, when he says that the faith, which
follows from the presupposed conviction of Jesus' resurrection and of its
meaning, is "not so much some greater confidence that these propositions
are true as it is confidence in the God who raised Jesus Christ and who
will raise all men" (p. 214). Instead of "all men" it should be "those
joined who are joined with Jesus," if resurrection in the sense of Paul
already mediates the gift of eternal life.

[81] Cf. above, p. 189.

tuted for the Holy Spirit,"[82] sets forth so crude a caricature of
my position, and one which, I hope, is so obviously a caricature to any unprejudiced judgment, that there is no need for
an answer to it. The difference between my conception and
Hamilton's presentation of it is especially evident in my repeated indications that it is not theoretical knowledge which
can create the fellowship with Jesus which alone assures salvation, and that such fellowship arises and lives only through
trust in Jesus and his message.[83] The knowledge of the history
on which faith is grounded has to do with the truth and reliability of that on which faith depends; these are presupposed
in the act of trusting, and thus logically precede the act of
faith in respect to its perceived content. But that does not
mean that the subjective accomplishment of such knowledge
would be in any way a condition of fellowship with God.
Hence this knowledge is not a pious "work" in the specific
theological sense of a condition for the attainment of salvation, as G. Klein has made out that I affirm. He who believes
in Jesus has salvation in Jesus whom he trusts, without regard
to the question how it stands with his historical and theological knowledge of Jesus. The presupposition is, of course, that
fellowship with Jesus really mediates and assures salvation.
The research and knowledge of theology, or at least of the
theoretical disciplines of theology, deal with the truth of this
presupposition of faith. Such knowledge is thus not a condition for participating in salvation, but rather it assures faith
about its basis. It thereby enables faith to resist the gnawing
doubt that it has no basis beyond itself and that it merely sat-
isfies a subjective need through fictions, and thus is only ac-
complishing self-redemption through self-deception. To this
suspicion, and to the trial which it must mean for faith which
understands itself from God's act, one cannot simply object
with Bultmann, that faith is "obedience" to an authority be-

[82] *Ibid.,* p. 188.
[83] Cf. *Offenbarung als Geschichte,* 1963 (2nd ed.), p. 145.

yond oneself.[84] For the question is why just *this* authority
should be accepted, while the claims of other positions are
rejected. Thinking which has appropriated the questions of
the Enlightenment can no longer be content with asserted
authorities. It must ask about the adequacy of the claims of
authority, and also about the reasons which are suited to be
convincing about the trustworthiness of such claims. It is at
this point that theological knowledge, for which the work of
theological research strives, makes its contribution to faith. It
is concerned that faith remain pure faith, which can trust the
antecedently given truth of the basis which supports it, and
which will not, as groundless "decision," deteriorate into the
"work" of an illusory redemption of oneself. The believer who
thinks that he can give the answer to the trial of gnawing
doubt through the act of faith itself is already on the road to
such a self-deceptive works-righteousness. In contradiction of
its own proper understanding of itself, even "obedient" acceptance of assertions on mere authority depends on a "decision" without a basis, if the truth-claim of the authority in
question is no longer certainly established in the general cultural situation, but has actually become fundamentally doubtful on account of the turning away from all authoritarian
thinking. Even the man who is more or less dimly conscious
that having his existence at his own disposal misses the real
possibility of life, is still far from being able to see clearly why
he should deny having himself at his own disposal for the
sake of *Jesus,* or for the sake of the authority of the Christian
kerygma which confronts him with an appeal to Jesus. In this
situation precisely the "obedient" decision to accept the Christian kerygma is transformed back into an act of putting oneself at one's disposal, as long as one cannot give any reasons
why one should not instead become a Buddhist, or a Marxist
atheist, or simply a secular humanist who does not find any
need for an appeal to Jesus. What is needed are the reasons

[84] Cited by Robinson above, n. 209. The problematical aspect of Bultmann's position is seen very much as I see it, though from a different
point of view and with a different accent, by K. Schwarzwäller, *Theologie oder Phänomenologie,* pp. 67 f., 63 f., also p. 142.

for the decision of faith. It is true that in order to be faith in the full sense of the word, faith does not need to be conscious of these reasons in every case and above all not in their ultimate clarity and form. It is sufficient that the decision of faith actually rests on reasons that will hold up. The question whether and to what extent this is the case forms the theme of theological reflection, in which the individual believer will take part to the extent that he finds necessary in order to confront the doubts that trouble him.

Therefore theology has to deal with the presupposition of faith, with the truth and reliability (already presupposed in the act of faith) of the "object" on which faith depends. Of course it can do this only in a provisional way. The truth or untruth of faith is not decided primarily in the act of faith; rather this decision depends on faith's object, which contains the promise in which faith trusts, and which is also the object of theological knowledge. Only in this way does faith depend on a truth *extra se*. It is the specific characteristic of knowledge that it insofar as possible perceives the object in its objectivity, in its difference from subjectivity (even that of the knower himself). Therefore it is the business of theological knowledge to confirm the truth which is presupposed for faith and on which it trusts. Theology has plainly exercised this function from the very beginning of Christianity, for all that its insights are provisional and subject to revision, and despite the resulting possibility and necessity that theological theses are debatable, and although knowledge, no less than faith, is an act of human subjectivity. This latter point of view was adduced by Klein as an argument against my thesis that the placing of the act of knowledge before the act of faith corresponded to the *extra me* on which faith depends.[85] His argument overlooks the fact that the distinctiveness of knowledge among all mental acts consists in its letting come to view the presupposed reality as such, in its difference from human subjectivity, even the subjectivity of the knower himself. This "objectivity" of the relation to the world forms the primary

[85] This objection of Klein is presented by Robinson above, p. 88.

anthropological meaning of the difference between subject and object,[86] and precedes all dialectic of a "power of disposal" over the object, a dialectic which it makes possible.[87] The other mental acts participate in this objectivity in that they relate themselves to something that is perceived as "objective" in the sense specified, and therefore to that element of consciousness which finds its specific development in knowledge. It is in this connection that it is theological knowledge, among human acts, that permits the decision of trust to catch sight of the antecedent givenness of its "object," and advocates this priority of the object over trust in it.

But does not any historical knowledge of Jesus remain hopelessly inadequate to the certainty of faith, even if the history of Jesus does in a certain sense bear the meaning of divine revelation? Does not historical knowledge attain probability at best, so that one must seek another rootage for the certainty of faith? This question has been raised again and again since

[86] M. Landmann, *Philosophische Anthropologie* (Berlin: de Gruyter, 1955), pp. 214 and 215 f., has rightly made this point against Heidegger.

[87] Disposability is made possible by the fact that the "object" remains identical with the change of subjective point of view or even, in communication by language with the change of subjects themselves. Insofar as the differences of subjective conception, which play a role in every case, can be ignored, the "object" can be treated as if it remained identical in the change of points of view and of its relationships with different subjects, and as if these changing relationships remained external to it. In this case the "object" can so be utilized as a means in appropriate projects of human action. But even when a power of disposal in this sense is not possible, because the particular subjective points of view in encountering the object cannot be ignored—and that is not only the case with knowledge of God, but with all historical knowledge—nevertheless the objectivity of knowledge is possible in this way, that each subject in his own way knows that the object is distinct from himself and is thus (in intention) the *same* object to which other subjects relate, although they describe it in other ways than he does. The self-identity of the object is indeed not unproblematically given; rather, there has to be a specific ascertaining of it. This takes place methodologically by the fact that the particular perspective mediates itself through critical discussion of previously given conceptions of "the same" object. Such discussion takes place, in turn, in subjective perspective, so that the ascertaining of the given common object of the subjects, which is in dispute among them, presents a task which can never be completed. The unfinishable task of historical research on ever-recurring themes offers the most impressive illustration of this situation.

the time of Lessing and Kierkegaard.[88] I have tried to answer it by distinguishing between historical certainty and certainty of faith. These two lie on different levels, and therefore there is no essential contradiction in basing a sure trust on an event which we can know historically only with probability. Historical research can never achieve definitive certainty in its results, but only greater or less probability. Formally that is true of all possible objects of historical examination, and has nothing to do with the special characteristic of a particular historical theme. But the certainty of faith, on the other hand, depends on the peculiarity of a particular historical event, namely, the history of Jesus. The special characteristic of this event consists in the fact that the final is here already present, and that the future, final salvation of each individual thus depends on the present stance toward Jesus. This special eschatological character of the history of Jesus demands and undergirds unrestricted trust: because in Jesus it is a question of the whole, here total trust is required, despite the relative uncertainty of our historical knowledge of Jesus. The certainty of faith consists in the completeness of trust, which in turn is grounded in the eschatological meaning of the history of Jesus. Of course our historical knowledge of this history of Jesus is only probable. In principle the possibility cannot be excluded that the historical probability of those traits of the history of Jesus in which its eschatological meaning is grounded will someday, from some points of view, become doubtful to the

---

[88] In his typology of answers to Lessing's question, Hamilton (pp. 190 ff.) ascribes to me the conception that a gulf could not possibly arise between past events and the present conviction of faith (or present binding truth in general), on account of the inseparability of fact and meaning (p. 192). He overlooks the fact that for me with each new understanding of the past the question is at stake what meaning the past event has for the present. That is always an open question. How little I indiscriminately unite present meaning and past event arises from my emphasis on historical difference, which cannot disappear with the hermeneutical bridging of past and present (*ZThK*, LX [1963], pp. 106 ff.). This point of view is my heaviest argument for the fact that only a plan of the history of the objects themselves (ultimately universal history) can adequately describe the scope of the hermeneutical task (*ibid.*, p. 118).

degree that a conception of the historical form of Jesus could or would have to seem probable, which would make the early Christian faith seem without support, without basis in the historical form of Jesus. I see no occasion for apprehension that such a position of research should emerge in the foreseeable future. But in principle it cannot be excluded. In such a case the foundation for the certainty of faith, trust in the eschatological power and meaning of the history of Jesus, would be removed. To be sure, the possibility would still remain that one could build on a future, "better," knowledge of Jesus, as over against the present judgment of historians.

Hence it is not at all my view, as Hamilton assumes,[89] that historical research could "only slightly affect" the certainty of faith. On the contrary, its results can far rather bring faith into dispute, and threaten it with the loss of its foundation; and where the conflict with knowledge is unequivocal and complete, hardly anyone could base faith on a future, better knowledge without the loss of his intellectual and personal integrity. For intellectual and personal integrity are bound up with the idea of the unity of truth. Therefore some present points of leverage would have to be available even for a confidence that directed itself to a future, better insight. If I had really asserted that faith was invulnerable to historical criticism, then Hamilton would have been right in casting the reproach against me that I had retreated into a theological

---

[89] Above, p. 185. He bases this conception on a sentence from my article, "Heilsgeschehen und Geschichte," *KuD*, V (1959), p. 278. But the translation of the sentence cited by Hamilton is misleading. It does not say in the original that historical knowledge could "only slightly impair" the certainty of faith, but that the *probabilistic character* of historical knowledge could not impair the peculiar *certainty* of faith, namely, just "as little" as on the other hand faith becomes superfluous through knowledge. (Instead of the expression used here, "as little as" [*so wenig wie*], the equivalent *"so wenig . . . so wenig* stands in the text, which would be translated, "as little as . . . just so little. . . ." Cobb (above, p. 215) was also misled by this incorrect translation. I fully concur in his sentence: "But it is hard to see how one can affirm in advance that the certainty of faith could be impaired only slightly by further developments in historical research" (*ibid.*). One could in fact only say that if one wanted to assert a "sheltered zone" of certainty of faith, and I have expressly rejected that.

circle, which I have criticized other positions for doing.[90] It seems that the point just touched on is the basis for Hamilton's mistrust of the methodological axiom that fact and meaning cannot be separated without falling into an abstract way of dealing with them. And in fact that thesis oriented to the history of the transmission of traditions would be a mere screen for a "sectarian theology,"[91] if it was misused to hold criticism at a distance. But the way of dealing with the history of the transmission of traditions which is sketched above, quite to the contrary, describes the process of the criticism and transformation of the contents of tradition, and can seek for the continuity of subject matter only in this process of criticism and transformation, and not in any supposed sheltered zone beyond it.

It is only in such a precarious and provisional way that knowledge is possible of that final reality which appeared in the history of Jesus. That is shown on the one hand by the ceaseless alteration of our historical picture of this history, and on the other, by the fact that the content and meaning of this event can only be expressed in language which anticipates that which has not yet appeared. Both aspects are part of the mystery of the incarnation, both the variability of our historical knowledge of the history of Jesus as well as the inexpressibility of its meaning, which makes us aware of the limits of our present knowledge and language. Both difficulties come to a focus in the question of the resurrection of Jesus, which forms the foundation of our confession of the incarnation. But even in the midst of such provisionalness and precariousness theology deals with the final reality, which has appeared in the midst of the relativity of our world. It is part of this situation that final reality appeared in a history that is now past for us.[92] This is what conditions the provisionalness and pre-

---

[90] Cf. above, p. 185.

[91] *Ibid.*, p. 187.

[92] I see this decisive element of the idea of the incarnation sacrificed by Altizer through his effort to cut off what he calls the living Christ from the historical Jesus (*The Gospel of Christian Atheism,* 1966, pp. 74 f., 83).

cariousness of theological knowledge. Nevertheless, the central meaning of the incarnation must not remain unspoken, but must be affirmed theologically, namely, that the final truth and the ultimate life have appeared in the midst of the finiteness of historical life. By reflection on its own particular limits in a given period, which means reflection on its finiteness, right theological knowledge is drawn into the mystery of its object, and thus, as a *reductio in mysterium*, it leads beyond itself into faith. Thus is accomplished the consciousness of the mystery of the incarnation, which I cannot express better than in the line of Eliot which Hamilton cites:

The hint half guessed, the gift half understood, is Incarnation.